Briefs

of

Leading Cases

in Law Enforcement

Rolando V. del Carmen
Sam Houston State University

Jeffery T. Walker
University of Arkansas-Little Rock

6th edition

Briefs of Leading Cases in Law Enforcement, Sixth Edition

Phone 877-374-2919
Web Site www.lexisnexis.com/anderson/criminaljustice

Library of Congress Cataloging-in-Publication Data

Del Carmen, Rolando V.
    Briefs of leading cases in law enforcement / Rolando V. del Carmen, Jeffery T. Walker.--6th ed.
        p. cm.
    Includes index.
    ISBN 1-59345-329-9 (soft bound)
    1. Criminal procedure--United States--Digests. 2. Law enforcement--United States--Digests.
3. Searches and seizures--United States--Digests. I. Walker, Jeffery T. II. Title.

KF9614.D45 2006
345.73'05--dc22

                                                                2006003214

Cover design by Tin Box Studio, Inc.

EDITOR Elisabeth Roszmann Ebben
ACQUISITIONS EDITOR Michael C. Braswell

Preface to the Sixth Edition

The Sixth Edition maintains the format of the previous editions. The cut-off date for this edition is September 30, 2005. This means that all significant United States Supreme Court cases up to the 2004-2005 term of the Court are included in this edition. A new term starts for the Court on October 3, 2005. Cases decided after that date will be included in the next edition.

This edition eliminates Chapter 19 (Forfeiture of Property), found in the fifth edition. This was done for two reasons. First, the topic is only peripherally relevant to law enforcement. Second, space is needed for the news cases that are added. The authors did not want the book to be unduly long.

A total of 15 new cases were added to this edition. Classified according to topics, these cases are:

Chapter 1 – Probable Cause: Maryland v. Pringle (2003)

Chapter 3 – Stop and Frisk: Hiibel v. Sixth Judicial District (2004)

Chapter 5 – Seizures – In General: Groh v. Ramirez (2004)

Chapter 6 – Searches – In General: United States v. Banks (2003)

Chapter 9 – Vehicle Stops and Searches:

Illinois v. Lidster (2004)
United States v. Flores-Montano (2004)
Thornton v. United States (2004)
Illinois v. Caballes (2005)

Chapter 14 – Confessions and Admissions: Cases Affirming *Miranda*:

Kaupp v. Texas (2003)
Fellers v. United States (2004)
Missouri v. Seibert (2004)

Chapter 15 – Confessions and Admissions: Cases Weakening *Miranda*:   United States v. Patane (2004)

Chapter 19 – Forfeiture of Property: This chapter is eliminated from the sixth edition.

New Chapter 19 – Legal Liabilities: Chavez v. Martinez (2004)
Muehler v. Mena (2005)
Town of Castle Rock v. Gonzales (2005)

The original decisions of the United States Supreme Court in these cases are readily available on the Internet by going to the Supreme Court's Web site at: www.supremecourtus.gov and clicking on "Opinions," then the year of the decision.

As in the past, the authors welcome suggestions to and comments on this edition. We hope this Sixth Edition continues to be of help to students and law enforcement officers.

Rolando V. del Carmen
Distinguished Professor of Criminal Justice
College of Criminal Justice
Sam Houston State University

Jeffery T. Walker
Professor of Criminal Justice
University of Arkansas, Little Rock

Contents

Chapter 4—Arrest   45

Chapter 5—Seizures—In General   65

Chapter 6—Searches—In General   77

Chapter 7—Searches After Arrest 97

Chapter 8—Searches with Consent 107

Chapter 9—Vehicle Stops and Searches 117

Chapter 19—Legal Liabilities   265

Index   289

List of Cases with Principle (Capsule) of Law

Chapter 1—Probable Cause

Chapter 2—The Exclusionary Rule

Chapter 3—Stop and Frisk

Chapter 4—Arrest

Chapter 5—Seizures—In General

Chapter 6—Searches—In General

Chapter 7—Searches After Arrest

Chapter 8—Searches with Consent

Chapter 9—Vehicle Stops and Searches

Chapter 10—Electronic Surveillance

Chapter 11—Plain View and Open Fields Searches

Chapter 12—Lineups and Other Pretrial Identification Procedures

Chaper 13—Use of Force

Chapter 14—Confessions and Admissions: Cases Affirming *Miranda*

Chapter 15—Confessions and Admissions: Cases Weakening *Miranda*

Chapter 16—What Constitutes Interrogation for *Miranda* Purposes?

Chapter 19—Legal Liabilities

Table of Cases

Probable Cause   1

Introduction

Probable cause is the most important and most often-used phrase in law enforcement. It is defined by the United States Supreme Court as more than bare suspicion; it exists when "the facts and circumstances within the officers' knowledge and of which they had reasonably trustworthy information are sufficient in themselves to warrant a man of reasonable caution in the belief that an offense has been or is being committed." *Brinegar v. United States*, 338 U.S. 160 (1949).

For purposes of day-to-day policing, probable cause is present if an officer has trustworthy evidence or information that is sufficient to make a "reasonable person" believe it is more likely than not that the proposed arrest or search is justified. In mathematical terms, probable cause exists if there is more than 50 percent certainty that the suspect has committed an offense or that the items sought can be found in a certain place.

Probable cause is used in four situations: arrests with a warrant, arrests without a warrant, searches of items with a warrant, and searches of items without a warrant. The definition of probable cause is the same in all four situations. The difference is that in arrests and searches with a warrant, probable cause has been determined by the judge or magistrate, thus the police officer does not have to prove it. In contrast, in arrests and searches without a warrant, the police officer has the burden of establishing probable cause in court if the validity of the arrest or search is later challenged.

The cases in this section contribute to an understanding of the meaning of probable cause. In reality, probable cause is subjective in that its precise meaning may vary from one person to another. In some cases, what constitutes probable cause to one judge or officer may not amount to probable cause to another. It is clear, however, that probable cause is likely to be strengthened by quantity, in addition to quality; meaning that the more articulable reasons an officer has, the greater the likelihood that probable cause will be found by the courts. Police officers are therefore advised to articulate as many specific reasons as they can to justify the arrest or search.

The leading cases briefed in this chapter on probable cause are *Draper v. United States* and *Illinois v. Gates*. A more recent case is *Maryland v. Pringle* (2003), which holds that an officer may make an arrest based on probable cause that a crime has been committed in a motor vehicle and it is unclear who committed it, as long as there is a reasonable inference from the circumstances that the person arrested *could have* committed it.

Draper v. United States
358 U.S. 307 (1959)

CAPSULE: Information from an informant that is corroborated by an officer may be sufficient to provide probable cause for an arrest even if such information is hearsay.

FACTS: A narcotics agent received information from an informant who had previously proven himself reliable, that Draper had gone to Chicago to bring three ounces of heroin back to Denver by train either the morning of September 8 or 9. The informant also gave a detailed physical description of Draper, the clothes he would be wearing, and that he habitually "walked real fast." Based on this information, police officers set up surveillance of all trains coming from Chicago. The morning of September 8 produced no one fitting the informant's description. On the morning of September 9, officers observed an individual, who matched the exact description the informant had supplied, get off of a train from Chicago and begin to walk quickly toward the exit. Officers overtook the suspect and arrested him. Heroin and a syringe were seized in a search incident to the arrest. The informant died prior to the trial and was therefore unable to testify. Draper was convicted of knowingly concealing and transporting drugs.

ISSUE: Can information provided by an informant, which is subsequently corroborated by an officer, provide probable cause for an arrest without a warrant? YES.

SUPREME COURT DECISION: Information received from an informant, which is corroborated by an officer, may be sufficient to provide probable cause for an arrest even though such information is hearsay and would not otherwise be admissible in a criminal trial.

REASON: The informant who provided information to the agent had provided reliable information in the past. When the agent personally verified each element of the informant's detailed description, except the part involving the possession of drugs, he developed probable cause to believe that the rest of the informant's description was true.

CASE SIGNIFICANCE: The evidence from the informant in this case could be considered hearsay, which ordinarily is inadmissible in a criminal trial. The Court said, however, that it could be used to show probable cause for purposes of a search; thus, evidence that may not be admissible in a trial may be used by the police to establish probable cause. This is important because all information from an informant is considered hearsay as the basis for police action, but the police can act on such information as long as it is good enough to establish probable cause. The Court held that there was probable cause in this case because the information came from "one employed for that purpose and whose information had always been found accurate and reliable." The Court added that "it is clear that [the police officer] would have been derelict in his duties had he not pursued it."

Spinelli v. United States
393 U.S. 410 (1969)

CAPSULE: To establish probable cause, an affidavit must meet the two-pronged test in *Aguilar v. Texas*. Failure to do so means that the warrant issued is invalid.

FACTS: The Federal Bureau of Investigation kept track of Spinelli's movements for five days. On four of the five days, Spinelli was seen going into St. Louis, Missouri between 11:00 A.M. and 12:15 P.M. Spinelli was also seen parking his car at a specific apartment complex between 3:30 P.M. and 4:45 P.M., where he was also observed entering an apartment there on at least one occasion. A check of phone records revealed that the phone numbers to the apartment Spinelli was seen entering were the same as those identified by an informant as the phone numbers Spinelli was using in a bookmaking operation. Based on the informant's tip, corroborated by the surveillance of Spinelli, the FBI filed an affidavit and secured a search warrant for the apartment. Spinelli was convicted of interstate travel in aid of racketeering based on evidence gathered pursuant to the warrant.

ISSUE: Did the affidavit by the FBI agent contain probable cause sufficient for the issuance of a search warrant? NO.

SUPREME COURT DECISION: The evidence of surveillance asserted in the affidavit is insufficient to constitute probable cause. Any information obtained from an informant must meet the two-pronged reliability test set down in *Aguilar*. This information did not meet either prong.

REASON: Government law enforcement officials must be allowed to use all available information at their disposal in identifying and apprehending criminal enterprises. "We believe, however, that the 'totality of circumstances' approach taken [here] . . . paints with too broad a brush. . . . There can be no question that the last item [the affidavit] mentioned, detailing the informant's tip, has a fundamental place in this warrant application. Without it, probable cause could not be established. The first two items reflect only innocent-seeming activity and data. . . . Can it be fairly said that the tip, even when certain parts of it have been corroborated by independent sources, is as trustworthy as a tip which would pass *Aguilar*'s tests without independent corroboration?" The Court said no.

CASE SIGNIFICANCE: This case illustrates the types of allegations in an affidavit that are insufficient to establish probable cause. It reiterates the two-pronged *Aguilar* test for probable cause if the information is given by an informant, namely: reliability of the informant and reliability of the informant's information. The *Aguilar* test, however, although still valid, has been modified by a subsequent case—*Illinois v. Gates*, 462 U.S. 213 (1983). Under *Gates*, the two-pronged independent test for establishing probable cause has been replaced by the "totality of circumstances test.

United States v. Chadwick
433 U.S. 1 (1977)

CAPSULE: The warrantless search of a movable container found in a motor vehicle is invalid in the absence of exigent circumstances.

FACTS: Railroad officials in San Diego observed defendants, who fit a "drug courier profile" (developed by the Drug Enforcement Administration), loading an unusually heavy footlocker, which was leaking talcum powder (often used to mask the smell of marijuana), onto a train. The officials notified federal narcotics agents, who had officers waiting in Boston, the destination of the defendants. The officers in Boston did not obtain a search warrant but brought a dog trained to detect marijuana. The dog signaled the presence of marijuana just before the footlocker was lifted into the trunk of the defendant's automobile. Before the trunk's lid could be closed or the car started, police arrested the three suspects. A search incident to the arrest revealed no weapons, but the keys to the footlocker were taken from one of the suspects. The defendants and the footlocker were taken to the Federal Building. One and one-half hours later, agents opened the footlocker without a search warrant or the defendants' consent. Large amounts of marijuana were found in the footlocker. The defendants were charged with and convicted of possession of marijuana with intent to distribute.

ISSUE: May the police, with probable cause but without a warrant, search a movable container found in a public place? NO.

SUPREME COURT DECISION: The warrantless search of a movable container (in this case, a 200-pound footlocker secured by padlocks) found in a public place is invalid, absent exigent circumstances.

REASON: "The factors which diminish the privacy aspects of an automobile do not apply to respondents' footlocker. . . . Unlike an automobile, whose primary function is transportation, luggage is intended as a repository of personal effects . . . [and] a person's expectations of privacy in personal luggage are substantially greater than in an automobile. . . . Nor does the footlocker's mobility justify dispensing with the added protections of the Warrant Clause . . . [Finally] warrantless searches of luggage or other property seized at the time of an arrest cannot be justified as incident to that arrest either if the 'search is remote in time or place from the arrest,' or no exigency exists."

CASE SIGNIFICANCE: In ruling that the warrantless search of the footlocker was unjustified, the Court reaffirmed the general principle that closed packages and containers may not be searched without a warrant. The Court said that "unlike an automobile, whose primary function is transportation, luggage is intended as a repository of personal effects." A footlocker, by virtue of its being a repository of personal effects, enjoys greater protection and its owner has greater expectations of privacy. The difference between the *Chadwick* case and the case of *United States v. Ross*, 456 U.S. 798 (1982) (in which pieces of evidence obtained without a warrant from a paper bag and a leather pouch were held admissible in court) is that *Chadwick* involved a footlocker, which was luggage and only incidentally loaded in a car when the seizure was made; whereas *Ross* involved a paper bag and a leather pouch, both of which were found in the trunk of the car and therefore could be opened by the police without a warrant.

Illinois v. Gates
462 U.S. 213 (1983)

CAPSULE: The two-pronged test for probable cause established in previous cases is abandoned in favor of the "totality of circumstances" test.

FACTS: On May 3, 1978, the Bloomingdale, Illinois Police Department received an anonymous letter containing the following statements: that Gates and his wife were engaged in selling drugs; that the wife would drive her car to Florida on May 3 to be loaded with drugs; that Gates would fly to Florida and drive the car back to Illinois; that the trunk would be loaded with drugs; and that Gates had more than $100,000 worth of drugs in his basement. Acting on the tip, a police officer obtained Gates' address and learned that he had made reservations for a May 5 flight to Florida. Arrangements for surveillance of the flight were made with an agent of the Drug Enforcement Administration. The surveillance disclosed that Gates took the flight, stayed overnight in a hotel room registered in his wife's name, and left the following morning with a woman in a car bearing an Illinois license plate, heading north. A search warrant for Gates' house and automobile was obtained on the basis of the officer's affidavit setting forth the foregoing facts and a copy of the anonymous letter. When Gates arrived at his home, the police were waiting. A search of the house and car revealed marijuana and other contraband. Gates was charged with violating state drug laws and was convicted.

ISSUE: Did the affidavit and the anonymous letter provide sufficient facts to establish probable cause for the issuance of a warrant? YES.

SUPREME COURT DECISION: The two-pronged test established under *Aguilar* and *Spinelli* is abandoned in favor of a "totality of circumstances approach. The task of an issuing magistrate is to make a practical decision whether, given all the circumstances, there is a fair probability that the evidence of a crime will be found in a particular place.

REASON: "Unlike a totality of circumstances analysis, which permits a balanced assessment of the relative weights of all the various indicia of reliability (and unreliability) attending an informant's tip, the 'two-pronged test' has encouraged an excessively technical dissection of informants' tips, with undue attention being focused on isolated issues that cannot sensibly be divorced from the other facts presented to the magistrate."

CASE SIGNIFICANCE: The two-pronged test for establishing probable cause in cases in which information is given by an informant is now replaced with the "totality of circumstances test, making it easier for police officers to establish probable cause for the issuance of a warrant. Under the two-pronged test as enunciated in *Aguilar v. Texas*, 378 U.S. 108 (1964), probable cause based on information obtained from an informant could be established only if the following were present: (1) reliability of the informant, and (2) reliability of informant's information. Both conditions must have been satisfied before probable cause could be established. In contrast, under the "totality of circumstances" test, probable cause may be established if, based on all the circumstances (including hearsay), there is a fair probability that contraband or evidence of crime will be found in a particular place. The *Gates* case still preserves the two-pronged test established in *Aguilar*, but it does not treat the two aspects separately and independently. Instead, the "totality of circumstances approach is used, meaning that whatever deficiencies there may be in one prong can be supplemented or overcome by the other, together with other available evidence.

United States v. Sokolow
490 U.S. 1 (1989)

CAPSULE: The totality of circumstances in this case established a reasonable suspicion that the suspect was transporting illegal drugs hence the investigative stop without a warrant was valid.

FACTS: Sokolow purchased two round-trip tickets for a flight from Honolulu to Miami under an assumed name. He paid for the tickets from a roll of $20 bills that appeared to contain about $4,000. He appeared nervous during the transaction. Neither he nor his companion checked their luggage.

Additional investigation revealed that Sokolow had scheduled a return flight for three days later. Based on these facts, which fit a "drug courier profile (developed by the Drug Enforcement Administration), officers stopped the pair and took them to the DEA office at the airport, where their luggage was examined by a narcotics detection dog. The examination indicated the presence of narcotics in one of Sokolow's bags. Sokolow was arrested and a search warrant was obtained for the bag. No narcotics were found in the bag, but documents indicating involvement in drug trafficking were discovered. Upon a second search with the narcotics detection dog, narcotics were detected in another of Sokolow's bags. Sokolow was released until a search warrant was obtained the next morning. A search of the bag revealed 1,063 grams of cocaine. Sokolow was again arrested and charged with possession with intent to distribute cocaine.

ISSUE: Were the factors matching Sokolow to a "drug courier profile" sufficient to justify his stop and subsequent search without a warrant? YES.

SUPREME COURT DECISION: Taken together, the circumstances in this case establish a reasonable suspicion that the suspect was transporting illegal drugs, and therefore the investigative stop without warrant was valid under the Fourth Amendment.

REASON: Under the decisions in *Terry v. Ohio*, 392 U.S. 1 (1968) and *United States v. Cortez*, 449 U.S. 411 (1981), the totality of circumstances must be evaluated to determine probable cause for an investigative stop. Police officers may stop and briefly detain an individual in order to determine whether they are involved in a criminal activity if the officer has reasonable suspicion, supported by articulable facts, that such activity is occurring.

CASE SIGNIFICANCE: This case addresses the issue of whether the use of "drug courier profiles" is valid under the Fourth Amendment. The Court said that there is nothing wrong with such use in this case because the facts, taken in totality, amounted to reasonable suspicion that criminal conduct was taking place. The Court indicated that whether the facts in this case fit a "profile" was less significant than the fact that, taken together, they establish a reasonable suspicion. In sum, the case appears to indicate that while a drug courier profile might be helpful, the totality of the circumstances is more important in establishing the legality of the stop and subsequent search.

Maryland v. Pringle
540 U.S. 366 (2003)

CAPSULE: An officer may make an arrest based on probable cause that a crime has been committed in a motor vehicle and it is not clear who committed it, as long as there is a reasonable inference from the circumstances that the person arrested could have committed the crime.

FACTS: A police officer stopped a car in which Pringle was riding for speeding. When the driver of the vehicle opened the glove compartment to retrieve the registration, the officer observed a large amount of rolled-up money. After issuing a warning to the driver, the officer sought and received consent to search the vehicle. The search yielded $763 and five plastic bags of cocaine. When none of the passengers in the vehicle admitted to ownership of the drugs and money, the officer arrested all of them and transported them to the police station. Later that morning, Pringle waived his *Miranda* rights and gave an oral and written confession in which he acknowledged that the cocaine belonged to him, that he intended to sell it, and that the other occupants did not know about the drugs. The trial court denied Pringle's motion to suppress his confession as the fruit of an illegal arrest, and he was convicted of possession with the intent to deliver illegal cocaine.

ISSUE: Is the arrest of a passenger in a car valid if there is probable cause to believe, from the standpoint of an objectively reasonable police officer, that the passenger was involved in the crime?

SUPREME COURT DECISION: The arrest of a passenger in a car is valid if the officer had probable cause to believe, based on the circumstances of the case, that the passenger could have committed the crime, even if it was not immediately clear who committed the crime.

REASON: "Maryland law authorizes police officers to execute warrantless arrests, *inter alia*, for felonies committed in an officer's presence or where an officer has probable cause to believe that a felony has been committed or is being committed in the officer's presence. . . . It is uncontested in the present case that the officer, upon recovering five glassine baggies containing the suspected cocaine, had probable cause to believe a felony had been committed. The sole question is whether the officer had probable cause to believe that Pringle committed the crime. . . . [W]e think it an entirely reasonable inference from these facts that any or all three of the occupants had knowledge of, and exercised dominion and control over, the cocaine. Thus a reasonable officer could conclude that there was probable cause to believe Pringle committed the crime of possession of cocaine, either solely or jointly."

CASE SIGNIFICANCE: This case addresses an issue police officers face when making vehicle arrests: Whether the officer may arrest all the passengers of the vehicle if there is probable cause to believe one or more of them is involved in the crime. The Court said yes, but based on the specific circumstances of the case. Here, the officer validly searched and seized a rolled-up case containing $763 and five glassine baggies of cocaine from between the backseat armrest and the back seat of the car. The three passengers denied ownership of the cocaine and money; all three were arrested. Pringle was a passenger in the front seat at the time the money and cocaine were discovered. (Pringle later "gave an oral and written confession in which he acknowledged that the cocaine belonged to him, that he and his friends were going to a party, and that he intended to sell the cocaine or use it for sex. But this confession was made after the arrest and therefore could not help determine probable cause.) When prosecuted for and convicted of possession with intent to distribute cocaine and possession of cocaine, he appealed, saying his arrest was illegal because there was no probable cause to arrest him. The Court concluded that Pringle's arrest was valid because probable cause was present at the time of arrest. The standard the Court used was: "To determine whether an officer had probable cause to make an arrest, a court must examine the events leading up to the arrest," and then make a decision. The presence of probable cause is determined by asking "whether . . . viewed from the standpoint of an objectively reasonable police officer," the facts amounted to probable cause. Given the circumstances of this case, the Court said, "it is an entirely reasonable inference from the facts here that any or all of the car occupants had knowledge of, and exercised dominion and control over, the cocaine . . . either solely or jointly." This case does not give police officers blanket authority to arrest passengers in a car. Instead, each case is different and must be judged based on whether "viewed from the standpoint of an objectively reasonable police officer," the circumstances amounted to probable cause. Given the facts of this case, the Court concluded that probable cause was a reasonable inference. What is a "reasonable inference" that could establish probable cause is ultimately for the courts to decide based on a case-by-case basis.

The Exclusionary Rule   2

Introduction

The exclusionary rule provides that any evidence obtained by the government in violation of the Fourth Amendment right against unreasonable searches and seizures is not admissible in a court of law. It is a judge-made rule whose purpose is to deter police misconduct; the assumption being that, if evidence obtained by the police in violation of the Fourth Amendment cannot be used in court, police misconduct will be minimized.

Evidence obtained by the police in violation of other rights under the Bill of Rights (such as the privilege against self-incrimination under the Fifth Amendment, or the right to counsel under the Sixth Amendment) is not admissible in court either, but that exclusion does not come under the exclusionary rule; rather, the evidence is excluded based on a violation of the constitutional right to due process. The exclusionary rule, therefore, is of limited application in that it applies only in cases involving violations of the prohibition against unreasonable searches and seizures under the Fourth Amendment.

The first exclusionary rule case decided by the United States Supreme Court was *Boyd v. United States* (116 U.S. 616) in 1886. In that case, the Court held that the forced disclosure of papers amounting to evidence of a crime violated the Fourth Amendment right of the suspect and, therefore, the evidence could not be used in court. In 1914, in *Weeks v. United States* (32 U.S. 383), the Court held that evidence illegally obtained by federal officers could not be used in federal criminal prosecutions. *Mapp v. Ohio*, 467 U.S. 643 (1961) is the leading and best-known case on the exclusionary rule. In *Mapp*, the Court held that the exclusionary rule also applied to state criminal prosecutions, thus extending the exclusionary rule to all federal and state criminal proceedings.

There are many exceptions to the exclusionary rule, as the cases briefed here show. The common theme in these cases is that the misconduct, mistake, or error was not committed by the police but by other government officials—in some cases judges, the legislature, or a court clerk. The evidence obtained can be used in court because the exclusionary rule was meant to deter police misconduct, not the misconduct of other government officials.

Although originally controversial, the exclusionary rule has been accepted and applied by the courts and is now an accepted part of policing. The United States Supreme Court continues to define exceptions, but the exclusionary rule is here to stay as a form of protection against violations by the police of the public's right against unreasonable searches and seizures.

The leading cases briefed in this chapter on the exclusionary rule are *Mapp v. Ohio* and *Weeks v. United States*.

Weeks v. United States
232 U.S. 383 (1914)

CAPSULE: Evidence illegally seized by federal law enforcement officers is not admissible in a federal criminal prosecution.

FACTS: Weeks was arrested for using the mail to transport tickets for a lottery. Other officers searched Weeks' home without a warrant and seized various articles and papers that were then turned over to the United States Marshals Service. Later in the day, police officers returned with a Marshal and again searched Weeks' home without a warrant and seized letters and other articles. Weeks was charged with and convicted of unlawful use of the mail.

ISSUE: Is evidence illegally obtained by federal law enforcement officers admissible in court? NO.

SUPREME COURT DECISION: Evidence illegally seized by federal law enforcement officers is not admissible in federal criminal prosecutions.

REASON: The Fourth Amendment freedom from unreasonable searches and seizures applies ". . . to all invasions on the part of the government and its employees of the sanctity of a man's home and the privacies of life. It is not the breaking of his doors and the rummaging of his drawers that constitutes the essence of the offense; but it is the invasion of his indefeasible right of personal security, personal liberty and private property."

CASE SIGNIFICANCE: This decision excluded illegally obtained evidence from use in federal prosecutions. This rule was extended to state criminal prosecutions in 1961 in *Mapp v. Ohio*, 367 U.S. 643 (1961), making illegally obtained evidence inadmissible in both state and federal courts. It is interesting to note that from 1914 to 1960, federal courts admitted evidence of a federal crime if it was obtained illegally by state officers, as long as there was no connivance with federal officers. This questionable practice was known as the "silver platter doctrine." In 1960, the Court rejected the "silver platter doctrine" (*Elkins v. United States*, 364 U.S. 206), holding that the Fourth Amendment prohibited the use of illegally obtained evidence in federal prosecutions whether it was obtained by federal or state officers.

Rochin v. California
342 U.S. 165 (1952)

CAPSULE: Some searches are so "shocking to the conscience" that they require exclusion of the evidence seized based on due process.

FACTS: Having information that Rochin was selling narcotics, police officers entered his home and forced their way into the bedroom. When asked about two capsules lying beside the bed, Rochin put them in his mouth. After an unsuccessful attempt to recover them by force, the officers took Rochin to the hospital where his stomach was pumped. Two capsules containing morphine were recovered. A motion to suppress this evidence was denied and Rochin was convicted in a California state court of possession of morphine.

ISSUE: Were the capsules recovered as a result of pumping Rochin's stomach admissible as evidence in court? NO.

SUPREME COURT DECISION: Although searches by state law enforcement officers are not governed by the exclusionary rule, some searches are so "shocking to the conscience" as to require exclusion of the evidence seized based on the due process (fundamental fairness) clause of the Constitution. These cases are limited to acts of coercion, violence, and brutality.

REASON: ". . . [T]he proceedings by which this conviction was obtained do more than offend some fastidious squeamishness or private sentimentalism about combating crime too energetically. This is conduct that shocks the conscience. Illegally breaking into the privacy of the petitioner, the struggle to open his mouth and remove what was there, the forcible extraction of his stomach's contents—this course of proceeding by agents of the government to obtain evidence is bound to offend even hardened sensibilities. They are methods too close to the rack and screw to permit of constitutional differentiation."

CASE SIGNIFICANCE: This case was decided prior to the extension of the exclusionary rule to the states in 1961. In this state prosecution, however, the Court decided that the evidence obtained could not be used in court, not because of the exclusionary rule, but because the conduct of the police officers was shocking and therefore violated Rochin's right to due process guaranteed by the Fourteenth Amendment. If the case were to be decided today, the evidence would be excluded under the exclusionary rule, not under the due process clause.

Mapp v. Ohio
367 U.S. 643 (1961)

CAPSULE: The exclusionary rule applies to all state criminal proceedings.

FACTS: Mapp was convicted of possession of lewd and lascivious books, pictures, and photographs in violation of Ohio law. Three Cleveland police officers went to Mapp's residence based on information that a person who was wanted in connection with a recent bombing was hiding out in her home. The officers knocked on the door and demanded entrance, but Mapp, telephoning her attorney, refused to admit them without a warrant. The officers again sought entrance three hours later, after the arrival of more police. When Mapp did not respond, the officers broke the door open. Mapp's attorney arrived but was denied access to his client. Mapp demanded to see the search warrant the police claimed to possess. When a paper supposed to be the warrant was held up by one of the officers, Mapp grabbed the paper and placed it in her bosom. A struggle ensued and the paper was recovered after Mapp was handcuffed for being belligerent. A search of the house produced a trunk that contained obscene materials. The materials were admitted into evidence at the trial and Mapp was convicted of possession of obscene materials.

ISSUE: Is evidence obtained in violation of the Fourth Amendment protection from unreasonable searches and seizures admissible in state criminal prosecutions? NO.

SUPREME COURT DECISION: The exclusionary rule, applicable in federal cases, which prohibits the use of evidence obtained as a result of unreasonable searches and seizures also applies to state criminal proceedings.

REASON: "Since the Fourth Amendment's right of privacy has been declared enforceable against the States through the Due Process Clause of the Fourteenth [Amendment], it is enforceable against them by the same sanction of exclusion as is used against the Federal Government. Were it otherwise, then just as without the *Weeks* rule the assurance against unreasonable searches and seizures would be 'a form of words,' valueless and undeserving of mention in a perpetual charter of inestimable human liberties, so too, without that rule the freedom from state invasions of privacy would be . . . ephemeral . . ."

CASE SIGNIFICANCE: *Mapp* is significant because the Court held that the exclusionary rule was thereafter to be applied to all states, thus forbidding both state and federal courts from accepting evidence obtained in violation of the constitutional protection against unreasonable searches and seizures. In the mind of the Court, the facts in *Mapp* illustrate what can happen if police conduct is not restricted. *Mapp* was therefore an ideal case for the Court to use in settling an issue that had to be addressed: whether the exclusionary rule should apply to state criminal proceedings. The Court answered with a definite yes.

Wong Sun v. United States
371 U.S. 471 (1963)

CAPSULE: Evidence obtained as a result of illegal acts by the police must be excluded. In addition, the "fruit of the poisonous tree of that illegal act must also be excluded. Evidence that has been purged of the primary taint, however, is admissible.

FACTS: Federal narcotics agents arrested Hom Way and found heroin in his possession. Although Way had not been an informant before, the agents went to "Oye's Laundry" based upon his statement that he had bought the heroin from "Blackie Toy," who owned the laundry. At the laundry, agent Wong got James Wah Toy to open the door by telling him that he was calling for dry cleaning. Upon announcing that he was a federal agent, Toy slammed the door and started running. The agents then broke open the door and began to chase Toy. Toy was placed under arrest in his bedroom. A search of the premises uncovered no drugs. There was nothing to link Toy to "Blackie Toy." Upon interrogation, he stated that he had not been selling narcotics but knew that an individual named Johnny had. He told the officers where Johnny lived, and described the bedroom where the heroin was kept and where he had smoked some of the heroin the night before. Based on this information, the agents went to the home of Johnny Yee and found him in possession of an ounce of heroin. Upon interrogation, Yee stated that he had bought the heroin from Toy and an individual named "Sea Dog." Further questioning of Toy revealed that "Sea Dog's" name was Wong Sun. Toy then took the agents to a multifamily dwelling where Wong Sun lived. After identifying himself, agent Wong was admitted by Wong Sun's wife who said he was in the back, asleep. Wong Sun was arrested by the agents. A search pursuant to the arrest found no narcotics. Each of the offenders was arraigned and released on his own recognizance. A few days later, Toy, Yee, and Wong Sun were interrogated again and written statements were made. Neither Toy nor Wong Sun signed their statements, but Wong Sun admitted to the accuracy of his statement. At the trial, the government's evidence consisted of: (1) the statements made by Toy at the time of his arrest; (2) the heroin taken from Yee; (3) Toy's pretrial statement; and (4) Wong Sun's pretrial statement. Wong Sun and Toy were convicted of transportation and concealment of heroin.

ISSUES: There were a number of issues in this case, but the important issues related to the exclusionary rule are:

1. Were the statements made by Toy after an unlawful arrest admissible? NO.
2. Were the narcotics taken from Yee after an unlawful arrest admissible? NO.
3. Was Wong Sun's statement admissible? YES.

SUPREME COURT DECISION: Statements or evidence obtained indirectly as a result of an unlawful arrest or search are not admissible in court because they are "tainted fruit of the poisonous tree." A suspect's intervening act of free will, however, breaks the chain of illegality, purges the evidence of the taint, and makes the evidence admissible.

REASON: The exclusionary rule has traditionally barred from trial physical, tangible materials obtained either during or as a direct result of an unlawful invasion. ". . . Thus, verbal evidence which derives so immediately from an unlawful entry and an unauthorized arrest as the officers' action in the present case is no less the 'fruit' of official illegality than the more common tangible fruits of the unwarranted intrusion . . ."

"We turn now to the case of . . . Wong Sun. We have no occasion to disagree with the finding of the Court of Appeals that his arrest, also, was without probable cause or reasonable grounds. For Wong Sun's unsigned confession was not the fruit of that arrest, and was therefore properly admitted at trial. On the evidence that Wong Sun had been released on his own recognizance after a lawful arraignment, and had returned voluntarily several days later to make the statement, we hold that the connection between the arrest and the statement had 'become so attenuated as to dissipate the taint.' "

CASE SIGNIFICANCE: This case addresses the "tainted fruit of the poisonous tree" aspect of the exclusionary rule. The exclusionary rule provides that evidence obtained in violation of the Fourth Amendment prohibition against unreasonable searches and seizures is not admissible in a court of law. The rule goes beyond that, however, and also says that any other evidence obtained directly or indirectly as a result of the illegal behavior is not admissible either. Hence, once an illegal act has been proved, any evidence obtained either directly or indirectly cannot be admitted in court either under the concept of the original illegality or as the "tainted fruit."

This case also carves out an exception to the exclusionary rule: the "purged taint" exception. What it says is that, despite the initial illegality, the evidence may nonetheless be admissible if it has been purged of the initial taint. An example is this case, in which the statement of Wong Sun, which initially was the product of unlawful behavior by the agents, was nonetheless admitted because of subsequent events. What happened was that after Wong Sun was released on his own recognizance and after lawful arraignment, he returned several days later and made a statement that was then admitted by the trial court. The Court said that the voluntary return by Wong Sun purged the evidence of the initial taint and therefore made the statement admissible.

United States v. Crews
445 U.S. 463 (1980)

CAPSULE: A pretrial identification is illegal if the arrest is illegal; however, an in-court identification is admissible if the victim's recollections are independent of the police misconduct.

FACTS: Immediately after being assaulted and robbed at gunpoint, the victim notified the police and gave them a full description of her assailant. Several days later, a man matching the description was seen by police near the scene of the crime. After an attempt to photograph him failed, he was taken to the police station, questioned briefly, photographed, and released. The victim identified the photograph as that of her assailant. Crews was then taken into custody and identified by the victim in a lineup. On a pretrial motion to suppress, the court ruled that the initial detention constituted an arrest without probable cause and that the photographs and lineup identifications were not admissible. The court, however, ruled that the courtroom identification by the victim was admissible. Crews was convicted of armed robbery.

ISSUE: Is the in-court identification of a suspect by a witness, when the identification is the result of a prior illegal arrest, admissible as evidence? YES.

SUPREME COURT DECISION: The pretrial identification of the suspect in a photograph and lineup are not admissible as evidence due to the illegal arrest. The in-court identification, however, is admissible because the victim's recollections were independent of the police misconduct.

REASON: The courtroom identification by the victim was wholly independent of any police misconduct. Aside from the fact that Crews was present in the courtroom, partially as the result of the illegal arrest, the prosecutor's case was established from the courtroom identification by the victim, which had nothing to do with the arrest. The conviction, independently established, was legal.

CASE SIGNIFICANCE: This case introduced the doctrine of "independent untainted source," an exception to the exclusionary rule. Under this exception, the police may use evidence related to an illegal search as long as it is not connected to the illegality. The Court said that the initial illegality (in this case the illegal detention of the suspect) could not deprive prosecutors of the opportunity to prove the defendant's guilt through the introduction of evidence wholly untainted by police misconduct. For example, a 14-year-old girl was found in the defendant's apartment during an illegal search. The girl's testimony that the defendant had sex with her was admissible because she was an independent source that predated the search of the apartment. Prior to the search, the girl's parents had reported her missing, and a police informant had already located her in the defendant's apartment (*State v. O'Bremski*, 70 Wash. 2d 425 [1967]). Note, however, that if the evidence has been tainted by police misconduct, such evidence cannot be admitted in court (*Wong Sun v. United States*, 371 U.S. 471 [1963]).

Nix v. Williams
467 U.S. 431 (1984)

CAPSULE: Illegally obtained evidence may be admissible if the police can prove that they would have discovered the evidence anyway through lawful means.

FACTS: On December 24, a 10-year-old girl disappeared from a YMCA building in Des Moines, Iowa. A short time later, Williams was seen leaving the YMCA with a large bundle wrapped in a blanket. A 14-year-old boy who helped him carry the bundle reported that he had seen "two legs in it and they were skinny and white." William's car was found the next day, 160 miles east of Des Moines. Items of clothing belonging to the missing child and a blanket like the one used to wrap the bundle were found at a rest stop between the YMCA in Des Moines and where the car was found. Assuming that the girl's body could be found between the YMCA and the car, a massive search was conducted. Meanwhile, Williams was arrested by police in a town near where the car was found and was arraigned. Williams' counsel was informed that Williams would be returned to Des Moines without being interrogated. During the trip, an officer began a conversation with Williams in which he said the girl should be given a Christian burial before a snowstorm which might prevent the body from being found. As Williams and the officer neared the town where the body was hidden, Williams agreed to take the officer to the child's body. The body was found about two miles from one of the search teams. At the trial, a motion to suppress the evidence was denied and Williams was convicted of first degree murder. Williams sought release on *habeas corpus* in U.S. District Court. That court ruled that the evidence had been wrongly admitted at Williams' trial. At his second trial, the prosecutor did not offer Williams' statements into evidence and did not seek to show that Williams had led the police to the body. The trial court ruled that the state had proved that, even if Williams had not led the police to the body, it would have been found by the searchers anyway. Williams was again convicted of murder.

ISSUE: Was the evidence (the body) admissible in court on the theory that the body would ultimately have been discovered anyway because of the ongoing search? YES.

SUPREME COURT DECISION: Evidence that is obtained illegally may be admissible if the police can prove that they would have discovered the evidence anyway through lawful means.

REASON: "The independent source doctrine teaches us that the interest of society in deterring unlawful police conduct and the public interest in having juries receive all probative evidence of a crime are properly balanced by putting the police in the same, not a worse, position than they would have been in if no police error or misconduct had occurred."

CASE SIGNIFICANCE: This case illustrates the "inevitable discovery exception to the exclusionary rule. "Fruit of the poisonous tree" is evidence obtained indirectly as a result of illegal police behavior (such as the illegal discovery of a map that tells where contraband is hidden). This evidence is usually inadmissible due to the illegality of police actions. The exception set out in this case states that evidence that is the "fruit of the poisonous tree is admissible if the police can prove that they would inevitably have discovered the evidence anyway by lawful means. In this case, no *Miranda* warnings were given to the suspect before he confessed; hence, the evidence obtained was excluded during the first trial. But because the evidence would have been discovered anyway as a result of the continued search, the Court said that the evidence could be admitted.

United States v. Leon
468 U.S. 897 (1984)

CAPSULE: The exclusionary rule allows the use of evidence obtained by officers who are acting in reasonable reliance on a search warrant that is later declared invalid.

FACTS: Acting on the basis of information from a confidential informant, officers initiated a drug trafficking investigation. Based on an affidavit summarizing the police officer's observation, a search warrant was prepared. The warrant was reviewed by three Deputy District Attorneys and issued by a state court judge. Ensuing searches produced large quantities of drugs. Leon was indicted on drug charges. Motions to suppress the evidence were granted in part because the affidavit was insufficient to establish probable cause. The court rejected the notion of good faith of the officer and acquitted the defendants.

ISSUE: Is evidence obtained as the result of a search conducted pursuant to a warrant that was issued by a neutral and detached magistrate admissible in court if the warrant is ultimately found invalid through no fault of the police officer? YES.

SUPREME COURT DECISION: The Fourth Amendment's exclusionary rule allows the use of evidence obtained by officers acting in reasonable reliance on a search warrant issued by a neutral and detached magistrate that is ultimately found invalid.

REASON: "In the ordinary case, an officer cannot be expected to question the magistrate's probable cause determination or his judgment that the form of the warrant is technically sufficient. '[O]nce the warrant issues, there is literally nothing more the policeman can do in seeking to comply with the law.' Penalizing the officer for the magistrate's error, rather than his own, cannot logically contribute to the deterrence of Fourth Amendment violations."

CASE SIGNIFICANCE: This case, together with *Massachusetts v. Sheppard*, 468 U.S. 981 (1984), which was decided on the same day, are arguably the most important cases decided on the exclusionary rule since *Mapp v. Ohio*, 367 U.S. 643 (1961). They represent a significant, although narrow, exception to that doctrine. In these two cases, the Court said that there were objectively reasonable grounds for the officers' mistaken belief that the warrants authorized the searches. The officers took every step that could reasonably have been taken to ensure that the warrants were valid. The difference between the *Leon* and *Sheppard* cases is that, in *Sheppard*, the issue was improper use of a search warrant form (the form used was used in another district to search for controlled substances, the judge telling the detective who filed the form that the necessary changes would be made by the judge), whereas in *Leon* the issue was the use of a questionable informant and stale information. The cases are similar, however, in that the mistakes were made by the judges, not the police. The Court said that the evidence in both cases was admissible because the judge, not the police, erred and the exclusionary rule is designed to control the conduct of the police, not the conduct of judges.

Massachusetts v. Sheppard
468 U.S. 981 (1984)

CAPSULE: Evidence obtained as a result of a search in which the police acted in reliance on a search warrant that was subsequently declared invalid by the court is admissible as an exception to the exclusionary rule.

FACTS: Based on evidence gathered in a homicide investigation, a police officer drafted an affidavit to support an application for a search warrant and an arrest warrant. The affidavit was reviewed and approved by the District Attorney. Because it was Sunday, the officer had difficulty finding a warrant application form. The officer ultimately found a used search warrant authorizing a search for controlled substances. After making some changes, the officer presented the warrant to a judge at his residence. The judge was informed that the warrant might need further changes. Concluding that the affidavit established probable cause for the search, the judge made some corrections and signed the warrant. He then returned the warrant to the officer with the assurance that it was sufficient authority to carry out the search. The ensuing search was limited to the items listed in the affidavit. Several pieces of incriminating evidence were found and Sheppard was arrested. At a pretrial motion to suppress, the judge ruled that the warrant was invalid, but the evidence was admitted based on the officer's good faith in executing what he believed to be a valid warrant. Sheppard was convicted of first degree murder.

ISSUE: Is evidence that is obtained from a search that is based on a warrant that is later declared invalid because of error by the issuing magistrate admissible in court? YES.

SUPREME COURT DECISION: Evidence obtained by the police acting in good faith, based on a search warrant that was issued by a neutral and detached magistrate, but that was later found to be invalid, is admissible in court as an exception to the exclusionary rule.

REASON: "Having already decided [in *Leon*] that the exclusionary rule should not be applied when the officer conducting the search acted in objectively reasonable reliance on a warrant issued by a detached and neutral magistrate that subsequently is determined to be invalid, the sole issue before us in this case is whether the officers reasonably believed that the search they conducted was authorized by a valid warrant. There is no dispute that the officers believed that the warrant authorized the search that they conducted. Thus, the only question is whether there was an objectively reasonable basis for the officers' mistaken belief. . . . The officers in this case took every step that could reasonably be expected of them. . . . [A] reasonable officer would have concluded, as O'Malley did, that the warrant authorized a search for the materials outlined in the affidavit. . . . Sheppard contends that since O'Malley knew the warrant form was defective, he should have examined it to make sure that the necessary changes had been made. However, that argument is based on the premise that O'Malley had a duty to disregard the judge's assurances that the requested search would be authorized and the necessary changes would be made. . . . [W]e refuse to rule that an officer is required to disbelieve a judge who has just advised him, by word and by action, that the warrant he possesses authorizes him to conduct the search he has requested."

CASE SIGNIFICANCE: As indicated in the *Leon* case, above, *Sheppard* was the second case involving the exclusionary rule decided by the Court on the same day. These cases dealt with incidents in which mistakes were made, not by the police, but by the magistrates who issued the warrants. Both cases carved out a significant exception to the exclusionary rule: that evidence is admissible if the mistake was made by a magistrate rather than by the police. Note, however, that this is a very narrow "good faith" exception. The police acted "in good faith" in these cases; but it cannot be said that evidence is admissible every time the police act "in good faith." For example, if the police acted illegally in obtaining evidence, they cannot later claim to have acted in good faith in arguing for the admissibility of the evidence obtained, even if they actually did act in good faith and can prove it. This is because the error was committed by the police, not a third person. In the *Sheppard* case, the error was committed by the magistrate, not the police This is an important difference.

Murray v. United States
487 U.S. 533 (1988)

CAPSULE: The exclusionary rule allows the use of evidence obtained by officers who act in reasonable reliance on a search warrant that is later declared invalid.

FACTS: Suspecting illegal drug activities, federal agents followed Murray and several co-conspirators. At one point, Murray drove a truck and another person drove a camper into a warehouse. Twenty minutes later, when the two emerged from the warehouse, law enforcement agents could see a tractor-trailer bearing a long, dark container. The truck and camper were later turned over to other drivers who were arrested and found in possession of marijuana.

Upon receiving this information, the law enforcement agents returned to the warehouse, without a warrant, and forced entry. The warehouse was unoccupied but the agents observed, in plain view, several burlap-wrapped bales of marijuana. The law enforcement agents left the warehouse without disturbing the bales and did not reenter until they had a valid search warrant. In applying for the warrant, the agents did not mention the forced entry into the warehouse and did not rely on any information obtained during that search. After obtaining the warrant, law enforcement agents returned to the warehouse and seized numerous bales of marijuana and a notebook listing the destinations of the bales. Murray was arrested and convicted of conspiracy to possess and distribute illegal drugs.

ISSUE: Is evidence first observed in an illegal entry by officers but subsequently seized through a valid, independent, search warrant admissible in court? YES.

SUPREME COURT DECISION: Even if the police illegally enter private property, evidence initially discovered during that illegal entry may be admissible in court if it is later discovered during a valid search that is wholly unrelated to the illegal entry.

REASON: The Court reasoned that the evidence ought not to have been excluded just because of unrelated illegal conduct by the police. If probable cause for a search warrant can be established apart from any illegal activity by the police, the evidence obtained in the subsequent search should be admissible.

CASE SIGNIFICANCE: This case illustrates the "independent source" exception to the exclusionary rule. In this case, the police illegally entered the warehouse and discovered bales of marijuana. The Court said that the marijuana would be admissible if the officers later searched the warehouse pursuant to a valid warrant that was issued based on information that was not obtained during the illegal entry. An initial illegal entry, therefore, does not automatically exclude the evidence if the evidence is not seized at the time of the illegal entry, but pursuant to a valid warrant that is later obtained without relying on information obtained during the illegal entry.

Minnesota v. Olson
495 U.S. 91 (1989)

CAPSULE: Warrantless nonconsensual entry of a residence by police to arrest an overnight guest violates the Fourth Amendment.

FACTS: The police suspected Olson of being the driver of the getaway car involved in a robbery-murder. Based on an anonymous tip, the police surrounded the home of two women with whom they believed Olson had been staying as a guest. A detective then telephoned the home and told one of the women that Olson should come outside, whereupon he heard a male voice saying, "Tell them I left." When the woman told the detective this, he ordered the police to enter. Without permission or a search warrant, and with their weapons drawn, the police entered the house and arrested Olson, who was hiding in a closet. Based on an incriminating statement made by Olson, he was convicted of murder, armed robbery, and assault.

ISSUE: Is the Fourth Amendment violated when the police make a warrantless, nonconsensual entry and arrest without exigent (emergency) circumstances? YES.

SUPREME COURT DECISION: The warrantless non-consensual entry by the police of a residence to arrest an overnight guest violates the Fourth Amendment, unless justified by exigent circumstances.

REASON: ". . . [W]e think that society recognizes that a houseguest has a legitimate expectation of privacy in his host's home." An overnight guest ". . . seeks shelter in another's home precisely because it provides him with privacy, a place where he and his possessions will not be disturbed by anyone except his host and those his host allows inside. . . . The houseguest is there with the permission of his host, who is willing to share his house and his privacy with the guest. . . . The host may admit or exclude from the house as he prefers, but it is unlikely that he will admit someone who wants to see or meet with the guest over the objection of the guest." Hosts, therefore, ". . . will more likely than not respect the privacy interests of their guests, who are entitled to a legitimate expectation of privacy despite the fact that they have no legal interest in the premises and do not have the legal authority to determine who may or may not enter the household." Because Olson's ". . . expectation of privacy in the host's home was rooted in 'understandings that are recognized and permitted by society,' it was legitimate, and respondent can claim the protection of the Fourth Amendment."

CASE SIGNIFICANCE: This case establishes the principle that the arrest of a suspect in another person's home requires a warrant for entry into the home, except: (1) if exigent circumstances are present, or (2) if consent is given by the owner of the house. In this case, suspect Olson was an overnight guest in the home. There was no reason to believe that he would flee the premises, hence exigent circumstances were not deemed present. The Court ruled that the police should have obtained a search warrant to enable them to enter the house legally. An overnight guest has an expectation of privacy that society is prepared to recognize as reasonable, hence a warrant should have been obtained. The statement made after his arrest was not admissible in court.

Arizona v. Evans
514 U.S. 1 (1995)

CAPSULE: The exclusionary rule does not require suppression of evidence seized in violation of the Fourth Amendment where the erroneous information resulted from clerical errors of court employees.

FACTS: Police officers saw Evans going the wrong way on a one-way street in front of the police station. When Evans was stopped, officers determined that his driver's license had been suspended. When Evans' name was entered into a computer data terminal in the officer's patrol car, it indicated that there was an outstanding misdemeanor warrant for Evans' arrest. While being handcuffed, Evans dropped a hand-rolled cigarette that turned out to be marijuana. A search of Evans' car revealed more marijuana under the passenger's seat. At trial, Evans moved to suppress the evidence as fruit of an unlawful arrest because the arrest warrant for the misdemeanor had been quashed 17 days prior to his arrest but was not entered into the computer due to a clerical error of a court employee. Evans also argued that the good faith exception to the exclusionary rule was inapplicable in this case. These motions were denied and Evans was convicted.

ISSUE: Does the exclusionary rule require suppression of evidence that is seized by an officer acting in reliance on erroneous information resulting from clerical errors of court employees? NO.

SUPREME COURT DECISION: "The exclusionary rule does not require suppression of evidence seized in violation of the Fourth Amendment where the erroneous information resulted from clerical errors of court employees."

REASON: "The exclusionary rule operates as a judicially created remedy designed to safeguard against future violations [by police officers] of Fourth Amendment rights through the rule's deterrent effect." The application of the exclusionary rule was for police officers rather than court employees (see *United States v. Leon*, 468 U.S. 897 [1974]). The Court found ". . . no sound reason to apply the exclusionary rule as a means of deterring misconduct on the part of judicial officers" because application of the exclusionary rule to court personnel could not be expected to alter the behavior of the arresting officer. Furthermore "[t]here [was] no indication that the arresting officer was not acting objectively reasonably when he relied upon the police computer record. Application of the *Leon* framework supports a categorical exception to the exclusionary rule for clerical errors of court employees."

CASE SIGNIFICANCE: This case extends an exception to the exclusionary rule when an error is committed by court employees rather than the police. The exclusionary rule was fashioned to deter police misconduct, hence the Court refused to apply it to cases in which the error was not made by the police. Previous cases have held that if the error is made by a magistrate (as in *Massachusetts v. Sheppard* and *United States v. Leon*), or by the legislature (as in *Illinois v. Krull*), the exclusionary rule does not apply. The theme in these cases is that if the error is not committed by the police, then the exclusionary rule should not apply because it was meant to control the behavior of the police. *Evans*, therefore, is consistent with the Court's holdings in previous cases and came as no surprise. The unanswered question is whether error by any public officer other than the police would be an addition to this rule. The dissent in *Evans* argued that the Fourth Amendment prohibition against unreasonable searches and seizures applies to the conduct of *all government officers*, not just the police. The majority in *Evans* disagreed, preferring instead to focus on the original purpose of the exclusionary rule—which is to control police conduct.

Stop and Frisk

3

Introduction

"Stop and frisk" is a term in policing that is best understood if construed as two separate acts rather than one continuous act. A stop is justified if the police have "reasonable suspicion" (less than probable cause) that an individual has committed or is about to commit a crime. The police then ask questions to determine whether the stop is justified based on reasonable suspicion. If the stop is not substantiated, the suspect should be released.

A frisk after a stop is valid if done for one purpose and one purpose only: officer protection. Any frisk conducted for any other purpose becomes a "fishing expedition" and is invalid. A valid stop does not always lead to a valid frisk, unless the officer fears for his or her safety. A frisk should not and cannot be used to look for evidence of a crime, unless that crime is the possession of a weapon that constitutes a danger to the officer.

The leading case on stop and frisk is *Terry v. Ohio*, 392 U.S. 1 (1968). In that case, the Supreme Court approved the practice in many states of the police stopping people without probable cause and then asking them questions to determine whether they have committed or are about to commit a crime. The Court held that the police can do this if they have "reasonable suspicion," and that a frisk may follow if there is fear for officer safety. There is no fixed time limit set for the length of an investigatory stop. Instead, it is decided on a case-by-case basis, using reasonableness as the standard. Stops cannot be for any time longer than is necessary for the police to ascertain whether a crime has taken place or is about to take place. A criminal profile alone does not constitute reasonable suspicion for a valid stop; instead, it is merely one factor to be considered in determining whether reasonable suspicion exists.

The extent of a frisk is strictly limited to a pat-down for weapons. Anything more than a pat-down is considered going beyond the allowable limits of a frisk. What starts as a frisk, however, may quickly turn into an arrest if probable cause develops. The suspect can then be subjected to a body search. In this case, the situation will have changed from a stop and frisk to an arrest based on probable cause.

More recent Court decisions hold that an anonymous tip that a person is carrying a gun is not, without more, sufficient to justify a stop and frisk. A more important recent case holds that presence in a high-crime area, combined with an unprovoked flight upon observing police officers, gives officers sufficient grounds to investigate further to determine whether criminal activity is about to take place. This is important because the police often face this situation in their work—individuals fleeing upon seeing the police. Flight alone will not likely justify a stop, but flight plus other circumstances, such as being in a high-crime area, establishes reasonable suspicion that will justify a stop. The most recent Supreme Court decision on stop and frisk holds that the determination of whether or not reasonable suspicion exists must be based on a totality of the circumstances rather than on individual factors that, taken individually, might not justify a legal stop.

The leading cases on stop and frisk are: *Terry v. Ohio, United States v. Sharpe*, and the more recent cases—*Illinois v. Wardlow* and *United States v. Arvizu*. A recently decided case, *Hiibel v. Sixth Judicial District Court of Nevada* (2004), holds that the Fourth Amendment allows officers, pursuant to a stop and frisk, to require a person to provide his or her name and that the person may be arrested for refusing to comply.

Terry v. Ohio
392 U.S. 1 (1968)

CAPSULE: A stop and frisk based on reasonable suspicion is valid.

FACTS: A plainclothes officer with 39 years of experience, 35 years of which were as a detective and 30 years of which were in the same patrol area, observed two men standing on a street corner. It appeared that the two men were "casing" a store because each walked up and down the street, peering into the store window, and then both returned to the corner to confer. At one point the two men were joined by a third man, who talked to them and then left swiftly. After the officer observed the two rejoining the same third man a couple of blocks away, he approached them, identified himself, and asked for identification. Receiving a mumbled response, the officer patted down the outside clothing of the men. The officer retrieved weapons from Terry and one other man. Terry and the other man were charged with and convicted of carrying concealed weapons.

ISSUE: Is "stop and frisk" valid under the Fourth Amendment? YES.

SUPREME COURT DECISION: The police have the authority to detain a person for questioning even without probable cause to believe that the person has committed a crime. Such an investigatory stop does not constitute an arrest and is permissible when prompted by both the observation of unusual conduct leading to a reasonable suspicion that criminal activity may be afoot and the ability to point to specific and articulable facts to justify the suspicion. Subsequently, an officer may frisk a person if the officer reasonably suspects that he or she is in danger.

REASON: ". . . [T]he police should be allowed to 'stop' a person and detain him briefly for questioning upon suspicion that he may be connected with criminal activity. Upon suspicion that the person may be armed, the police should have the power to 'frisk' him for weapons. If the 'stop' and the 'frisk' give rise to probable cause to believe that the suspect has committed a crime, then the police should be empowered to make a formal 'arrest,' and a full incident 'search' of the person. This scheme is justified in part by the notion that a 'stop' and a 'frisk' amount to a mere 'minor inconvenience and petty indignity,' which can properly be imposed upon the citizen in the interest of effective law enforcement on the basis of a police officer's suspicion." [Footnotes omitted.]

CASE SIGNIFICANCE: The *Terry* case made clear that the stop and frisk practice is valid. Prior to *Terry*, police departments regularly used stop and frisk either by law or by judicial authorization, but its validity was doubtful because the practice was based on *reasonable suspicion* rather than *probable cause*, which is necessary in arrest and search cases. The Court held that stop and frisk is constitutionally permissible despite the lack of probable cause for either full arrest or full search, and despite the fact that a brief detention not amounting to full arrest is a "seizure," requiring some degree of protection under the Fourth Amendment.

Adams v. Williams
407 U.S. 143 (1972)

CAPSULE: A stop and frisk may be based on information provided by another individual.

FACTS: While patrolling a high-crime area of the city in the early hours of the morning, an officer was approached by an informant who had provided him with reliable information in the past. The informant told the officer that Adams, in a nearby automobile, was carrying narcotics and had a gun in his waistband. The officer proceeded to the car, tapped on the window, and asked Adams to open the door. When Adams rolled down the window instead, the officer reached inside the car and removed a revolver from the precise place the informant had said it would be (although it was not visible to the officer). Adams was arrested for unlawful possession of a weapon. A search incident to the arrest revealed more weapons and a quantity of heroin. Adams' motion to suppress the evidence was denied and he was convicted on a weapons and a narcotics charge.

ISSUE: May an officer make a "stop and frisk" under the doctrine set down in *Terry v. Ohio*, based on information provided by an informant? YES.

SUPREME COURT DECISION: Reasonable grounds for a stop and frisk do not rest solely on an officer's personal observations—rather, they may be based on information provided by another individual.

REASON: "The Fourth Amendment does not require a policeman who lacks the precise level of information necessary for probable cause to arrest to simply shrug his shoulders and allow a crime to occur or a criminal to escape. On the contrary, *Terry* recognizes that it may be the essence of good police work to adopt an intermediate response."

CASE SIGNIFICANCE: This case settles the issue of whether information leading to a "stop and frisk" situation can come from an informant and not from direct police observation. It is clear that the police can make an arrest based on information from an informant as long as such information constitutes probable cause. It follows that if the police can make an arrest based on information from a third person (an informant), the police should also be able to effect a "stop and frisk" (a less intrusive act by the police) based on third-party information—as long as such information constitutes reasonable suspicion.

United States v. Hensley
469 U.S. 221 (1985)

CAPSULE: Reasonable suspicion based on a "wanted poster" is sufficient for a valid stop.

FACTS: Hensley was wanted for questioning about an armed robbery in St. Bernard, Ohio. The police issued a "wanted" flyer to other police departments in the area. Knowing of the flyer, and after inquiring without success as to the existence of an arrest warrant, officers in Covington, Kentucky stopped the automobile that Hensley was driving. Firearms were found in the car and Hensley was arrested. Hensley was ultimately convicted of being a convicted felon in possession of a handgun. He appealed the conviction, claiming that the stop was illegal because there was no probable cause and the evidence should have been excluded.

ISSUE: May the police stop and briefly detain an individual who is the subject of a "wanted" flyer from another jurisdiction? YES.

SUPREME COURT DECISION: When the police have a reasonable suspicion, grounded in specific and articulable facts (in this case the "wanted" flyer), that an individual was involved in or is wanted in connection with a completed felony, a *Terry* stop may be made to investigate that suspicion.

REASON: "[W]here police have been unable to locate a person suspected of involvement in a past crime, the ability to briefly stop that person, ask questions, or check identification in the absence of probable cause promotes the strong government interest in solving crimes and bringing offenders to justice. Restraining police action until after probable cause is obtained would not only hinder the investigation, but might also enable the suspect to flee in the interim and remain at large. . . . The law enforcement interests at stake in these circumstances outweigh the individual's interest to be free of a stop and detention that is no more extensive than permissible in the investigation of imminent or ongoing crimes."

CASE SIGNIFICANCE: *Terry v. Ohio*, 392 U.S. 1 (1968), the leading case on stop and frisk, has been applied primarily in instances when the police have reasonable suspicion that criminal activity may be afoot and when the suspect may be armed and dangerous. *Hensley* authorizes a *Terry*-type stop in cases in which the stop is based on the issuance of a "wanted" flyer by a police department in another city and not on the possible commission of a criminal offense. Moreover, the Court publicly recognized the need among law enforcement agencies for communication and cooperation, saying:

> In an era when criminal suspects are increasingly mobile and increasingly likely to flee across jurisdictional boundaries, this rule is a matter of common sense: it minimizes the volume of information concerning suspects that must be transmitted to other jurisdictions and enables police in one jurisdiction to act promptly in reliance on information from another jurisdiction.

United States v. Sharpe
470 U.S. 675 (1985)

CAPSULE: There is no rigid time limit for the length of an investigatory stop; instead, specific circumstances should be taken into account.

FACTS: An agent of the U.S. Drug Enforcement Administration (DEA) was patrolling in an area under surveillance for suspected drug trafficking when he observed Sharpe's automobile driving in tandem with an apparently overloaded truck that was driven by Savage. After following the two vehicles for 20 miles, the agent radioed for a marked car to assist him in making an investigatory stop. The two officers followed the vehicles several more miles at speeds in excess of the speed limit. The DEA agent stopped the car driven by Sharpe, but the officer was forced to chase the truck, which he stopped a half-mile later.

The DEA agent radioed for additional uniformed officers to detain Sharpe while the situation was investigated. These officers arrived 10 minutes later. The DEA agent arrived at the location of the truck approximately 15 minutes after it had been stopped. The agent's requests to search the truck were denied, but after he smelled marijuana, he took the keys from the ignition, opened the back of the truck, and found marijuana. Savage was then placed under arrest and the officers returned to arrest Sharpe approximately 40 minutes after his car had been stopped. Sharpe and Savage were charged with and convicted of possession of a controlled substance.

ISSUE: Can a suspect be detained for a period of 20 minutes while officers conduct a limited investigation of suspected criminal activity? YES.

SUPREME COURT DECISION: Detaining a driver for 20 minutes is considered reasonable in view of the circumstances surrounding this case. There is no rigid time limit for the length of an investigatory stop; instead, the following should be taken into account:
1. the purpose of the stop;
2. the reasonableness of the time used for the investigation that the officers want to conduct; and
3. the reasonableness of the means of investigation used by the officers.

REASON: "While it is clear that 'the brevity of the invasions of the individual's Fourth Amendment interests is an important factor in determining whether the seizure is so minimally intrusive as to be justifiable in reasonable suspicion,' we have emphasized the need to consider the law enforcement purposes to be served by the stop as well as the time reasonably needed to effectuate those purposes." [Citations omitted.]

"Clearly this case does not involve any delay unnecessary to the legitimate investigation of the law enforcement officers. Respondents presented no evidence that the officers were dilatory in their investigation. The delay in this case was attributable almost entirely to the evasive actions of Savage . . ."

CASE SIGNIFICANCE: This case answers the question, "How much time is allowed in cases of investigative stops?" The answer: there is no fixed time allowed; instead, it depends upon the purpose to be served by the stop and the time reasonably needed to carry it out. In this case, the circumstances were such that the detention for 20 minutes was considered reasonable. The Court added that judges should refrain from second-guessing police officers' decisions, particularly when the police are faced with a swiftly developing situation, as was the case here. This means that the benefit of the doubt must be given to the police on questions of how much time is sufficient for an investigative stop. Police officers must be ready to justify the amount of time used for an investigative stop, based on the purpose of the stop and the investigative method used, because an arbitrary delay would be considered unduly intrusive and unreasonable by the courts.

Alabama v. White
496 U.S. 325 (1990)

CAPSULE: Reasonable suspicion is a less demanding standard than probable cause.

FACTS: Acting on an anonymous phone call, police responded to a call that White would be leaving her apartment at a particular time in a brown Plymouth station wagon with the right taillight lens broken, in the process of going to Dobey's motel, and that she would be in possession of approximately one ounce of cocaine inside a brown attaché case. The police saw White leave her apartment without an attaché case, but she got in a car matching the description given in the telephone call. When the car reached the area where the motel was located, a patrol unit stopped the car and told White that she was suspected of carrying cocaine. After obtaining her permission to search the car, the police found the brown attaché case. Upon request, White provided the combination to the lock; the officers found marijuana and subsequently arrested her. At the station, the officers also found cocaine in her purse. White was charged with and convicted of possession of marijuana and cocaine. She sought to reverse her conviction, saying that the police did not have the necessary reasonable suspicion required by *Terry v. Ohio*, 392 U.S. 1 (1968) for such stops.

ISSUE: Did the anonymous tip, corroborated by independent police work, constitute reasonable suspicion to justify a stop? YES.

SUPREME COURT DECISION: Reasonable suspicion is a less demanding standard than probable cause. It can be established with information different in quantity or content from that required to establish probable cause; it may also be established with the help of an anonymous tip. The stop made by the police in this case was based on reasonable suspicion, therefore the evidence obtained was admissible in court.

REASON: When ". . . an informant is shown to be right about some things, he is probably right about other facts that he has alleged, including the claim that the object of the tip is engaged in criminal activity." It is, thus, not unreasonable in this case to conclude ". . . that the independent corroboration by the police of significant aspects of the informer's predictions imparted some degree of reliability to the other allegations made by the caller. . . . What was important was the caller's ability to predict [White's] *future behavior*, because it demonstrated inside information. . . . When significant aspects of the caller's predictions were verified, there was reason to believe not only that the caller was honest but also that he was well informed, at least well enough to justify the stop." Under the totality of circumstances, the anonymous tip, as corroborated, showed sufficient grounds of reliability to justify the investigatory stop of White's car.

CASE SIGNIFICANCE: This case is significant because it categorically states that "reasonable suspicion" is not as demanding a standard as probable cause and that it can be established with information that may be different in quality and quantity from that required for probable cause. The information may also be less reliable. It is important to note, however, that the anonymous tip by telephone given to the police in this case would not, in and of itself, have established reasonable suspicion. The Court said that "although it is a close question, the totality of the circumstances demonstrates that significant aspects of the informant's story were sufficiently corroborated by the police to furnish reasonable suspicion." What established reasonable suspicion in this case, therefore, was a combination of the anonymous telephone tip and corroboration by the police.

Minnesota v. Dickerson
508 U.S. 366 (1993)

CAPSULE: A frisk that goes beyond that allowed in *Terry* is invalid.

FACTS: During routine patrol, two police officers spotted Dickerson leaving an apartment building that one of the officers knew was a "crack house." Dickerson began walking toward the police, but, upon making eye contact with them, walked in the opposite direction and into an alley. Because of his evasive actions, the police decided to stop Dickerson and investigate further. They pulled into the alley and ordered Dickerson to stop and submit to a patdown search. The search revealed no weapons, but the officer found a small lump in Dickerson's pocket, which he said he examined with his fingers and determined that it felt like a lump of cocaine in cellophane. The officer reached into Dickerson's pocket and retrieved a small plastic bag of crack cocaine. Dickerson was arrested and charged with possession of a controlled substance.

ISSUE: Was the seizure of the crack cocaine valid under the stop and frisk rule of *Terry v. Ohio*? NO.

SUPREME COURT DECISION: A frisk that goes beyond that allowed under *Terry* is not valid. In this case, the search went beyond the "patdown search" allowed by *Terry* because the officer "squeezed, slid, and otherwise manipulated the packet's content" before knowing it was cocaine.

REASON: The court ruled in *Terry* that a protective search, ". . . permitted without a warrant and on the basis of reasonable suspicion less than probable cause, must be strictly 'limited to that which is necessary for the discovery of weapons which might be used to harm the officer or others nearby.' . . . If the protective search goes beyond what is necessary to determine if the suspect is armed, it is no longer valid under *Terry* and its fruits will be suppressed." If an officer, however, ". . . lawfully pats down a suspect's outer clothing and feels an object whose contour or mass makes its identity immediately apparent, there has been no invasion of privacy beyond that already authorized by the officer's search for weapons . . ." In this case, though, the ". . . officer's continued exploration of respondent's pocket after having concluded that it contained no weapon was unrelated to '[t]he sole justification of the search [under *Terry*:] . . . the protection of the police officer and others nearby.'" It therefore amounted to the sort of evidentiary search that is unauthorized by *Terry*.

CASE SIGNIFICANCE: This stop and frisk case further clarifies what is allowed under *Terry v. Ohio*, 392 U.S. 1 (1968). The Court said that the officer's actions in this case went beyond that allowed in *Terry*, saying the officer did not merely conduct a frisk (a pat-down), but instead "squeezed, slid, and otherwise manipulated the pocket's content." During the initial pat-down, the officer felt a "small lump" in suspect's jacket pocket, but admitted it was not a weapon. He believed it to be contraband only after he "squeezed, slid, and otherwise manipulated" it. This goes beyond *Terry*, which authorizes a pat-down only for one purpose: officer safety. That was absent here because the officer admitted that what he felt was not a weapon. The Court's decision might have been different, however, had the officer testified that he knew it was not a weapon when he felt the lump, but that he had probable cause to believe—from his experience as a police officer and the circumstances of this case—that the lump was cocaine. If those were the circumstances, the seizure may have been valid, not under stop and frisk, but under probable cause. A frisk in stop and frisk cases can quickly turn into a valid warrantless search if the officer establishes probable cause (through experience, surrounding circumstances, etc.) that, although the item felt is not a weapon, he or she believes it is in fact contraband, and that belief is reasonable.

Illinois v. Wardlow
528 U.S. 119 (2000)

CAPSULE: Presence in a high crime area, combined with unprovoked flight upon observing police officers gives officers sufficient grounds to investigate further to determine if criminal activity is about to take place.

FACTS: Narcotics officers were caravanning to make arrests in an area known for heavy narcotics trafficking. One officer noticed Wardlow standing next to a building holding an opaque bag. Wardlow looked toward the officers then fled; the officers followed him. When the officers stopped Wardlow, one officer conducted a *Terry* type pat-down search based on the officer's experience that it was common for there to be weapons in the area of the narcotics trafficking. The officer found a handgun and arrested Wardlow.

ISSUE: Did Wardlow's actions of fleeing in a high crime area upon seeing police officers create a reasonable suspicion sufficient to justify a *Terry* stop and frisk? YES.

SUPREME COURT DECISION: Wardlow's presence in a high crime area, combined with unprovoked flight upon observing police officers gives officers sufficient grounds to investigate further to determine if criminal activity is afoot. The determination of reasonable suspicion must be based on commonsense judgments and inferences of human behavior.

REASON: "While 'reasonable suspicion' is a less demanding standard than probable cause . . . the Fourth Amendment requires at least a minimal level of objective justification for making the stop." "An individual's presence in an area of expected criminal activity, standing alone, is not enough to support a reasonable, particularized suspicion that the person is committing a crime," "but a location's characteristics are relevant in determining whether the circumstances are sufficiently suspicious to warrant further investigation". "In this case, moreover, it was not merely respondent's presence in an area of heavy narcotics trafficking that aroused the officers' suspicion, but his unprovoked flight upon noticing the police." "We conclude that [the officer] was justified in suspecting that Wardlow was involved in criminal activity, and, therefore, in investigating further."

CASE SIGNIFICANCE: This case is significant because it addresses the issue whether the police may stop and frisk a person who flees upon seeing the police. The Court ruled that such flight, under the circumstances of this case, gave the police sufficient reason to stop and frisk. The Court did not answer whether it would have made the same decision if the flight happened in another place not known for heavy narcotics trafficking. Instead the Court concluded that "it was not merely respondent's presence in an area of heavy narcotics trafficking that aroused the officers' suspicion but his unprovoked flight upon noticing the police," implying that these two factors combined to establish reasonable suspicion. The Court ruled that a "reasonable suspicion determination must be based on commonsense judgments and inferences about human behavior." The strong implication in this case is that the place where the flight took place was taken into consideration by the Court in giving the police authority to stop. A safe interpretation would be that the Court would look into the "totality of the circumstances" to determine if flight upon seeing the police constitutes reasonable suspicion for a stop and frisk. The police should be prepared to identify "flight plus" factors to be able to establish reasonable suspicion in flight-from-police cases.

Florida v. J.L.
529 U.S. 266 (1999)

CAPSULE: "An anonymous tip that a person is carrying a gun is not, without more, sufficient to justify a police officer's stop and frisk if that person."

FACTS: Police responded to an anonymous tip that a young black male was standing at a particular bus stop wearing a plaid shirt and carrying a gun. When officers observed a person matching that description standing at the bus stop with two other persons, they frisked J.L. and found a pistol. The two other persons were also frisked, but nothing was found. The officers did not see a gun, and had no reason to suspect any of the three of any illegal conduct.

ISSUE: Is an anonymous tip that a person is carrying a gun, without more, sufficient to justify a stop and frisk of the person? NO.

SUPREME COURT DECISION: "An anonymous tip that a person is carrying a gun is not, without more, sufficient to justify a police officer's stop and frisk of that person." The anonymous tip alone in this case did not amount to reasonable suspicion.

REASON: "Here, the officers' suspicion that J.L. was carrying a weapon arose not from their own observations but solely from a call made from an unknown location by an unknown caller. The tip lacked sufficient indicia of reliability to provide reasonable suspicion to make a *Terry* stop: It provided no predictive information and therefore left the police without a means to test the informant's knowledge or credibility." Without some indication of criminal wrongdoing, the police did not possess sufficient reasonable suspicion to warrant the search.

CASE SIGNIFICANCE: This case clarifies what the Court ruled in *Alabama v. White*, 496 U.S. 325 (1991). In *White*, the Court held that reasonable suspicion can be established with the help of an anonymous tip, but more is needed. In *J.L.*, the Court reaffirmed this principle, arguing that an anonymous tip in itself does not amount to reasonable suspicion. What is needed is more indication that would establish that the tip itself was reliable. In *White*, the Court also said that "when significant aspects of the caller's predictions were verified, there was reason to believe not only that the caller was honest but also that he was well informed, at least well enough to justify the stop." Even then, *White* was considered a "close case." In contrast, the anonymous tip in *J.L.* was made from an unknown location by an unknown caller that "a young black male standing at a particular bus stop and wearing a plaid shirt was carrying a gun." There was nothing else beyond that. The Court held this alone did not amount to reasonable suspicion and was not as reliable as the information received by the officers in *White* where "the police received an anonymous tip asserting that a woman was carrying cocaine and predicting that she would leave an apartment building at a specified time, get into a car matching a particular description, and drive to a named motel." This tip alone in *White* would not have justified a stop. But based on this tip, the police went to the place and observed the suspect's movements, which confirmed what the anonymous tip provided. Taken together, the tip plus observation by the police established reasonable suspicion. In sum, the test for reasonable suspicion should be "tip plus more" that would indicate the information given in the tip was reliable. It should be of interest that in this case, the State of Florida and the federal government argued that the Court should create a "firearm exception" to *Terry v. Ohio*, the original stop and frisk case. They suggested that a tip alleging that the suspect had an illegal gun (as in the *J.L.* case) should justify a stop and frisk even if the information did not amount to reasonable suspicion. The Court rejected this exception, thus holding the same level of standard for stop and frisk in weapons and non-weapons cases.

United States v. Arvizu
534 U.S. 266 (2001)

CAPSULE: "In making reasonable-suspicion determinations, reviewing courts must look at the totality of the circumstances of each case to see whether the detaining officer has a particularized and objective basis for suspecting legal wrongdoing."

FACTS: The U.S. Border Patrol operated a checkpoint in an isolated area of Arizona. A limited number of roads circumvented the checkpoint, and were routinely used by smugglers to avoid the checkpoint. Because of this, sensors were placed along those roads to detect vehicular traffic. When one of the sensors indicated traffic, an officer responded. While following the vehicle for several miles, the officer observed several indicators of suspicious behavior, including: the time the vehicle was on the road coincided with shift change for roving patrols in the area, the roads taken by the vehicle were remote and not well suited for the vehicle type, the vehicle slowed dramatically upon first observing the officer, the driver of the vehicle would not look at the officer when passing, children in the vehicle seemed to have their feet propped up on some cargo, the children waved mechanically at the officer as if being instructed, and the vehicle made turns that would allow it to completely avoid the checkpoint. Based on these observations, the officer stopped the vehicle. After obtaining consent from Arvizu, the officer searched the vehicle and found drugs. The Court of Appeals ruled to suppress the evidence of the search based on an analysis of what it determined to be ten factors related to the stop. Each of the factors was examined individually, and seven were found to not present sufficient ground for reasonable suspicion. Since the majority of these factors were not found in themselves to be sufficient to support reasonable suspicion, the Court of Appeals ruled the search unconstitutional.

ISSUE: What is the proper standard for evaluating the factors used in an officer's decision to make an investigatory stop: consideration of each factor individually, or totality of the circumstances? Totality of the circumstances.

SUPREME COURT DECISION: "In making reasonable-suspicion determinations, reviewing courts must look at the totality of the circumstances of each case to see whether the detaining officer has a particularized and objective basis for suspecting legal wrongdoing."

REASON: "The court's evaluation and rejection of seven of the listed factors in isolation from each other does not take into account the totality of the circumstances, as our cases have understood that phrase. The court appeared to believe that each observation by [the officer] that was by itself readily susceptible to an innocent explanation was entitled to no weight. *Terry*, however, precludes this sort of divide-and-conquer analysis." "When discussing how reviewing courts should make reasonable-suspicion determinations, we have said repeatedly that they must look at the totality of circumstances of each case to see whether the detaining officer has a particularized and objective basis for suspecting legal wrongdoing." "Having considered the totality of the circumstances and given due weight to the factual inferences drawn by the law enforcement officer and District Court Judge, we hold that [the officer] had reasonable suspicion to believe that respondent was engaged in illegal activity."

CASE SIGNIFICANCE: This case settles an issue in stop and frisk cases: how an officer determines the existence of reasonable suspicion. Is it by considering each factor individually, or by focusing on the totality of the circumstances? The Court of Appeals in this case had ruled that seven out of the ten factors cited by the officer, if taken individually, did not establish reason suspicion because they were innocent activities and were not in themselves illegal. The Court disagreed, saying that previous decisions on this issue have always held that totality of the circumstances was the test to follow. This means that even if the factors identified by the officer individually did not establish reasonable suspicion, taken together they were sufficient to legally stop the vehicle. This case involved stop and search rather than stop and frisk. What was at issue, though, was the legality of the stop, not the legality of the search. The search itself was considered legal because there was valid consent. However, if the stop was illegal because of the absence of reasonable suspicion, the search would also have been illegal because of the illegal stop and, therefore, the evidence would have been excludible. The decision is significant in two ways: (1) it makes it generally easier for officers to establish reason suspicion since they can rely on a number of factors to establish reasonable suspicion, and (2) the statement by the Court that in determining reasonable suspicion, the process "allows officers to draw on their own experiences and specialized training to make inferences from and deductions about the cumulative information available." This means that what may appear innocent to an untrained person may in fact appear suspicious to a police officer because of his or her training. This reemphasizes an original principle enunciated by the Court in the *Terry*, the original stop and frisk case, that an officer's training and expertise can be taken into account in determining reasonable suspicion.

Hiibel v. Sixth Judicial District Court of Nevada et al. 542 U.S. 177 (2004)

CAPSULE: The Fourth Amendment allows officers, pursuant to a stop and frisk, to require a person to provide his or her name. The person may be arrested for refusing to comply.

FACTS: The Humbolt County Sheriff's Office received a telephone call from a person who had seen a man assault a woman in a red and silver GMC truck on Grass Valley Road. When an officer arrived at the scene, he found a truck matching the description parked on the side of the road where the caller described. The officer observed skid marks in the gravel behind the vehicle, indicating a sudden stop. The officer also observed a man standing by the truck and a woman sitting inside. The officer approached the man and explained he was investigating the report of an assault. The man appeared intoxicated. The officer asked if he had any identification, but the man refused. After repeated requests and refusals to identify himself, the man began to taunt the officer by putting his hands behind his back and telling the officer to arrest him. After warning the man he would be arrested if he refused to comply, the officer placed Hiibel under arrest pursuant to a Nevada law allowing officers to detain a person suspected of committing a crime to ascertain his or her identity. The law states that "any person so detained shall identify himself, but may not be compelled to answer any other inquiry of any peace officer."

ISSUE: Can a person be arrested for refusing to identify himself or herself to a police officer? YES, but only under certain circumstances.

SUPREME COURT DECISION: Requiring a suspect to disclose his or her name in the course of a stop and frisk does not violate the Fourth or the Fifth Amendment.

REASON: Hiibel argued that his Fourth Amendment rights were violated because he could not be compelled to give his name, and his Fifth Amendment rights were violated because his response was testimonial and could incriminate him. The Court rejected both of these arguments. On the Fourth Amendment issue, the Court held that, ordinarily, an "officer is free to ask a person for identification without implicating the Fourth Amendment" as a part of a *Terry* stop. "Here, there is no question that the initial stop was based on reasonable suspicion, satisfying the Fourth Amendment requirements noted in *Brown*." Also, the Nevada statute is more precise than previous laws and only requires the person to provide his or her name, not produce a driver's license or other document. "The Nevada statute is consistent with Fourth Amendment prohibitions against unreasonable searches and seizures because it properly balances the intrusion on the individual's interests against the promotion of legitimate government interest. . . . Hiibel's contention that his conviction violates the Fifth Amendment's prohibition on self-incrimination fails because disclosure of his name and identity presented no reasonable danger of incrimination. The Fifth Amendment prohibits only compelled testimony that is incriminating, and protects only against disclosures that the witness reasonably believes could be used in a criminal prosecution or could lead to other evidence that might be so reasonably used. . . . In this case, [Hiibel's] refusal to disclose his name was not based on any articulated real and appreciable fear that his name would be used to incriminate him, or that 'it would furnish a link in the chain of evidence needed to prosecute' him." [internal citations omitted]

CASE SIGNIFICANCE: This case is significant because it resolves an important issue in law enforcement: whether or not "stop and identify" laws can be constitutional. An earlier California law that required a suspect to furnish an officer "credible and reliable" identification when asked to identify himself or herself was declared unconstitutional because of vagueness or overbreadth. What was at issue in this case was whether the Nevada stop and identify law, which was more specific, is constitutional. The Nevada law (Nev. Rev. Stat.[NRS] Section 199.280 (2003) provides as follows:

"1. Any peace officer may detain any person whom the officer encounters under circumstances which reasonably indicate that the person has committed, is committing, or is about to commit a crime."

. . .

"3. The officer may detain the person pursuant to this section only to ascertain his identity and the suspicious circumstances surrounding his presence abroad. Any person so detained shall identify himself, but may not be compelled to answer any other inquiry of any peace officer."

Hiibel claimed that this law violated his Fourth and Fifth Amendment rights, not simply because they were vague or overly broad. The Court rejected these claims, saying that the "Nevada statute is consistent with Fourth Amendment prohibitions against unreasonable searches and seizures because it properly balances the intrusion on the individual's interest against the promotion of legitimate government interests." The alleged violation of the Fifth Amendment privilege against self-incrimination was also rejected by the Court, saying that the "Fifth Amendment prohibits only compelled testimony that is incriminating, and protects only against disclosures that the witness reasonably believes could be used in a criminal prosecution or could lead to other evidence that might be so used." In this case, "Hiibel's refusal to disclose was not based on any articulated real and appreciable fear that his name would be used to incriminate him, or that it would furnish evidence needed to prosecute him." He refused to identify himself "because he thought his name was none of the officer's business," and not because he feared subsequent prosecution; therefore, the Fifth Amendment privilege against self-incrimination could not be successfully invoked.

Arrest 4

Introduction

The law of arrest is of great importance to law enforcement officers. An illegal arrest violates the constitutional rights of an individual and can lead to lawsuits against the police. An arrest is defined as the taking of a person into custody against his or her will for the purpose of criminal prosecution or interrogation (*Dunaway v. New York*, 442 U.S. 200 [1979]). Not all detentions constitute an arrest. An arrest occurs only when there is governmental termination of freedom of movement through means intentionally applied (*Brower v. County of Inyo*, 486 U.S. 593 [1989]).

Police arrests may be classified into two general categories: with a warrant and without a warrant. In both categories, probable cause is required. The difference is that, in arrests with a warrant, probable cause has already been determined by a judge or magistrate. In arrests without a warrant, probable cause must be established by the police.

An arrest has four elements. These are: (1) seizure and detention, (2) intention to arrest, (3) arrest authority, and (4) understanding by the person arrested. Seizure and detention can be actual or constructive. Actual seizure takes place when the police take the person into custody with the use of hands or firearms, or by merely touching the individual without the use of force. Constructive seizure takes place without any physical touching, grabbing, holding, or use of force. It occurs when the person peacefully submits to the will and control of the officer. The intent to arrest exists in the mind of the police officer and is therefore difficult for the arrested person to prove. But actions often speak louder than words. For example, if an officer places handcuffs on a suspect or takes the suspect to the police station in a police car, intent to arrest may be present although the police officer may not have said: "You are under arrest." Arrest authority is inherent in policing in that every police officer is authorized to make an arrest unless there are specified limitations otherwise. Some jurisdictions limit this authority to the time during which an officer is on duty; other jurisdictions authorize officers to arrest a person even while off-duty if there is probable cause to believe that a crime has been or is being committed.

When a person is under arrest has been addressed by the Supreme Court in a number of cases, starting with *Michigan v. Chesternut*, 486 U.S. 567 (1988), in which the Court ruled that the test to determine whether a seizure occurs is whether a reasonable person viewing the police conduct would conclude that he or she is free to leave. In *Brower v. County of Inyo*, 489 U.S. 593 (1989), the Court held that a seizure occurs when there is a "governmental termination of freedom of movement through means intentionally applied." Then, in *California v. Hodari D.*, 499 U.S. 621 (1991), the Court held that no seizure occurs when an officer seeks to arrest a suspect through a show of authority, but applies no physical force, and the subject does not willingly submit (therefore there was no actual or constructive seizure). Finally, in *Florida v. Bostick*, 501 U.S. 429 (1991), the Court ruled that the test to determine whether a police-citizen encounter on a bus is a seizure is whether a reasonable passenger would feel free to decline the officers' request or otherwise terminate the encounter. In sum, not every encounter with the police is an arrest. The general test is that it is an arrest only if a reasonable person under the same circumstances would have considered the encounter with the police to be an arrest.

Two recent cases have further clarified the authority of the police in arrest cases. In *Atwater v. City of Lago Vista*, 532 U.S. 318 (2001), the Court held that the Fourth Amendment does not forbid a warrantless arrest for a minor criminal offense, such as a misdemeanor seatbelt violation, which is punishable only by a fine. This settles an issue that the Court had not addressed before. At present, all 50 states authorize the police to make an arrest even for non-jailable offenses. Another recent case holds that under emergency circumstances, and where there is need to preserve evidence until the police can obtain a warrant, they may temporarily restrain a person's movement without violating his or her Fourth Amendment rights (*Illinois v. McArthur*, 531 U.S. 326 (2001). This gives the police more power to limit the movement of a suspect who has not been arrested and where the police are sure they have probable cause to obtain a warrant and are in the process of obtaining it.

The leading cases briefed in this section on arrest are *United States v. Watson*, *Payton v. New York*, and *Atwater v. City of Lago Vista*.

Frisbie v. Collins
342 U.S. 519 (1952)

CAPSULE: An unlawful arrest does not deprive the court of jurisdiction to try a criminal case.

FACTS: Acting as his own lawyer, Collins brought a *habeas corpus* action in federal court seeking release from a Michigan state prison where he was serving a life sentence for murder. He alleged that, while he was living in Chicago, officers from Michigan forcibly handcuffed, blackjacked and abducted him, and took him back to Michigan. He claimed that the trial and conviction under such circumstances violated his due process rights under the Fourteenth Amendment and the Federal Kidnapping Act and were therefore void.

ISSUE: Does the unlawful arrest of a defendant affect the validity of a court's jurisdiction in a criminal proceeding? NO.

SUPREME COURT DECISION: An unlawful arrest has no impact on a subsequent criminal prosecution. An invalid arrest, therefore, does not deprive the court of jurisdiction to try a criminal case.

REASON: "This Court has never departed from the rule announced in *Ker v. Illinois*, 119 U.S. 436 (1886), that the power of a court to try a person for crime is not impaired by the fact that he had been brought within the court's jurisdiction by reason of a 'forcible abduction.' No persuasive reasons are now presented to justify overruling this line of cases. They rest on sound basis that due process of law is satisfied when one present in court is convicted of crime after having been fairly apprised of the charges against him and after a fair trial in accordance with constitutional procedural safeguards. There is nothing in the Constitution that requires a court to permit a guilty person rightfully convicted to escape justice because he was brought to trial against his will."

CASE SIGNIFICANCE: The *Collins* decision constitutes what might seem to be a surprising exception to the exclusionary rule. It would seem logical to think that if items subject to illegal search and seizure are not admissible in evidence, then defendants illegally arrested ought not to be subject to court jurisdiction (for purposes of a trial) either. The Court disagrees, stating that "the power of the court to try a person for crime is not impaired by the fact that he had been brought within the court's jurisdiction by reason of a 'forcible abduction.'" It then added that "[t]here is nothing in the Constitution that requires a court to permit a guilty person rightfully convicted to escape justice because he was brought to trial against his will." Note that the *Collins* case was decided in 1952, before the exclusionary rule was applied to the states in *Mapp v. Ohio*. Nonetheless, the ruling is still valid today.

United States v. Santana
427 U.S. 38 (1975)

CAPSULE: A warrantless arrest that begins in a public place is valid even if the suspect retreats to a private place and is arrested there.

FACTS: An undercover police officer arranged a heroin buy from Patricia McCafferty. After meeting with the officer and driving to the residence of Santana, McCafferty took the officer's $115 of marked bills, went into Santana's house and returned shortly thereafter. The officer asked McCafferty for the heroin; she gave several envelopes of heroin to him. The officer then placed McCafferty under arrest. When asked where the money was, McCafferty replied that Santana had it. While McCafferty was being taken to the police station, other officers drove to Santana's house where they saw her standing in the doorway with a brown paper bag in her hand. After they identified themselves as police officers, Santana attempted to escape into her house. The officers chased and caught her. During the ensuing scuffle, two bundles of heroin fell to the floor, which the police recovered. Told to empty her pockets, Santana produced $135, of which $70 was the undercover officer's marked money. Santana and others were later charged with possession of heroin with intent to distribute.

ISSUE: Is the warrantless arrest of a suspect in a public place valid if the suspect retreats from a public place to a private place? YES.

SUPREME COURT DECISION: A warrantless arrest that begins in a public place is valid even if the suspect retreats to a private place and is arrested there.

REASON: "While it may be true under common law of property that the threshold of one's dwelling is 'private,' as is the yard surrounding the house, it is nonetheless clear that under the cases interpreting the Fourth Amendment, Santana was in a 'public' place, . . . not in an area where she had any expectation of privacy . . . She was not merely visible to the public but was exposed to public view, speech, hearing, and touch as if she had been standing completely outside her house." The police, therefore, had probable cause to arrest her and did so in the proper manner. Santana could not, furthermore, thwart her arrest by retreating into her private home. "The District Court was correct in concluding that 'hot pursuit' means some sort of a chase, but it need not be an extended hue and cry 'in and about [the] public streets.' The fact that the pursuit ended almost as soon as it began did not render it any less a 'hot pursuit' sufficient to justify the warrantless entry into Santana's house."

CASE SIGNIFICANCE: In *United States v. Watson,* 423 U.S. 411 (1976), the Court held that the police are not required to obtain a warrant before arresting a person in a public place even if there was time and opportunity to obtain a warrant, as long as there is probable cause. The *Santana* case extends that principle to instances in which the arrest begins in a public place, but ends up in a private place (in this case, the suspect's home) because the suspect goes there. Santana was in a public place when she was standing in the doorway of her house, but ended up in a private place when she retreated. The Court considered what happened as a case of "hot pursuit" and therefore did not require a warrant. Note, however, that as in the case of *Watson*, a warrantless arrest in a public place—even if based on probable cause—may be invalid if prohibited by state law or agency policy.

United States v. Watson
423 U.S. 411 (1976)

CAPSULE: An arrest without a warrant in a public place is valid as long as there is probable cause, even if there is time to obtain a warrant.

FACTS: A reliable informant telephoned the postal inspector and informed him that he was in possession of a stolen credit card provided by Watson and that Watson had agreed to furnish the informant with additional cards. The informant agreed to meet with Watson and give a signal if he had additional stolen cards. When the signal was given, officers arrested Watson and took him from the restaurant where he was sitting to the street, where he was given his *Miranda* warnings. When a search revealed no stolen credit cards on Watson, the postal inspector asked if he could look inside Watson's automobile. The inspector told Watson that "if I find anything, it is going to go against you." Watson agreed to the search. Using keys furnished by Watson, the car was searched and an envelope containing stolen credit cards was found. Watson was charged with and convicted of possession of stolen credit cards.

ISSUE: Can officers arrest an individual in a public place with probable cause but without an arrest warrant even if there was time to obtain a warrant? YES.

SUPREME COURT DECISION: An officer may arrest a suspect in a public place without a warrant, even if there is time and opportunity to obtain one, if there is probable cause to believe that a criminal act has been committed.

REASON: "The usual rule is that a police officer may arrest without a warrant one believed by the officer upon reasonable cause to have been guilty of a felony. . . . Just last term, while recognizing that maximum protection of individual rights could be assured by requiring a magistrate's review of the factual justification prior to any arrest, we stated that 'such a requirement would constitute an intolerable handicap for legitimate law enforcement' and noted that the Court 'has never invalidated an arrest supported by probable cause solely because the officers failed to secure a warrant.'" [Citations omitted.]

"The cases construing the Fourth Amendment thus reflect the ancient common-law rule that a peace officer was permitted to arrest without a warrant for a misdemeanor or felony committed in his presence as well as for a felony not committed in his presence if there was reasonable grounds for making the arrest . . ."

CASE SIGNIFICANCE: This case states that police officers can make an arrest in a public place, without a warrant, based on probable cause, hence dispensing with the warrant requirement even if the police have time to obtain a warrant. The general rule is that a warrant must be obtained before making an arrest, unless the arrest falls under one of the many exceptions to the warrant requirement. This is one of those exceptions—arrest in a public place based on probable cause. The suspect in this case argued that the police should have obtained a warrant because they had time to do so. The Supreme Court ruled that the common law and the laws of most states do not require a warrant to be obtained under these circumstances.

Watson is a federal case involving postal service officers. These officers acted in accordance with a federal law that authorizes officers to "make arrest without warrant for felonies cognizable under the laws of the United States if they have reasonable grounds to believe that the person to be arrested has committed or is committing such a felony." Watson sought to have this law declared unconstitutional, in effect saying that an arrest warrant was constitutionally required whenever there was time to obtain it, even if the arrest is made in a public place. The Court disagreed, saying that this has never been required under common law, the laws of many states, or previous Supreme Court decisions. Note that this case simply says that an arrest warrant is not constitutionally required for arrests made in a public place that are based on probable cause. If a state statute requires that a warrant be obtained, then the statute must be followed. The Court noted, however, that state statutes usually do not require an arrest warrant. The rule stands, therefore, that unless a state statute or case law provides otherwise, the police can make a warrantless arrest in a public place, based on probable cause, even if they have time to obtain a warrant.

Dunaway v. New York
442 U.S. 200 (1979)

CAPSULE: Probable cause is needed for the stationhouse detention of a suspect if such detention is accompanied by an interrogation.

FACTS: An informant implicated Dunaway in a murder but could not provide sufficient information to justify the issuance of a warrant. The police, however, ordered Dunaway to be picked up and brought to the police station, where he was taken into custody. Although he was never told that he was under arrest, there was evidence that "he would have been physically restrained if he had attempted to leave." At the station, Dunaway made statements implicating himself in the murder after receiving his *Miranda* warnings. Dunaway was charged with and convicted of murder.

ISSUE: May the police take any suspects into custody, transport them to a police station, and detain them there for interrogation without probable cause to make an arrest? NO.

SUPREME COURT DECISION: The taking of a person into custody against his or her will for the purpose of criminal prosecution or interrogation constitutes an arrest for which probable cause is needed. Probable cause is therefore necessary for the stationhouse detention of a suspect when such detention is accompanied by interrogation (as opposed to just fingerprinting), even if no formal arrest is made.

REASON: ". . . [T]he detention of petitioner was in important respects indistinguishable from a traditional arrest. Petitioner was not questioned briefly where he was found. Instead, he was taken from a neighbor's home to a police car, transported to a police station, and placed in an interrogation room. He was never informed that he was 'free to go'; indeed, he would have been physically restrained if he had refused to accompany the officers or had tried to escape their custody."

"The central importance of the probable cause requirement to the protection of a citizen's privacy afforded by the Fourth Amendment guarantees cannot be compromised in this fashion. . . . Hostility to seizures based on mere suspicion was a prime motivation for the adoption of the Fourth Amendment, and decisions immediately after its adoption affirmed that 'common rumor or report, suspicion, or even "strong reason to suspect" was not adequate to support a warrant for arrest.'"

CASE SIGNIFICANCE: This case resolves the issue of whether the stationhouse detention of a suspect, accompanied by interrogation, is so restrictive of a person's freedom as to be the equivalent of an arrest, which is illegal without probable cause. In this case, there was no probable cause to arrest Dunaway, but there were reasons for the police to consider him a suspect in connection with a crime being investigated. Dunaway was therefore asked to come to police headquarters. He was never told that he was under arrest, but probably would have been physically restrained had he attempted to leave. He received his *Miranda* warnings, was questioned, and ultimately confessed. The Court held that, because Dunaway was in fact taken into custody by the police and not simply stopped on the street, probable cause was required to take him to the police station. Because probable cause was absent, Dunaway's detention at the stationhouse was illegal and the evidence obtained from him, despite the fact that he was given the *Miranda* warnings, was inadmissible.

Payton v. New York
445 U.S. 573 (1980)

CAPSULE: The police may not validly enter a private home to make a routine, warrantless felony arrest, unless justified by exigent circumstances.

FACTS: After two days of intensive investigation, police officers assembled sufficient evidence to establish probable cause to believe that Payton had murdered the manager of a gas station. Officers went to Payton's apartment to arrest him. They had no warrant, although they had time to obtain one. Although light and music emanated from the apartment, there was no response to their knock on the metal door. They summoned emergency assistance and used crowbars to break open the door and enter the apartment. There was no one in the apartment, but in plain view was a .30-caliber shell casing that was seized and later admitted into evidence at Payton's trial. Payton later surrendered to the police and was indicted for murder. In a motion to suppress the evidence, the court ruled that the search of the house was illegal and suppressed the evidence, but also said that the shell casing was in plain view and admitted it into evidence. Payton was ultimately convicted.

ISSUE: Does the Fourth Amendment guarantee against unreasonable search and seizure require officers to obtain a warrant if making a routine felony arrest when there is time to obtain a warrant? YES.

SUPREME COURT DECISION: In the absence of exigent circumstances or consent, the police may not enter a private home to make a routine, warrantless felony arrest. The evidence was not admissible because there was time to obtain a warrant and there were no exigent circumstances to justify a warrantless search.

REASON: "In terms that apply equally to seizures of property and to seizures of persons, the Fourth Amendment has drawn a firm line at the entrance to the house. Absent exigent circumstances, that threshold may not reasonably be crossed without a warrant."

CASE SIGNIFICANCE: The *Payton* case settled the issue of whether the police can make a warrantless arrest in a routine felony case. The practice was authorized by the state of New York and 23 other states at the time *Payton* was decided. These authorizations are now unconstitutional and officers must obtain a warrant before making a routine felony arrest. If the arrest is not routine (meaning exigent circumstances are present), a warrantless arrest can be made.

Michigan v. Chesternut
486 U.S. 567 (1988)

CAPSULE: The test to determine whether a seizure occurs is whether a reasonable person, viewing the police conduct and surrounding circumstances, would conclude that he or she is not free to leave.

FACTS: Chesternut began to run after observing the approach of a police car. Officers followed him to "see where he was going." As the officers drove alongside Chesternut, they observed him pull a number of packets from his pocket and throw them away. The officers stopped and seized the packets, concluding that they might be contraband. Chesternut was then arrested. A subsequent search revealed more drugs. Chesternut was charged with felony narcotics possession.

ISSUE: Did the officer's investigatory pursuit of Chesternut to "see where he was going" constitute a seizure under the Fourth Amendment? NO.

SUPREME COURT DECISION: The appropriate test to determine whether a seizure has occurred is whether a reasonable person, viewing the police conduct and surrounding circumstances, would conclude that he or she is not free to leave. There is no seizure *per se* in police investigatory pursuits.

REASON: "No bright-line rule applicable to all investigatory pursuits can be fashioned. Rather, the appropriate test is whether a reasonable man, viewing the particular police conduct as a whole and within the setting of all the surrounding circumstances, would have concluded that the police had in some [manner] restrained his liberty so that he was not free to leave. . . . Under this test, respondent [Chesternut] was not 'seized' before he discarded the drug packets. . . . The record does not reflect that the police activated a siren or flashers; commanded respondent to halt or displayed any weapons; or operated the car aggressively to block his course or to control his direction or speed. Thus, respondent could not reasonably have believed that he was not free to disregard the police presence and go about his business. The police, therefore, were not required to have a particularized and objective basis for suspecting him of criminal activity, in order to pursue him."

CASE SIGNIFICANCE: This case provides guidelines to a persistent and difficult question in police work: When is a person considered seized by the police? The question is important because seizure by the police involves the Fourth Amendment and sets in motion constitutional guarantees, particularly the requirements of probable cause and, whenever possible, a warrant. Absent seizure, the police do not have to abide by constitutional guarantees. The Court stated that there is no definitive test to determine seizure; rather, it sets the following guideline: "whether a reasonable man, viewing the particular police conduct as a whole and within the setting of all the surrounding circumstances, would have concluded that the police had in some way restrained his liberty so that he was not free to leave." The standard is not whether the police intended to make a seizure, but whether the suspect would have concluded (as a reasonable person would have) that the police had in some way restrained his or her liberty so that he or she was not free to leave. This is ultimately a question of fact for the judge or jury to decide. Such determination, however, must be made by taking all surrounding circumstances into account; i.e., use of siren or flashers, commands to halt, etc. If the behavior of the police is passive rather than active, chances are that there is no seizure.

Brower v. County of Inyo
489 U.S. 593 (1989)

CAPSULE: A seizure occurs when there is a "governmental termination of freedom of movement through means intentionally applied."

FACTS: In an effort to stop Brower, who had stolen a car and eluded the police in a chase of more than 20 miles, police placed an 18-wheeled truck across both lanes of a highway, behind a curve, with a police car's headlights pointed in a manner that would blind Brower. Brower was killed in the crash as a result of the roadblock. Brower's heirs and estate brought a civil rights action (42 U.S.C. § 1983) for damages against the police, alleging a violation of Brower's constitutional right against unreasonable search and seizure.

ISSUE: Is a roadblock set up by the police to stop a fleeing suspect a form of seizure under the Fourth Amendment? YES.

SUPREME COURT DECISION: A seizure occurs when there is a "governmental termination of freedom of movement through means intentionally applied." Because Brower was stopped through means intentionally designed to stop him, the stop constituted a seizure.

REASON: "Consistent with the language, history, and judicial construction of the Fourth Amendment, a seizure occurs when governmental termination of a person's movement is effected through means intentionally applied. Because the complaint alleges that Brower was stopped by the instrumentality set in motion or put in place to stop him, it states a claim of Fourth Amendment 'seizure.'"

CASE SIGNIFICANCE: The importance of this case lies in the Court's definition of a "seizure" under the Fourth Amendment. Under the Court's definition of seizure, a roadblock is a form of seizure; and, because the roadblock in this case was set up in such a manner that it was likely to kill Brower, the Court decided that there was possible civil liability for his death. The Court did not say, however, that the police were automatically liable. Instead, it remanded the case to the Court of Appeals to determine whether the District Court erred in concluding that the roadblock was reasonable. If the roadblock was reasonable, then no liability could be imposed on the police. If, however, the roadblock was unreasonable, liability could be imposed.

California v. Hodari D.
499 U.S. 621 (1991)

CAPSULE: No seizure occurs when an officer seeks to arrest a suspect through a show of authority, but applies no physical force, and the subject does not willingly submit.

FACTS: Two police officers were patrolling a high-crime area in Oakland, California, late one evening. They saw four or five youths huddled around a small red car parked at the curb. When the youths saw the police car approaching, they fled. One officer, who was wearing a jacket with the word "Police" embossed on its front, left the car to give chase. The officer did not follow one of the youths, who turned out to be Hodari, directly; instead, the officer took another route that brought them face to face on a parallel street. Hodari was looking behind as he ran and did not turn to see the officer until they were upon each other; whereupon Hodari tossed away a small rock. The officer tackled Hodari and recovered the rock, which turned out to be crack cocaine. This was used as evidence against Hodari in a subsequent juvenile proceeding.

ISSUE: Had Hodari been "seized" within the meaning of the Fourth Amendment at the time he dropped the crack cocaine? NO.

SUPREME COURT DECISION: No "seizure" occurs under the Fourth Amendment when a law enforcement officer seeks to arrest a suspect through a show of authority, but applies no physical force, and the suspect does not willingly submit. "Seizure" under the Fourth Amendment occurs only when there is either use of physical force or submission by the suspect to the authority of the officer.

REASON: "To say that an arrest is effected by the slightest application of physical force, despite the arrestee's escape, is not to say that for Fourth Amendment purposes there is a continuing arrest during the period of fugitivity. If, for example, Pertoso [the officer] had laid his hands upon Hodari to arrest him, but Hodari had broken away and had then cast away the cocaine, it would hardly be realistic to say that disclosure had been made during the course of an arrest. The present case, however, is even one step further removed. It does not involve the application of any physical force; Hodari was untouched by Officer Pertoso at the time he discarded the cocaine. His defense relies instead upon the proposition that a seizure occurs 'when the officer, by means of physical force or show of authority, has in some way restrained the liberty of a citizen.' Hodari contends that Pertoso's pursuit qualified as a 'show of authority' calling upon Hodari to halt. The narrow question before us is whether, with respect to a show of authority as with respect to application of physical force, a seizure occurs even though the subject does not yield. We hold that it does not."

"The language of the Fourth Amendment, of course, cannot sustain respondent's contention. The word 'seizure' readily bears the meaning of a laying on of hands or application of physical force to restrain movement, even when it is ultimately unsuccessful. It does not remotely apply, however, to the prospect of a policeman yelling 'Stop, in the name of the law!' at a fleeing form that continues to flee. That is no seizure. Nor can the result respondent wishes to achieve be produced—indirectly, as it were—by suggesting that Pertoso's uncomplied-with show of authority was a common-law arrest, and then appealing to the principle that all common-law arrests are seizures. An arrest requires either physical force or, where that is absent, submission to the assertion of authority."

CASE SIGNIFICANCE: There are four elements for an arrest to take place: intention to arrest, authority to arrest, seizure and detention, and the understanding of the individual that he or she is being arrested. This case clarifies one of these elements—seizure and detention. The issue here was whether, at the time Hodari threw away the crack cocaine, he had been arrested. Had he been arrested before throwing away the crack cocaine, the evidence would have been excluded because at that time there was no probable cause for his arrest. On the other hand, if he had not been arrested, the evidence would be admissible because what Hodari did would constitute abandonment.

The Court held that, at the time Hodari dropped the drugs, he had not been "seized" within the meaning of the Fourth Amendment. This is because for "seizure" to be present under the Fourth Amendment, there must be "either the application of physical force, however slight, or, where that is absent, submission to an officer's 'show of authority' to restrain the subject's liberty." There are generally two types of seizures: actual and constructive. Actual seizure is accomplished by taking the person into custody with the use of hands or firearms (denoting use of force without touching the individual) or by merely touching the individual without the use of force. Constructive seizure is accomplished without any physical touching, grabbing, holding, or the use of force. It occurs when the individual peacefully submits to the officer's will and control.

The facts show that Hodari was untouched by the officer before he dropped the cocaine, hence no physical force had been applied. The officer had told Hodari to "halt," but Hodari did not comply and, therefore, he was not seized until he was tackled. There was, therefore, no actual or constructive seizure; hence, one of the elements of an arrest under the Fourth Amendment was missing. Because no illegal arrest had taken place at the time the crack cocaine was tossed away, the evidence recovered by the police was admissible in court.

County of Riverside v. McLaughlin
500 U.S. 413 (1991)

CAPSULE: Detention of a suspect for 48 hours is presumptively reasonable. If the time-to-hearing is longer, the burden of proof shifts to the police to prove reasonableness. If the time-to-hearing is shorter, the burden of proof of unreasonable delay shifts to the suspect.

FACTS: A lawsuit was brought challenging Riverside County, California's process of determining probable cause for warrantless arrests. The county's policy was to combine probable cause determinations with arraignment proceedings. The policy was close to the California Penal Code, which says that arraignments must be conducted without unnecessary delay and within two days (48 hours) of arrest, excluding weekends and holidays. The U.S. District Court issued a preliminary injunction requiring the county to provide all persons arrested without a warrant with a probable cause hearing within 36 hours. The Ninth Circuit Court of Appeals affirmed, saying that the county policy of providing a probable cause hearing at arraignment within 48 hours was not in accord with *Gerstein*'s [*v. Pugh*, 420 U.S. 103 (1975)] requirement of promptly providing the probable cause determination after arrest because no more than 36 hours were needed to complete the administrative steps incident to arrest.

There was conflict among the Circuit Courts of Appeals on this issue. The Ninth, Fourth, and Seventh Circuit Courts of Appeals all required a probable cause determination immediately following completion of the administrative procedures incident to arrest. The Second Circuit Court of Appeals allowed flexibility and permitted states to combine probable cause determinations with other pretrial proceedings.

ISSUE: Does the Fourth Amendment require a judicial determination of probable cause immediately after completing the administrative steps incident to arrest (within 36 hours after arrest)? NO.

SUPREME COURT DECISION: If a probable cause determination is combined with arraignment, it is presumptively reasonable for the arrest-to-hearing period to last up to 48 hours. If more time than that elapses, the government bears the burden of showing that the delay is reasonable. Conversely, if the release is made before 48 hours after arrest, the burden of showing unreasonable delay shifts to the person arrested.

REASON: "Our task in this case is to articulate more clearly the boundaries of what is permissible under the Fourth Amendment. Although we hesitate to announce that the Constitution compels a specific time limit, it is important to provide some degree of certainty so that States and counties may establish procedures with confidence that they fall within constitutional bounds. Taking into account the competing interests articulated in *Gerstein*, we believe that a jurisdiction that provides judicial determinations of probable cause within 48 hours of arrest will, as a general matter, comply with the promptness requirement of *Gerstein*. For this reason, such jurisdictions will be immune from systemic challenges."

"This is not to say that the probable cause determination in a particular case passes constitutional muster simply because it is provided within 48 hours. Such a hearing may nonetheless violate *Gerstein* if the arrested individual can prove that his or her probable cause determination was delayed unreasonably. Examples of unreasonable delays are delays for the purpose of gathering additional evidence to justify the arrest, a delay motivated by ill will against the arrested individual, or delay for delay's sake. In evaluating whether the delay in a particular case is unreasonable, however, courts must allow a substantial degree of flexibility. Courts cannot ignore the often unavoidable delays in transporting arrested persons from one facility to another, handling late-night bookings where no magistrate is readily available, obtaining the presence of an arresting officer who may be busy processing other suspects or securing the premises of an arrest, and other practical realities."

CASE SIGNIFICANCE: This case defines the allowable time a suspect may be detained by the police without a hearing when a warrantless arrest occurs. In *Gerstein v. Pugh*, the Court held that "the Fourth Amendment requires a prompt judicial determination of probable cause as a prerequisite to an extended pretrial detention following a warrantless arrest." In this case, the Court clarified what the term "prompt" in *Gerstein* means. The Court said that it is presumptively reasonable for the detention to last up to 48 hours. If more than 48 hours elapse, the government bears the burden of showing that the delay was reasonable. On the other hand, release within 48 hours does not necessarily mean that there was no unreasonable delay, but the burden of showing that the delay was unreasonable shifts to the person who has been detained. In the words of the Court, "although we hesitate to announce that the Constitution compels a specific time limit, it is important to provide some degree of certainty so that States and counties may establish procedures with confidence that they fall within constitutional bounds." The Court added that, in evaluating whether the delay in a particular case is unreasonable, courts must allow a substantial degree of flexibility, taking into account practical realities. This includes unavoidable delays in transporting arrested persons, handling late-night bookings, and obtaining the presence of an arresting officer who may be busy doing other jobs. Determinations of unreasonable or reasonable delay are made by lower courts on a case-by-case basis, but using the principle laid out in *McLaughlin* as a standard. This puts more substance and meaning into the word "prompt."

United States v. Alvarez-Machain
504 U.S. 655 (1992)

CAPSULE: The abduction of a foreigner that is not in violation of a treaty does not deprive a U.S. court of jurisdiction in a criminal trial.

FACTS: Alvarez-Machain, a citizen and resident of Mexico, was indicted in the United States for participating in the kidnapping and murder of a U.S. Drug Enforcement Administration (DEA) agent, Enrique Camarena-Salazar, and his pilot. Alvarez-Machain was subsequently abducted from his medical office in Guadalajara, Mexico and flown to El Paso, Texas, where he was arrested by DEA officials. In court, Alvarez-Machain moved to dismiss the indictment, claiming that the U.S. District Court did not have jurisdiction to try him because he was abducted in violation of an extradition treaty between the U.S. and Mexico.

ISSUE: Can a criminal defendant, forcibly abducted and brought to the United States from Mexico, be tried by a United States court? YES.

SUPREME COURT DECISION: Alvarez-Machain's abduction did not violate the Extradition Treaty between the United States and Mexico; therefore, the abduction did not deprive the U.S. court of jurisdiction in a criminal trial.

REASON: "This Court has never departed from the rule announced in *Ker* [*v. Illinois*, 119 U.S. 436 (1886)] that the power of a court to try a person for [a] crime is not impaired by the fact that he had been brought within the court's jurisdiction by reason of a 'forcible abduction.' No persuasive reasons are newly presented to justify overruling this line of cases. They rest on the sound basis that due process of law is satisfied when one present in court is convicted of [a] crime after having been fairly apprised of the charges against him and after a fair trial in accordance with constitutional procedural safeguards. There is nothing in the Constitution that requires a court to permit a guilty person rightfully convicted to escape justice because he was brought to trial against his will" (citing *Frisbie v. Collins*, 342 U.S. 519 [1952]).

CASE SIGNIFICANCE: The decision in this case was based on provisions of the Extradition Treaty between the United States and Mexico. The Court said that a defendant cannot be prosecuted in violation of the terms of an extradition treaty, but that the Extradition Treaty between the United States and Mexico did not contain any prohibition against kidnapping. Said the Court: "[n]either the Treaty's language nor the history of negotiations and practice under it supports the proposition that it prohibits abductions outside its terms."

The greater significance of this case, however, lies in the Court's implied reaffirmation of the principle that "the power of a court to try a person for crime is not impaired by the fact that [a defendant] had been brought within the court's jurisdiction by reason of a 'forcible abduction'" (*Frisbie v. Collins*, 342 U.S., at 522 [1952]). In *Frisbie*, a defendant alleged that while he was living in Chicago, Michigan officers forcibly seized, handcuffed, blackjacked, and then abducted him back to Michigan. He sought release from the Michigan state prison in a *habeas corpus* case. The Court denied his release, saying that an unlawful arrest has no impact on a subsequent criminal prosecution and that an invalid arrest does not deprive the court of jurisdiction to try a criminal case. This leads to an interesting situation: evidence illegally seized is not admissible in a court of law, but a defendant who has been unlawfully arrested can nonetheless be lawfully tried in criminal court.

Illinois v. McArthur
531 U.S. 326 (2001)

CAPSULE: Under exigent circumstances, and where there is a need to preserve evidence until the police can obtain a warrant, they may temporarily restrain a person's movements without violating his or her Fourth Amendment right.

FACTS: A woman asked police officers to accompany her to the trailer where she lived with her husband, McArthur, while she removed her belongings. The woman went inside where McArthur was present, and the officers remained outside. When the woman emerged, she told one of the officers that McArthur had drugs in the trailer. This established probable cause and so the officer knocked on the door and asked permission to search the trailer, which McArthur denied. One officer left to obtain a warrant. When McArthur stepped onto his porch, the other officer prevented him from reentering his trailer unaccompanied. McArthur did reenter the trailer on three occasions while the officer stood in the doorway and observed him. When the other officer returned with a warrant, the officers searched the trailer and found drugs and paraphernalia.

ISSUE: Was the temporary seizure of a suspect while officers obtained a warrant to search his trailer valid? YES

SUPREME COURT DECISION: Under exigent circumstances, and where there is a need to preserve evidence until the police obtain a warrant, they may temporarily restrain a suspect without violating his or her Fourth Amendment right against unreasonable searches and seizures. The minimal nature of the intrusion and the law enforcement interest at stake justified the brief seizure.

REASON: "When faced with special law enforcement needs, diminished expectations of privacy, minimal intrusions, or the like, the Court has found that certain general, or individual, circumstances may render a warrantless search or seizure reasonable." "Temporarily keeping a person from entering his home, a consequence whenever police stop a person on the street, is considerably less intrusive than police entry into the home itself in order to make a warrantless arrest or conduct a search." "We have found no case in which this Court has held unlawful a temporary seizure that was supported by probable cause and was designed to prevent the loss of evidence while the police diligently obtained a warrant in a reasonable period of time."

CASE SIGNIFICANCE: The Court gave four reasons for this decision:

1. The police had probable cause to believe that the trailer home contained evidence of a crime and unlawful drugs;
2. The police had good reasons to fear that, unless restrained, the suspect would destroy the drugs before they could return with a warrant;
3. The police made reasonable effort to reconcile their law enforcement needs with the demands of suspect's personal privacy; and
4. The police imposed the restraint for a limited time—two hours.

The Court concluded: the police officers in this case had probable cause to believe that a home contained contraband, which was evidence of a crime. They reasonably believed that the home's resident, if left free of any restraint, would destroy that evidence. And they imposed a restraint that was both limited and tailored reasonably to secure law enforcement needs while protecting privacy interests. In our view, the restraint met the Fourth Amendment's demands.

This case is enlightening because although the Court allowed the temporary restraint of the suspect while another officer went to obtain a warrant, the decision carefully pointed out the circumstances that justified the restraint. The implication is that temporary restraints by officers must be justified by circumstances similar to this case for the restraint to be valid. How similar is difficult to determine; that will have to be decided on a case-by-case basis. It is safe to say, however, that the closer the circumstances are to this case, the greater is the likelihood that the police restraint will be deemed valid.

Atwater v. City of Lago Vista
532 U.S. 318 (2000)

CAPSULE: "The Fourth Amendment does not forbid a warrantless arrest for a minor criminal offense, such as a misdemeanor seatbelt violation, punishable only by a fine."

FACTS: A Texas law requires all front seat passengers to wear a seatbelt, a crime punishable by a fine of not more than $50. Texas law also expressly authorizes a police officer to arrest without a warrant if a person is found in violation of the law, although the police may issue a citation in lieu of arrest. Atwater was driving a vehicle with her two young children in the front seat; none was wearing a seatbelt. An officer observed the violation and stopped Atwater—telling her as he approached the vehicle that she was going to jail. Following the release of Atwater's children to a neighbor, the officer handcuffed Atwater, placed her in his police car, and took her to the police station where she was made to remove her shoes, jewelry, eyeglasses, and empty her pockets. Officers later took her mug shot and placed her in a cell for about an hour. She was then taken before a magistrate and released on bond. She later pleaded no contest and paid a $50 fine.

ISSUE: Does the Fourth Amendment forbid a warrantless arrest for a minor criminal offense punishable only by a fine? NO.

SUPREME COURT DECISION: "The Fourth Amendment does not forbid a warrantless arrest for a minor criminal offense, such as a misdemeanor seatbelt violation, punishable only by a fine."

REASON: At common law, commentators disagreed on the ability of police officers to make a warrantless arrest of an individual if the crime committed was not a felony or a misdemeanor involving a breach of the peace. However, during the time of the framing of the Bill of Rights, the states regularly authorized police officers to make warrantless misdemeanor arrests without the requirement of a breach of the peace. When combined with the fact that each of the states currently has laws authorizing arrest for misdemeanors not involving a breach of the peace, Atwater's argument of a constitutional proscription against warrantless arrests for minor violations was not persuasive. Atwater also argued that, even if there was not a constitutional provision against such arrests, the Court should create one, drawing a distinction between crimes for which a sentence of jail time could accrue from those punishable only by a fine. The latter, then, could not result in an arrest without a warrant. "The trouble with this distinction, of course, is that an officer on the street might not be able to tell [if the crime carries a jail sentence]" ". . . [because] penalties for ostensibly identical conduct can vary on account of facts difficult (if not impossible) to know at the scene of the arrest." "For all these reasons, Atwater's various distinctions between permissible and impermissible arrests for minor crimes strike us as very unsatisfactory lines to require police officers to draw on a moment's notice."

CASE SIGNIFICANCE: This case is important because it settles an issue of concern to the police: whether the police can arrest persons who violate laws or ordinances that are not punishable with jail or prison time. At present, all 50 states and the District of Columbia have laws authorizing such warrantless arrests. Texas allows a warrantless arrest even for a minor criminal offense, such as not wearing a seatbelt, which is punishable only by a $50 fine. Atwater paid the fine, but later challenged the constitutionality of the law, arguing that it violated her Fourth Amendment right. She maintained that no such arrests were authorized under common law and that the history and intent of the framers of the Constitution did not allow such arrests. The Court disagreed, saying that it was unclear whether or not such arrests were authorized under common law, and also found that "there is no historical evidence that the framers or proponents of the Fourth Amendment, outspokenly opposed to the infamous general warrants and writs of assistance, were at all concerned about warrantless arrests by local constables and other peace officers." The Court then concluded that: "We simply cannot conclude that the Fourth Amendment, as originally understood, forbade peace officers to arrest without warrant for misdemeanors not amounting to or involving breach of the peace." Given these, the Court held that warrantless arrests for nonjailable offenses are constitutional.

Seizures—In General 5

Introduction

The Fourth Amendment provides that "The right of the people to be secure in their persons, houses, papers, and effects, against unreasonable searches and seizures, shall not be violated, and no Warrants shall issue, but upon probable cause, supported by Oath or affirmation, and particularly describing the place to be searched, and the person or things to be seized." This provision governs the constitutionality of searches and seizures conducted by the police.

A seizure is defined as the exercise of dominion or control by the government over a person or thing because of a violation of law. The seizure discussed in this chapter is a seizure of things or items, as opposed to the seizure of a person, which is an arrest. The items subject to police seizures fall into four general categories: (1) contraband, such as drugs, counterfeit money, and gambling paraphernalia; (2) fruits of a crime, such as stolen goods; (3) instrumentalities of a crime, such as robbery tools and weapons; and (4) "mere evidence" of a crime, such as clothing containing bloodstains, masks, wigs, etc., that are related to criminal activity.

State law may list specific items the police can seize, but those items generally fall under one or more of the four categories listed above. Seizures of these items may either be with a warrant or without a warrant. In both instances, probable cause must be present, or the seizure is unconstitutional.

The cases briefed in this section begin with *Schmerber v. California*, 384 U.S. 757 (1966), in which the Court held that drawing blood from a suspect without his or her consent is not a violation of any constitutional right, as long as it is done under certain circumstances and using accepted medical methods. There are limits, however, to what the police can seize, even with court permission. For example, in *Winston v. Lee*, 470 U.S. 753 (1985), the Court held that surgery requiring general anesthesia to remove a bullet lodged near a suspect's heart cannot be allowed, even with court permission, unless the government demonstrates a compelling need for it.

The leading cases briefed in this chapter on seizures in general are *Schmerber v. California* and *Winston v. Lee*. A significant recent decision, *Groh v. Ramirez* (2004), holds that a search warrant that does not comply with the requirement that the warrant particularly describe the person or things to be seized is unconstitutional. The fact that the application for the warrant (but not the warrant itself) adequately described the things to be seized does not make the warrant valid.

Schmerber v. California
384 U.S. 757 (1966)

CAPSULE: Drawing blood from a suspect without his or her consent is not a violation of any constitutional right, as long as it is done by medical personnel using accepted medical methods.

FACTS: Schmerber was arrested for driving under the influence of alcohol, which resulted in an automobile accident. After reading Schmerber his *Miranda* warnings, and while Schmerber was in a hospital being treated for injuries suffered in the accident, an officer directed a physician to draw a blood sample for purposes of chemical analysis. This was completed over the objection of Schmerber and against the advice of his counsel. Evidence of the chemical analysis, which indicated intoxication, was admitted in court over Schmerber's objection and he was convicted.

ISSUE: Does the drawing of blood from a defendant over his or her objection violate the Fifth Amendment protection from self-incrimination or the Fourth Amendment protection from unreasonable searches and seizures? NO.

SUPREME COURT DECISION: The drawing of blood from a suspect, without his or her consent, to obtain evidence is not a violation of any constitutional right as long as the removal is done by medical personnel using accepted medical methods.

REASON: "*Breithaupt* [*v. Abram*, 352 U.S. 432 (1957)] was also a case in which police officers caused blood to be drawn from the driver of an automobile involved in an accident, and which there was ample justification for the officer's conclusion that the driver was under the influence of alcohol. There, as here, the extraction was made by a physician in a simple, medically accepted manner in a hospital environment. There, however, the driver was unconscious at the time the blood was withdrawn and hence had no opportunity to object to the procedure. We affirmed the conviction there resulting from the use of the test in evidence, holding that under such circumstances the withdrawal did not offend 'that "sense of justice" of which we spoke in *Rochin v. California*, 342 U.S. 165.' 352 U.S. at 435. *Breithaupt* thus requires the rejection of petitioner's due process argument and nothing in the circumstances of this case or in supervening events persuades us that this aspect of *Breithaupt* should be overruled."

CASE SIGNIFICANCE: *Schmerber* addressed and settled four constitutional issues that suspects usually raised during pretrial identification: right against self-incrimination, right to counsel, right to due process, and right against unreasonable search and seizure. On the self-incrimination claim, the Court said that the seizure of "real or physical" evidence does not violate Fifth

Amendment guarantees because the amendment applies only to testimonial evidence. This implies that a suspect cannot refuse to appear in a police lineup or showup. The issue of right to counsel was dismissed by the Court, saying that there was no right to counsel at this stage. On the right to due process, the Court concluded that the extraction of blood in this case was valid because it was made by a doctor in a hospital and followed a medically accepted procedure. On the issue of unreasonable search and seizure (*Schmerber* alleging that the police could have obtained a warrant prior to blood removal), the Court ruled that the presence of exigent circumstances (the alcohol would be processed through the body and be lost in a short time) justified the warrantless seizure.

Cupp v. Murphy
412 U.S. 291 (1973)

CAPSULE: The police may make a warrantless seizure of evidence that is likely to disappear before a warrant can be obtained.

FACTS: Upon learning of his estranged wife's death, Murphy voluntarily went to the police station for questioning. After arriving at the station, where he was met by his lawyer, the police noticed a dark spot on Murphy's finger that they suspected might be dried blood from the murder. Murphy refused an officer's requests to take a sample of scrapings from his fingernails, placed his hands behind his back and in his pockets, and appeared to rub them to remove the spot. Under protest and without a warrant, the police took the fingernail samples. The samples were determined to have traces of skin, blood cells, and fabric from the victim's nightgown. Murphy was tried and convicted of second degree murder.

ISSUE: Does seizing evidence that is likely to disappear without consent or formal arrest violate the Fourth Amendment protection from unreasonable searches and seizures? NO.

SUPREME COURT DECISION: The police may seize, without a warrant, evidence that is likely to disappear before a warrant can be obtained. Given the facts of this case—the existence of probable cause, limited intrusion caused by the stationhouse detention, and the destructibility of the evidence—the warrantless seizure by the police did not violate the right against unreasonable search and seizure.

REASON: "Where there is no formal arrest, as in the case before us, a person might [be] . . . less likely to take conspicuous, immediate steps to destroy incriminating evidence on his person." A full search of Murphy without formal arrest would have been unconstitutional under *Chimel v. Cali-*

fornia, 395 U.S. 752 (1969); but the limited intrusion on Murphy was justified here because of probable cause.

CASE SIGNIFICANCE: This case illustrates the "evanescent evidence" exception to the warrant requirement. The general rule is that searches and seizures must be by virtue of a warrant. This rule, however, is subject to many exceptions. One of those exceptions is the "evanescent evidence" rule, which means that the absence of a warrant does not invalidate the seizure if the evidence sought is likely to disappear unless immediately obtained. In this case, the blood on the suspect's fingernails could easily have been rubbed off by the suspect, and the evidence would have disappeared, had the police not acted immediately. The likelihood of disappearance of the evidence constituted an emergency that justified the warrantless seizure.

Welsh v. Wisconsin
466 U.S. 740 (1984)

CAPSULE: The warrantless nighttime entry of a suspect's home to effect an arrest for a nonjailable offense violates the Fourth Amendment.

FACTS: A witness saw Welsh's automobile being driven erratically, eventually swerving off the road and stopping in a field. Before the police could arrive, Welsh walked away from the accident. Upon arrival at the scene, the police were told that the driver was either drunk or very sick. The police checked the registration of the car and went to the owner's house without obtaining a warrant. The police gained entry to the house when Welsh's stepdaughter answered the door. Welsh was arrested and convicted for driving while under the influence of intoxicants.

ISSUE: Is a warrantless nighttime entry of a person's home to make an arrest for a nonjailable traffic offense constitutional under the Fourth Amendment? NO.

SUPREME COURT DECISION: The warrantless nighttime entry of a suspect's home to effect an arrest for a nonjailable offense is prohibited by the Fourth Amendment.

REASON: "Before government agents may invade the sanctity of the home, it must demonstrate exigent circumstances that overcome the presumption of unreasonableness that attaches to all warrantless home entries. An important factor to be considered when determining whether any exigency exists is the gravity of the underlying offense for which the arrest is being made. Moreover, although no exigency is created simply because there is probable cause to believe that a serious crime has been committed, application of the exigent circumstances exception in the context of home entry should rarely be sanctioned when there is probable cause that only a minor offense has been committed."

CASE SIGNIFICANCE: Probable cause and exigent circumstances almost always justify a warrantless search or seizure. This means that as long as probable cause and exigent (emergency) circumstances that justify immediate action by the officer are present, a warrantless search or seizure is valid. This case adds a third dimension to this general rule. The Court said that the gravity of the offense must be considered when determining whether a warrantless search or seizure can be undertaken. If the offense is minor and nonjailable, a warrantless entry into a home is not justified, particularly at night. There are, however, unanswered questions in this case. For example, what if the offense is minor but carries a jail term? Or suppose the incident takes place during the day? Or how might current DWI laws with more severe sentences change this ruling? What is clear from this case is that a warrantless night-time entry into a person's home to make an arrest for a nonjailable traffic offense is invalid under the Fourth Amendment.

Winston v. Lee
470 U.S. 753 (1985)

CAPSULE: Surgery requiring a general anesthetic to remove a bullet from a suspect for use as evidence constitutes an intrusion into the suspect's privacy and security that violates the Fourth Amendment. It cannot be allowed unless the government demonstrates a compelling need for it.

FACTS: In a shoot-out resulting from a robbery, a store owner was wounded in the legs and the assailant appeared to be wounded in the left side of the body. Some time later, officers responding to another call saw the suspect (Lee) eight blocks from the store. He told the officers that he had been wounded when he himself was robbed. The suspect was taken to the same hospital as the store owner. While at the hospital, Lee was identified by the store owner as the man who had shot him. The state asked a court for an order directing Lee to undergo surgery to have the bullet removed. The doctors first said that there was some danger involved in the operation, but later testified that the bullet was lodged near the surface of the skin and could be easily removed with no danger. While Lee was being prepared for surgery, it was discovered that the bullet was deeper than originally thought and would require surgery under general anesthesia with some risk involved. Lee then moved for a rehearing in the state court which was denied. The case eventually went to the United States Supreme Court.

ISSUE: May a state compel an individual to undergo surgery in a search for evidence of a crime? NO.

SUPREME COURT DECISION: Compelled surgical intrusions into an individual's body may be of such a magnitude that the intrusion is unreasonable even if it may produce evidence of a crime.

REASON: "A compelled surgical intrusion into an individual's body for evidence . . . implicates expectations of privacy and security of such magnitude that the intrusion may be 'unreasonable' even if likely to produce evidence of a crime. . . . The unreasonableness of surgical intrusions beneath the skin depends on a case-by-case approach, in which the individual's interests in privacy and security are weighed against society's interests in conducting the procedure. In a given case, the question whether the community's need for evidence outweighs the substantial privacy interest at stake is a delicate one admitting of few categorical answers."

CASE SIGNIFICANCE: This case is significant because it indicates that there are limits to what the government can do in an effort to solve a crime. In this case, the government sought a court order to recover a bullet lodged in the chest of a suspect. The evidence would have been conclusive against the suspect, but the Court held that not even a court of law could order that such surgery be performed because it would have been too intrusive into the suspect's body. In an earlier case (*Schmerber v. California*, 384 U.S. 757 [1966]), the Court held that a state may, over the suspect's protest, have a physician extract blood without violating the suspect's rights. However, according to the *Schmerber* decision, the holding that the Constitution does not forbid minor intrusions into an individual's body under stringently limited conditions in no way indicates that it permits more substantial intrusions or intrusions under other conditions. The Court in *Lee* concluded that the procedure sought was an example of the "more substantial intrusion" cautioned against in *Schmerber*, and therefore held that to permit the procedure would violate the suspect's right to be secure in his person, as guaranteed by the Fourth Amendment, unless a compelling need for it was established by the government. That was not done in this case.

City of West Covina v. Perkins
525 U.S. 234 (1999)

CAPSULE: The due process clause does not require the police to provide the owner of property seized with notice of remedies specified by state law for the property's return and the information necessary to use those procedures.

FACTS: Pursuant to a valid search warrant, police officers searched Perkins' home and seized a number of items. The suspect in the crime (March) was a boarder in the Perkins' house. Items seized by the police incriminated March, but some belonged to Perkins. Upon completing the seizure, officers left notice of the search and other information such as the judge who issued the warrant, officers to contact for information and an itemized list of property seized. The officers did not leave the warrant number because the case was ongoing and the information was sealed; however, that information was maintained by the court clerk in a file indexed by the address of the home searched. After attempts to secure the return of the property, Perkins filed suit.

ISSUE: When seizing property for a criminal investigation, does the due process clause require that the person from whom property is taken be provided with a detailed notice of the procedures for the return of the seized property and the information needed to use those procedures? NO.

SUPREME COURT DECISION: The Due Process Clause does not require the police to provide the owner of property seized with notice of remedies specified by state law for the property's return and the information necessary to use those procedures.

REASON: "A primary purpose of the notice required by the Due Process Clause is to ensure that the opportunity for a hearing is meaningful. . . . It follows that when law enforcement agents seize property pursuant to [a] warrant, due process requires them to take reasonable steps to give notice that the property has been taken so the owner can pursue available remedies for its return. . . . No similar rationale justifies requiring individualized notice of state-law remedies which, like those at issue here, are established by published, generally available state statutes and case law. Once the property owner is informed that his property has been seized, he can turn to these public sources to learn about the remedial procedures available to him. The City need not take other steps to inform him of his options."

CASE SIGNIFICANCE: In this case, the Ninth Circuit had held that the owner of the property seized must be given by the police a "detailed notice of the state procedures for the return of the seized property and the information necessary to invoke those procedures, including the search warrant number or a method of obtaining it." The Supreme Court rejected this as a requirement under the due process clause, saying that this interpretation by the Ninth Circuit lacked precedent. The Court added that "individualized notice that officers have taken property is necessary in a case such as this one because the owner has no other reasonable means of ascertaining who is responsible for his loss," but that the other requirements specified by state law (such as detailed notice of the state procedures for the return of the seized property and the information necessary to use those procedures, including the search warrant number or a method of obtaining it, as required by California law) are not required by the due process clause.

Groh v. Ramirez et al.
540 U.S. 551 (2004)

CAPSULE: A search warrant that does not comply with the requirement that the warrant particularly describe the person or things to be seized is unconstitutional. The fact that the application for the warrant (but not the warrant itself) adequately described the things to be seized does not make the warrant valid.

FACTS: Groh, an agent of the Bureau of Alcohol, Tobacco, and Firearms (ATF) prepared an application for a search warrant based on information that weapons and explosives were located on Ramirez's farm. The application was supported by a detailed affidavit listing the items to be seized and describing the basis for his belief that the items were concealed on the property. Groh presented these documents, along with a warrant form he had completed, to a magistrate. The magistrate signed the warrant form. Although the application and affidavit described the contraband expected to be discovered, the warrant form only indicated that the place to be searched was Ramirez's home. The warrant did not incorporate any reference to the itemized list contained in the application or affidavit. The day after the magistrate signed the warrant, officers searched Ramirez's home but found no illegal weapons or explosives. Groh left a copy of the warrant at the home but did not leave a copy of the application. The following day, in response to a request from Ramirez's attorney, Groh faxed a copy of the application. No charges were filed against Ramirez, but he later filed suit claiming his Fourth Amendment rights were violated by the non-specific warrant.

ISSUE: Does a search warrant that does not particularly describe the persons or things to be seized, but has those in the application that was filed with the judge, violate the Fourth Amendment? YES.

SUPREME COURT DECISION: A search and seizure warrant that does not contain a particular description of the things to be seized is unconstitutional even if the application for the warrant contains such descriptions.

REASON: "The Fourth Amendment states unambiguously that 'no Warrants shall issue, but upon probable cause, supported by Oath or affirmation, and particularly describing the place to be searched, and the persons or things to be seized.' The warrant in this case complied with the first three of these requirements: It was based on probable cause and supported by a sworn affidavit, and it described with particularity the place of the search. On the fourth requirement, however, the warrant failed altogether." The Court relied upon previous cases, including *Massachusetts v. Sheppard*, 468 U.S. 981 (1984), where they stressed that a warrant that does not particularly describe the items to be seized is unconstitutional. The Court then addressed the argument by Groh that the search was based on a particular description because it was in the supporting documents. To this, the Court responded, "The fact that the *application* adequately described the 'things to be seized' does not save the *warrant* from its facial invalidity." The Fourth Amendment by its terms requires particularity in the warrant, not the supporting documents" [emphasis in original]. The reason given by the Court for this requirement is, "unless the particular items described in the affidavit are also set forth in the warrant itself (or at least incorporated by reference, and the affidavit present at the search), there can be no written assurance that the Magistrate actually found probable cause to search for, and to seize, every item mentioned in the affidavit." The Court did concede that the particular description could be addressed in supporting documents, however, with the statement that "We do not say that the Fourth Amendment forbids a warrant from cross-referencing other documents. Indeed, most Courts of Appeals have held that a court may construe a warrant with references to a supporting application or affidavit if the warrant uses appropriate words of incorporation, and if the supporting document accompanies the warrant."

CASE SIGNIFICANCE: In this case, the application submitted by the officer to the judge clearly specified the items to be seized; however, the warrant itself did not specify those, and neither did the warrant incorporate by reference the application's itemized list. The Court concluded that the warrant was "plainly invalid." The purpose for the specificity requirement is to have "written assurance" that the judge "actually found probable cause for a search as broad as the affiant requested." The Court also said that "the particularity requirement's purpose is not limited to preventing general searches; it also assures the individual whose property is searched and seized of the executing officer's legal authority, his need to search, and the limits of his power to do so." For purposes of civil liability, the Court held that the officer was "not entitled to qualified immunity despite the constitutional violation because it would be clear to a reasonable officer that his conduct was unlawful in the situation he confronted." It added that: "Given that the particularity requirement is stated in the Constitution's text, no reasonable officer could believe that a warrant that did not comply with that requirement was valid." The Court, however, refused to specifically address two other issues that were involved in the case: (1) whether the warrant would have been valid if the warrant itself mentioned that the application listed the items to be seized, but without such list being available during the search; and (2) whether orally describing the items to the defendant during the search complied with the specificity requirement.

This case presents a common dilemma for police officers. Many search warrant forms are computer generated, which are often cumbersome to fill out and do not provide sufficient space for some descriptions. To overcome these problems with search warrant forms, officers often include references to other documents (affidavits or applications for the warrant), or they provide a brief description and rely on the supporting documents to meet the particularity requirement of the Fourth Amendment. Although the Supreme Court appears to support the procedure of including references to other documents in the search warrant, as long as the documents then accompany the warrant, the Court firmly rejected instances in which the warrant itself does not particularly describe "the place to be searched, and the persons or things to be seized." Officers must be careful, therefore, to make sure the items to be seized are adequately described in the search warrant, or are at least referenced in the warrant and the supporting documents attached to the warrant.

Searches—In General 6

Introduction

A search is different from a seizure, although both are governed by the same rules. A search is defined as the exploration or examination of an individual's house, premises, or person, to discover things or items that may be used by the government for evidence in a criminal prosecution.

In contrast, a seizure is defined as the exercise of dominion or control by the government over a person or thing because of a violation of law. Searching is looking; seizing is taking. If the search yields items that may lawfully be seized, then a seizure takes place. A search usually precedes a seizure.

A search is not limited to homes, buildings, apartments, or other enclosed places. It can take place anywhere, even in a public place (as in a parking lot or a telephone booth, or even a person's computer or Internet account), if the person has a reasonable expectation of privacy. The rule is that searches (and seizures) must be authorized by a warrant issued by a judge or magistrate—with exceptions, of course. There are four basic requirements for a search warrant to be valid. These are: probable cause, supporting oath or affirmation, particular description of the place to be searched and the things to be seized, and the signature of a magistrate. In reality, however, most seizures, as well as arrests, are made without a warrant. In searches without a warrant, the police bear the burden of establishing probable cause. A more recent case holds that a warrantless search by an officer of a probationer's apartment supported by reasonable suspicion and authorized by a condition of probation is valid under the Fourth Amendment.

The scope of a search is governed by the rule of reasonableness, given the object sought. The following rule succinctly delineates what an officer can and cannot do: Do not look for an elephant in a matchbox.

The "knock and announce" issue has recently generated several decisions from the Supreme Court. In *Wilson v. Arkansas*, 514 U.S. 927 (1995), the Court said that the reasonableness requirement of the Fourth Amendment requires officers to knock and announce before entering a place, subject to exceptions determined by state courts. In a subsequent case, the Court held that the Fourth Amendment does not allow a blanket exception to the knock and announce requirement in felony drug investigations. The rule on no-knock entries holds even if the entry results in the destruction of property, *United States v. Ramirez*, 523 U.S. 65 (1998).

The leading cases briefed in this chapter on searches in general are: *Steagald v. United States, Maryland v. Garrison*, and *Wilson v. Arkansas. United States v. Banks* (2003) gives more certainty to the time factor in searches when it held that after knocking and announcing their presence and intention to search, 15 to 20 seconds is sufficient time for officers to wait before forcing entry into a home to execute a search warrant for drugs.

Coolidge v. New Hampshire
403 U.S. 443 (1971)

CAPSULE: A warrant is valid only if issued by a neutral and detached magistrate.

FACTS: A 14-year-old girl left her home in response to a man's request for a baby-sitter. Thirteen days later, her body was found by the side of a major highway. On January 28, the police questioned Coolidge in his home concerning the ownership of guns, and asked if he would take a lie detector test concerning his whereabouts on the night of the girl's disappearance. He produced three guns voluntarily and agreed to the lie detector test. The following Sunday, Coolidge was called to the police station to take the lie detector test and for further questioning. While he was being questioned, two officers (not those who had questioned him earlier) went to his house and questioned his wife. During the course of the questioning, she voluntarily produced four of Coolidge's guns and the clothes he was believed to have been wearing on the night of the girl's disappearance. After a meeting involving the officers working on the case and the Attorney General, the Attorney General signed an arrest warrant for Coolidge and search warrants for his house and car. Pursuant to those warrants, Coolidge was arrested and his cars impounded. The car was searched two days later and twice after that. Evidence presented over Coolidge's objection included gunpowder residue, microscopic particles taken from the car and from the clothes provided by Coolidge's wife, and a .22 caliber rifle also provided by her. Coolidge was charged with and convicted of murder.

ISSUES:
1. Was the warrant authorizing the search of Coolidge's house and car valid? NO.
2. If the warrant was not valid, could the seizure of the evidence in Coolidge's house and car be justified as an exception to the warrant requirement? NO.
3. Were the guns and clothes given to the officers by Coolidge's wife prior to the issuance of the warrant admissible as evidence? YES.

SUPREME COURT DECISIONS:
1. The warrant issued by the state's chief investigator and prosecutor (the state attorney general) was not issued by a neutral and detached magistrate; hence, the warrant was invalid.
2. The evidence seized from Coolidge's house (vacuum sweepings of the clothes taken from the house) and from the car (particles of gunpowder) could not be admissible as exceptions to the warrant requirement.
3. The guns and clothes given by Coolidge's wife to the police were given voluntarily; hence, they were admissible.

REASONS:
1. "When the right of privacy must reasonably yield to the right of search is, as a rule, to be decided by a judicial officer, not by a policeman or government enforcement agency." A warrant must, therefore, be issued by a neutral and detached magistrate.
2. "Since the police knew of the presence of the automobile and planned all along to seize it, there was no 'exigent circumstance' to justify their failure to obtain a warrant." Such warrantless seizures could not be justified under any of the exceptions to the warrant requirement.
3. "[T]he policemen were surely acting normally and properly when they asked her [Coolidge's wife], as they had asked those questioned earlier in the investigation, including Coolidge himself, about any guns there might be in the house. The question concerning the clothes Coolidge had been wearing the night of the disappearance was logical and in no way coercive. Indeed, one might doubt the competence of the officers involved had they not asked exactly the questions they did ask. And surely when Mrs. Coolidge of her own accord produced the guns and clothes for inspection, rather than simply describing them, it was not incumbent on the police to stop her or avert their eyes."

CASE SIGNIFICANCE: The *Coolidge* case is best known for the principle that a warrant is valid only if issued by a *neutral and detached magistrate*. If issued by any person who has an interest in the outcome of the case (such as the state attorney general who was also the state's chief investigator and prosecutor in the case), the warrant is invalid. In this case, because the warrant was invalid, the state sought to justify the admission of the evidence under the various exceptions to the warrant requirement. The Court said that the evidence here did not come under such exceptions as "search incident to an arrest," "automobile exception," or the "instrumentality of the crime." The evidence (guns and clothes) given by Coolidge's wife, however, were admissible because they were given not as the result of improper conduct on the part of the police, but because she wanted to help clear her husband of the crime.

Zurcher v. Stanford Daily
436 U.S. 547 (1978)

CAPSULE: Searches of property belonging to third parties are permissible as long as probable cause exists to believe that evidence of someone's guilt or other items subject to seizure will be found.

FACTS: Responding to a call to quell a disturbance, police were attacked by a group of the demonstrators, resulting in several injuries to the officers. There were no police photographers in the vicinity of the attack. Two days later, a special edition of a student newspaper carried articles and photographs of the clash. The District Attorney's Office obtained a warrant to search the newspaper offices. The warrant affidavit contained no allegation that members of the newspaper staff were suspects in the disturbance. The search was conducted pursuant to the warrant and no locked rooms or drawers were opened. The search revealed only the photographs already published and no materials were removed from the paper's offices. Members of the staff filed suit, seeking to have the court declare the issuance of the warrant illegal and unconstitutional.

ISSUE: Is it constitutional under the Fourth Amendment for a court to issue a warrant for a search of the premises of a third party when the police have probable cause to believe that fruits, instrumentalities, or evidence of a crime are on the premises but do not have probable cause to believe that the possessor of the property is involved in the crime? YES.

SUPREME COURT DECISION: Searches of property belonging to persons not suspected of crime are permissible as long as probable cause exists to believe that evidence of someone's guilt or other items subject to seizure will be found.

REASON: "A state is not prevented by the Fourth and Fourteenth Amendments from issuing a warrant to search for evidence simply because the owner or possessor of the place to be searched is not reasonably suspected of criminal involvement. The critical element in a reasonable search is not that the property owner is suspected of crime but that there is reasonable cause to believe that the 'things' to be searched for and seized are located on the property to which entry is sought."

CASE SIGNIFICANCE: This case is significant in that it expands the authority of the courts and the police to obtain warrants to search places or property of third parties, meaning people who are not involved in the commission of a particular crime. Without this decision, it would have been difficult for the police to obtain evidence other than directly from the scene of the crime or from people nearby. This authority, however, cannot be used to conduct a "fishing expedition" for evidence in the home of a third person. The Court stressed that the search warrant can be issued only if there is probable cause to believe that evidence of someone's guilt or other items subject to seizure will be found.

Mincey v. Arizona
437 U.S. 385 (1978)

CAPSULE: A warrantless murder scene search, where there is no indication that evidence would be lost, destroyed, or removed during the time required to obtain a search warrant and there is no suggestion that a warrant could not easily be obtained, is inconsistent with the Fourth Amendment because the situation does not create exigent circumstances of the kind that would justify a warrantless search.

FACTS: During a narcotics raid on Mincey's apartment, an undercover officer was shot and killed and Mincey and others were wounded. Pursuant to police department policy that officers should not investigate incidents in which they are involved, officers at the scene took no action other than to look for other wounded people and to render medical assistance. About ten minutes after the shooting, homicide investigators arrived at the scene and took charge of the investigation. These officers conducted an extensive search of the apartment that lasted four days, included opening drawers and ripping up carpets, and resulted in the seizure of 200 to 300 objects. The items seized were admitted into evidence during trial. Mincey was convicted of murder, assault, and narcotics offenses.

ISSUE: Does the scene of a homicide represent exigent circumstances that would create an additional exception to the warrant requirement of the Fourth Amendment? NO.

SUPREME COURT DECISION: "The 'murder scene exception' created by the Arizona Supreme Court to the warrant requirement is inconsistent with the Fourth and Fourteenth Amendments, and the warrantless search of petitioner's apartment was not constitutionally permissible simply because a homicide had occurred there."

REASON: ". . . [W]hen the police come upon the scene of a homicide they may make a prompt warrantless search of the area to see if there are other victims or if a killer is still on the premises . . . [a]nd the police may seize any evidence that is in plain view during the course of their legitimate emergency activities. . . . But a warrantless search must be 'strictly circumscribed by the exigencies which justify its initiation.' *Terry v. Ohio*, 392 U.S., at 25-26. And it simply cannot be contended that this search was justified by any emergency threatening life or limb." "We decline to hold that the seriousness of the offense under investigation itself creates exigent circumstances of the kind that under the Fourth Amendment justify a warrantless search."

CASE SIGNIFICANCE: This case is best understood as an issue under the "exigent circumstances" exception to the warrant requirement. The general rule is that a search warrant must be obtained prior to a search. Among the many exceptions, however, is the presence of exigent circumstances. In this case, the Arizona Supreme Court in previous decisions had carved out a "murder scene" exception, saying that investigations of murder scenes did not need a warrant because of the seriousness of the offense. The police conducted a warrantless search based on this exception. The importance of this case lies in the Court's statement that "the seriousness of the offense under investigation did not itself create exigent circumstances of the kind that under the Fourth Amendment justify a warrantless search, where there is no indication that evidence would be lost, destroyed, or removed during the time required to obtain a search warrant and there is no suggestion that a warrant could not easily and conveniently have been obtained." In sum, the Court said that a warrant must be obtained for crime scene investigations, regardless of the seriousness of the offense. The only exception to this rule is if obtaining a warrant would mean that the evidence would be lost, destroyed, or removed during the time required to obtain a search warrant.

Steagald v. United States
451 U.S. 204 (1981)

CAPSULE: An arrest warrant does not authorize entry into another person's residence where the suspect may be found.

FACTS: Acting on an arrest warrant issued for a person named Lyons, Drug Enforcement Administration agents entered the home of Steagald to search for Lyons. The entry was made without a warrant. While searching the home of Steagald, the agents found cocaine and other incriminating evidence, but did not find Lyons. Steagald was arrested and convicted on federal drug charges.

ISSUE: May an officer search for the subject of an arrest warrant in the home of a third party, absent exigent circumstances, without a search warrant? NO.

SUPREME COURT DECISION: An arrest warrant is valid for entry into a suspect's place of residence. It does not authorize entry into another person's residence. If the suspect is in another person's home, a search warrant is needed to gain entry into that home, unless there is consent or emergency circumstances that would justify a warrantless search.

REASON: "Two distinct interests were implicated by the search in this case—Lyons' interest in being free from an unreasonable seizure and petitioner's [Steagald's] interest in being free from an unreasonable search of his home. Because the arrest warrant for Lyons addressed only the former interest, the search of petitioner's home was no more reasonable from petitioner's perspective than it would have been if conducted in the absence of any warrant." The search therefore violated the Fourth Amendment.

CASE SIGNIFICANCE: Having an arrest warrant does not authorize the police to enter a third person's home without a search warrant. This is because such an entry violates the Fourth Amendment rights of the third person who may not be involved in the crime. This rule, however, is subject to two exceptions: "exigent circumstances" and consent of the third person. Exigent circumstances means that the police do not have to obtain a search warrant if circumstances are such that to obtain one would jeopardize the arrest. For example, if the police can establish that obtaining a warrant would allow the suspect to leave the premises and escape arrest, a warrantless arrest would be justified. Another example would be cases of hot pursuit. If a suspect being pursued by the police enters a third person's home, the police may enter the home without a warrant to capture the suspect. Consent of the third person makes the warrantless search valid as long as the consent is intelligent and voluntary.

Michigan v. Summers
452 U.S. 692 (1981)

CAPSULE: A search warrant carries with it the limited authority to detain the occupants of the premises while the search is conducted.

FACTS: While officers were executing a warrant to search a house for drugs, they encountered Summers descending the front steps of the house. They requested his assistance in gaining entry to the house. He replied that he did not have keys to the front door, but that he would ring someone in over the intercom. Another occupant of the house answered the door but refused to admit the police. The officers gained entry to the house by forcing the door open. Officers detained Summers and eight others in the house while the premises were searched. When narcotics were found in the house, the police determined that Summers was, in fact, the owner of the house and arrested him. During a search of Summers incident to the arrest, officers discovered heroin in his coat pocket.

ISSUE: May the police detain a person on the premises while a search is conducted? YES.

SUPREME COURT DECISION: A warrant to search carries with it the limited authority to detain the occupants of the premises while the search is conducted.

REASON: "The detention of one of the residents while the premises were searched, although admittedly a significant restraint on his liberty, was surely less intrusive than the search itself. Indeed, we may safely assume that most citizens, unless they intend flight to avoid arrest, would elect to remain in order to observe the search of their possessions."

CASE SIGNIFICANCE: This case expands, to a limited extent, the search and seizure power of the police, enabling them to detain persons on the premises while a search is being conducted. A warrant to search for certain items may be used by the police to temporarily deprive a person found on the premises of liberty; such detention being merely a minimal intrusion of the person's Fourth Amendment rights.

Maryland v. Garrison
480 U.S. 79 (1987)

CAPSULE: A warrant that is overbroad in describing the place to be searched, but is based on a reasonable, although mistaken, belief of the officer, is valid.

FACTS: Police officers obtained a warrant to search "the premises known as 2036 Park Avenue third floor apartment," for drugs and drug paraphernalia that supposedly belonged to a person named McWebb. The police reasonably believed that there was only one apartment at the location; in fact, there were actually two apartments on the third floor, one belonging to McWebb and one belonging to Garrison. Before the officers became aware that they were in Garrison's apartment instead of McWebb's, they discovered contraband that provided the basis for Garrison's conviction for violating a Controlled Substance Act.

ISSUE: Is a search of the wrong apartment valid if conducted pursuant to a search warrant issued on a reasonable but mistaken belief on the part of the officers that the address was correct? YES.

SUPREME COURT DECISION: The validity of a warrant must be judged in light of the information available to officers when the warrant is sought; thus, a warrant that is overbroad in describing the place to be searched based on a reasonable but mistaken belief of the officer is not in violation of the Fourth Amendment. In this case, the search warrant was valid even though the warrant proved to be too broad to authorize the search of both apartments.

REASON: "On the basis of the information that the officers disclosed, or had a duty to discover and to disclose, to the issuing magistrate, the warrant, insofar as it authorized a search that turned out to be ambiguous in scope, was valid when it [was] issued. The validity of the warrant must be judged in light of the information available to the officers at the time they obtained the warrant. The discovery of facts demonstrating that a valid warrant was unnecessarily broad does not retroactively invalidate the warrant."

CASE SIGNIFICANCE: One of the elements of a valid search is that the warrant must contain a "particular description of the place to be searched." This means that the warrant must remove any doubt or uncertainty about which premises are to be searched. The *Garrison* case appears to soften the demands of that requirement. Here was a case of mistaken place description, leading to a mistake in the execution of the warrant. Despite this mistake, which stemmed from a warrant that was characterized as "ambiguous in scope," the Court said that the "validity of the warrant must be judged in light of the information available to the officers at the time they obtained the warrant." The fact that later discovery found the warrant to be unnecessarily overbroad did not invalidate the warrant; neither did it affect the admissibility of evidence obtained. It is important to note that the Court found the warrant to be valid on its face although its broad scope led to an error in the place of execution. There was reasonable effort on the part of the officers to ascertain and identify the place that was the target of the search; nonetheless, a mistake took place. This case should not be interpreted as validating all search warrants when there is a mistake made in the description of the place to be searched. The test as to the validity of search warrants that are "ambiguous in scope" appears to be "whether the officers' failure to realize the overbreadth of the warrant was objectively understandable and reasonable . . ."

California v. Greenwood
486 U.S. 35 (1988)

CAPSULE: A warrantless search and seizure of trash left for collection in an area accessible to the public is valid.

FACTS: Upon receiving information that Greenwood was engaged in drug trafficking, police set up surveillance of his home. Officers observed several vehicles make brief stops at the house during late-night and early morning hours, one of which was followed to another residence suspected of drug trafficking. Officers then asked the trash collector to pick up the trash bags Greenwood had left to be collected and turn them over to the police. Once in police possession, officers searched the trash bags and found items indicating drug use. Based on this information, the police obtained a search warrant for Greenwood's home. There police discovered quantities of cocaine and hashish. Greenwood and a co-conspirator were arrested and charged with felony narcotics charges. After receiving reports of continued drug trafficking, police once again seized Greenwood's garbage and again found evidence of drug use. This resulted in a second search of Greenwood's home, which revealed additional evidence of drug trafficking. Greenwood was arrested again and additional narcotics charges were brought against him.

ISSUE: Are warrantless searches of garbage left outside the curtilage of the home for regular collection valid under the Fourth Amendment? YES.

SUPREME COURT DECISION: The Fourth Amendment does not prohibit a warrantless search and seizure of trash left for collection in an area accessible to the public.

REASON: "The warrantless search and seizure of the garbage bags left at the Greenwood house would violate the Fourth Amendment only if respondents [Greenwood] manifested a subjective expectation of privacy in their garbage that society accepts as objectively reasonable. . . . It may well be that respondents did not expect that the contents of their garbage bags would become known to the police or other members of the public. An expectation of privacy does not give rise to Fourth Amendment protection, however, unless society is prepared to accept that expectation as objectively reasonable. . . . Here we conclude that respondents exposed their garbage to the public sufficiently to defeat their claim to Fourth Amendment protection. It is common knowledge that plastic garbage bags left on or at the side of a public street are readily accessible to animals, children, scavengers, snoops, and other members of the public . . ."

CASE SIGNIFICANCE: This case settles an issue that divided federal appellate courts: whether garbage left outside the curtilage of a home for collection is deemed abandoned, and therefore can be seized by the police without a warrant. The Court made it clear that garbage left in that condition no longer enjoys the protection of the Constitution and, therefore, may be seized without a warrant. The test used was whether the original owner of the trash nonetheless enjoyed a "reasonable expectation of privacy" despite its being left outside the curtilage. The Court answered no, saying that "having deposited their garbage 'in an area particularly suited for public inspection and in a manner of speaking, public consumption, for the express purpose of having strangers take it,' respondents could have no reasonable expectation of privacy in the inculpatory items that they discarded." [Citations omitted.] This case, therefore, allows officers to delve into a person's garbage left at the curb so as to gather evidence of criminality without a warrant. It is logical to assume that newspaper reporters and other individuals may also do so without violating the original owner's property rights.

Wilson v. Arkansas
514 U.S. 927 (1995)

CAPSULE: The Fourth Amendment requires officers to knock and announce before entering a dwelling unless there are exigent circumstances.

FACTS: Wilson conducted several narcotics transactions with an informant over a period of several months. Based on these transactions, police officers obtained an arrest warrant for Wilson and a search warrant for her home. At Wilson's residence, officers identified themselves and stated that they had a warrant as they entered the home through an unlocked door. Once inside the home, officers seized various drugs, a gun, and ammunition. They also found Wilson in the bathroom, flushing marijuana down the toilet. At trial, Wilson moved for suppression of the evidence, asserting that the search was invalid because the officers did not follow the common law procedure of "knock and announce" before they entered her home.

ISSUE: Does the Fourth Amendment reasonableness requirement require officers to "knock and announce" before entering a home? YES, absent exigent circumstances.

SUPREME COURT DECISION: The reasonableness requirement of the Fourth Amendment requires officers to knock and announce before entering a dwelling unless there are exigent circumstances.

REASON: "An examination of the common law of search and seizure . . . leaves no doubt that the reasonableness of a search of a dwelling may depend in part on whether law enforcement officers announce their presence and authority prior to entering." This common law rule of knock and announce dates to at least 1603 and the decision in *Semayne's Case*, 77 Eng. Rep 194, which held: "But before he breaks it, he ought to signify the cause of his coming, and to make request to open doors." "Our own cases have acknowledged that the common-law principle of announcement is embedded in Anglo-American law, but we have never squarely held that this principle is an element of the reasonableness inquiry under the Fourth Amendment. We now so hold." [Citations omitted.]

CASE SIGNIFICANCE: This case holds that, absent exigent circumstances, officers are required to "knock and announce" to meet the reasonableness requirements of the Fourth Amendment. The announcement requirement is based on common law practice that was woven quickly into the fabric of early American law. The Court stressed, however, that the ". . . Fourth Amendment's flexible requirement of reasonableness should not be read to mandate a rigid rule of announcement that ignores countervailing law enforcement interest." The Court considers "countervailing law enforcement interest" as justifying entries without announcement. Such interest, said the Court, includes threats of physical harm to police, pursuit of recently escaped arrestees, and when there is reason to believe that evidence would be likely to be destroyed if advance notice was given. The Court refrained from presenting a "comprehensive catalog of the relevant countervailing factors," saying instead that "we leave to the lower courts the task of determining the circumstances under which unannounced entry is reasonable under the Fourth Amendment." The rule may be summarized as follows: Announcement prior to entry must be made unless there are exigent circumstances; whether an unannounced entry is reasonable is left to the discretion of lower courts.

Richards v. Wisconsin
520 U.S. 385 (1997)

CAPSULE: The Fourth Amendment does not permit a blanket exception to the knock and announce requirement when executing a felony drug warrant. Exceptions must be decided by the court on a case-by-case basis.

FACTS: Police officers obtained a warrant to search Richards' hotel room for drugs and paraphernalia based on an investigation that Richards was one of several individuals dealing drugs out of hotel rooms. The officer's request for a no-knock entry was explicitly denied by the magistrate. One officer knocked on Richard's door and identified himself as a maintenance worker. When Richards opened the door, he saw one of the uniformed officers and slammed the door. At that point, officers identified themselves and began to break down the door. Upon entering the room, officers caught Richards trying to escape through a window. A search of the room revealed cash and cocaine hidden in plastic bags above the bathroom ceiling tiles. The no-knock entry was later justified by the officer based on the rule, in place before *Wilson*, that "police officers are never required to knock and announce when executing a search warrant in a felony drug investigation because of the special circumstances of today's drug culture."

ISSUE: Does the Fourth Amendment allow ". . . a blanket exception to the knock-and announce requirement for felony drug investigations?" NO.

SUPREME COURT DECISION: The Fourth Amendment does not allow a blanket exception to the knock and announce requirement in felony drug investigations. The fact that felony drug investigations may frequently involve threats of physical violence or destruction of evidence (either or both of which *may* justify not having to knock and announce) does not automatically exempt it from the review of a court to determine the reasonableness of the police decision not to knock and announce in a particular case.

REASON: ". . . the fact that felony drug investigations may frequently present circumstances warranting a no-knock entry cannot remove from the neutral scrutiny of a reviewing court the reasonableness of the police decision not to knock and announce in a particular case. Instead, in each case, it is the duty of a court confronted with the question to determine whether the facts and circumstances of the particular entry justified dispensing with the knock-and-announce requirement. . . . In order to justify a 'no knock' entry, the police must have a reasonable suspicion that knocking and announcing their presence, under the particular circumstances, would be dangerous or futile, or that it would inhibit the effective investigation of the crime by, for example, allowing the destruction of evidence."

CASE SIGNIFICANCE: This case clarifies an issue that was not clearly addressed in the case of *Wilson v. Arkansas*, 514 U.S. 927 (1995). *Wilson* held that the knock and announce rule is required by the Fourth Amendment, but that there were numerous exceptions to it; such exceptions to be determined by lower courts. The police in this case sought a blanket exception from this requirement in felony drug investigations, saying that these cases frequently involved threats of physical violence or possible destruction of evidence. The Court rejected this based on two grounds. First, it said that there will be situations in which "the asserted governmental safety may not outweigh the individual privacy interests" involved in a particular case. Second, "the blanket exception would threaten to swallow the rule." In other words, if a blanket exception were allowed in felony drug investigations, it might lead to other exceptions (such as in bank robbery cases) that might then completely negate the rule.

United States v. Ramirez
523 U.S. 65 (1998)

CAPSULE: The Fourth Amendment does not impose a higher standard when officers destroy property during a no-knock entry than the requirement that the police have a reasonable suspicion that knocking and announcing would be dangerous or futile, or would inhibit the effective investigation of the crime.

FACTS: Based on probable cause that an escaped and violent felon was staying at Ramirez's residence, federal agents obtained a no-knock warrant. Early in the morning, officers announced over a loudspeaker that they had a warrant, and simultaneously broke a window in the garage and pointed a weapon through the opening to prevent anyone from obtaining weapons that an informant had suggested were there. After awakening, and believing that he was being burglarized, Ramirez obtained a pistol and shot it through the ceiling of the garage. After police returned fire and announced their presence,

Ramirez threw his pistol down and surrendered. The escaped prisoner the agents sought was not found, but Ramirez was taken into custody and charged with being a felon in possession of firearms.

ISSUE: Does the Fourth Amendment hold law enforcement officers to a higher standard when a no-knock entry includes the destruction of property? NO.

SUPREME COURT DECISION: The Fourth Amendment does not impose a higher standard when officers destroy property during a no-knock entry than the requirement that the police have a reasonable suspicion that knocking and announcing would be dangerous or futile, or would inhibit the effective investigation of the crime.

REASON: "Under *Richards*, a no-knock entry is justified if police have a 'reasonable suspicion' that knocking and announcing would be dangerous, futile, or destructive to the purposes of the investigation. Whether such a 'reasonable suspicion' exists depends in no way on whether police must destroy property in order to enter."

CASE SIGNIFICANCE: This case extended the decisions in *Wilson v. Arkansas* and *Richards v. Wisconsin* concerning knock and announce entries. The standard set by the Supreme Court in knock and announce cases is that a no-knock entry is reasonable if officers have reasonable suspicion that obeying the rule would be dangerous or futile or would hamper effective investigation. The trial court in this case had ruled that the search was invalid because there were "insufficient exigent circumstances" to justify the officer's destruction of property. The Court rejected that interpretation and held that reasonable suspicion that obeying the rule would be dangerous or futile or would hamper effective investigation is sufficient to justify entry without knocking and announcing. This decision wiped out a long line of cases from the United States Court of Appeals for the Ninth Circuit that required "a more compelling showing of an exigency to justify a destructive no-knock entry than when a no-knock entry was effected without property damage."

Minnesota v. Carter
525 U.S. 83 (1998)

CAPSULE: A person who is in a home for a short period, although with the consent of the owner, has no expectation of privacy under the Fourth Amendment.

FACTS: A law enforcement officer went to an apartment based on information from an informant that he had seen through a ground floor window people putting a white powder into bags. The officer observed the same activity for several minutes through a gap in a closed blind in the apartment. When Carter and an accomplice, Johns, left the apartment, police stopped the car. After observing a handgun in the automobile, officers arrested Carter and Johns. A subsequent search of the automobile revealed drugs and drug paraphernalia. Based on the arrest of Carter and Johns, and pursuant to a search warrant based on the officer's observations, police returned to the apartment and arrested the lessee, Thompson. A search of the apartment pursuant to the warrant revealed additional drugs and drug paraphernalia. Police later learned that Carter and Johns had come to the apartment from another city for the sole purpose of packaging the drugs, that they had never been to the apartment previously, they were only in the apartment for approximately two and one-half hours, and that in return for using the apartment, they gave Thompson one-eighth of an ounce of cocaine.

ISSUE: Is there an expectation of privacy sufficient to invoke the Fourth Amendment for persons who are in a home for a short period of time at the request of the owner? NO.

SUPREME COURT DECISION: ". . . [A]n overnight guest in a home may claim the protection of the Fourth Amendment, but one who is merely present with the consent of the owner may not."

REASON: "Respondents here were obviously not overnight guests, but were essentially present for a business transaction and were only in the home a matter of hours. There is no suggestion that they had a previous relationship with Thompson, or that there was any other purpose to their visit. Nor was there anything similar to the overnight guest relationship in [*Minnesota v.*] *Olson* [495 U.S. 91 (1990)] to suggest a degree of acceptance into the household. While the apartment was a dwelling place for Thompson, it was for these respondents simply a place to do business."

CASE SIGNIFICANCE: This case makes clear previous gaps in Supreme Court decisions concerning the expectation of privacy that persons enjoy in certain places. The expectation of privacy concerns the ability of law enforcement officials to make searches within the guidelines of the Fourth Amendment. The Court had previously stated in *Olson* that overnight guests in a person's house have an expectation of privacy under the Fourth Amendment. The Court had also held that a person had an expectation of privacy in a personal office at work. The Court ruled here, however, that a person does not have that same privilege as an invited guest in a person's house for a short period of time.

United States v. Knights
534 U.S. 112 (2001)

CAPSULE: A warrantless search by an officer of a probationer's residence supported by reasonable suspicion and authorized by a condition of probation is valid under the Fourth Amendment.

FACTS: A court imposed as a condition of probation that probationer Knight submit to searches by probation or law enforcement officers of his person, vehicle, and house without a search warrant. An officer investigating vandalism and arson suspected Knights and an accomplice, Simoneau, were involved in the crime. When the officer observed Simoneau's vehicle at Knights' residence, he set up surveillance. Later, Simoneau left Knights' residence with three cylindrical tubes the officer believed to be pipe bombs and threw them in the river. When Simoneau left Knights' residence, the officer followed him. When Simoneau stopped, the officer looked in Simoneau's truck and saw explosive materials and two padlocks matching the description of those taken during the vandalism. Based on this and knowledge of the probation order permitting searches, the officer conducted a search of Knights' apartment. The search revealed more arson and bomb-making materials and a padlock with the vandalized company's name stamped on it.

ISSUE: Is a warrantless search by an officer of a probationer's residence pursuant to a probation condition and supported by reasonable suspicion (but not probable cause) constitutional? YES.

SUPREME COURT DECISION: A warrantless search by an officer of a probationer's residence supported by reasonable suspicion and authorized by a condition of probation is valid under the Fourth Amendment.

REASON: "The degree of individualized suspicion required of a search is a determination of when there is a sufficiently high probability that criminal conduct is occurring to make the intrusion on the individual's privacy interest reasonable." "Although the Fourth Amendment ordinarily requires the degree of probability embodied in the term 'probable cause,' a lesser degree satisfies the Constitution when the balance of governmental and private interests makes such a standard reasonable." Based on these principles, the Court held that "the search of Knights was reasonable under our general Fourth Amendment approach of 'examining the totality of the circumstances' with the probation search condition being a salient circumstance" [citations omitted].

CASE SIGNIFICANCE: This case is significant for probationers and parolees. It resolved the issue of whether law enforcement officers can search the residence of a probationer with less than probable cause. The Court held that it could, as long as: (1) there is reasonable suspicion and (2) the search is authorized by the condition of probation. One of the most frequently imposed conditions of probation is that the probationer submit to a search by a probation officer. The Court had earlier decided in *Griffin v. Wisconsin* (483 U.S. 868 [1987]) that a warrantless search by a probation officer of a probationer's home based on reasonable grounds (less than probable cause) is valid because of "special needs," meaning the need to supervise a probationer to accomplish the purpose of probation. The *Griffin* case, however, did not involve a law enforcement officer. In *Knights*, the search was conducted by a sheriff's detective who was authorized by the judge to conduct a search of the probationer. The probationer claimed his Fourth Amendment rights were violated because the search by the officer was investigatory rather than probationary in nature and therefore needed probable cause, like all police searches. The Court disagreed, holding the search was reasonable based on the totality of circumstances. There was a condition of probation imposed by the judge, the probationer was informed of such a condition, and the condition of probation was justified. Given the purposes of probation (reintegration back into the community) and since the probationer was more likely to engage in criminal activity than an ordinary member of the community, the search by the police here was reasonable.

Probation conditions are often enforced by the probation officer, not by the police. Prior to this case, it was unclear whether or not the judge may authorize police officers to enforce conditions of probation other than those involving arrests for criminal acts. The Court in this case implied that law enforcement can also be authorized by the judge to search probationers' dwellings based on less than probable cause. Note, however, that here the officer was authorized by the judged to conduct a search of the probationer's residence. Without such an authorization, the search here on less than probable cause would likely have been unconstitutional. Also, this case involved a probationer, but it can likely be extended to parolees as long as there is reasonable suspicion and authorization to search by the parole board that sets the conditions of parole.

United States v. Banks
540 U.S. 31 (2003)

CAPSULE: After knocking and announcing their presence and intention to search, 15 to 20 seconds is sufficient time for officers to wait before forcing entry into a home to execute a search warrant for drugs.

FACTS: With information that Banks was selling cocaine from his apartment, officers obtained and executed a search warrant. Upon reaching his apartment, officers announced "police search warrant" and knocked on the door loud enough to be heard by officers at the back door. After waiting 15 to 20 seconds, officers broke down the door with a battering ram. Banks was in the shower and testified he did not hear the officers until they broke the door. The search of the apartment produced weapons, crack cocaine, and other evidence of drug dealing. Banks moved to suppress the evidence, arguing that the officers waited an unreasonably short time before forcing entry, violating the Fourth Amendment.

ISSUE: Does a 15- to 20-second wait before a forcible entry by police violate the Fourth Amendment? NO.

SUPREME COURT DECISION: After knocking and announcing their presence and intention to search, 15 to 20 seconds is sufficient time for officers to wait before forcing entry into a home to execute a search for drugs.

REASON: In this case, the Court rejected the Ninth Circuit Court of Appeals method of using a list of requirements for forcing entry following a knock and announce, and instead reemphasized that such cases are to be decided on totality of the circumstances. The Court then turned its intention to the circumstances that might require forced entry. They noted that most people keep their doors locked, necessitating use of force when no one answers the knock. The critical issue, then, is what constitutes an exigency. The Court noted that it is exigency that creates a situation authorizing a no-knock warrant; but that same exigency will exist when officers announce their presence and intention to search. The knock and announce essentially "starts the clock" on the potential destruction of evidence. The exigency in this case is that the suspect will attempt to destroy the evidence, typically by flushing it down a drain or toilet. Not answering a knock by police would further indicate this possibility because the bathroom or kitchen will not be near the door but in the interior of the home. The Court recognized that 15 to 20 seconds would be sufficient for a person to begin to destroy evidence such as drugs, but noted that something like a search for a stolen piano would require more time for a person to respond to a knock because of the difficulty in disposing of the evidence.

CASE SIGNIFICANCE: This case is significant because it addresses an important issue of policing: what is a reasonable time in drug cases, after knocking, when officers may gain a valid forcible entry to a dwelling. The officers here had a valid warrant and knocked and announced their presence. After a 15- to 20-second wait, with no response, they used a battering ram and forcibly entered the dwelling. Banks claimed that a 15- to 20-second wait before entry was too short, was unreasonable, and therefore violated the Fourth Amendment. He said he was in the shower and did not hear the officers, and that in any case it might have taken him more time than that to reach the door. The Court disagreed, saying that "the facts known to the police are what count in judging a reasonable waiting time, and there is no indication that they knew Banks was in the shower and thus unaware of an impending search." The assertion that it would have taken Banks more time to reach the door was also rejected, the Court saying that "it is not unreasonable to think that someone could get in a position to destroy the drugs within 15 to 20 seconds." The 15- to 20-second wait considered sufficient in this case may not necessarily suffice in cases other than those involving drugs. An important factor in this case was that the defendant could easily have disposed of the drugs within that short time. Had they waited longer, the suspect could easily have flushed the drugs down the toilet. The Court adhered to a totality of circumstances analysis, in effect saying that whether the time to wait before any forcible entry was too short depends on an analysis of all surrounding circumstances. In this case, those circumstances favored the government agents.

Searches after Arrest 7

Introduction

Searches after arrest require a separate chapter because of their importance in everyday policing. Although the constitutional rule is that arrests are to be made with a warrant, most arrests are made without a warrant. After a valid arrest, the police may conduct a full search of the arrested person and of the vicinity around him or her. The cases briefed in this chapter define the extent of that search.

The two major cases on searches after an arrest are *United States v. Robinson* (414 U.S. 218 [1973]) and *Chimel v. California* (395 U.S. 752 [1969]). In *Robinson*, the Court said that a body search is valid when a full-custody arrest occurs. In *Chimel*, the Court authorized the search of the area within a person's immediate control after an arrest. The Court has authorized officers to search the area of immediate control for two reasons: (1) officer safety and (2) to prevent the destruction of evidence. The problem with *Chimel*, however, is that it does not clearly indicate what is meant by the "area of immediate control." It is clear that this includes the area covered by an arrested person's "wingspan"; however, how much further beyond the wingspan has not been addressed by the Court, other than saying that it is that area from which the arrested person may obtain weapons or destroy evidence.

Most of the cases briefed in this chapter extend the authority of the police to search after an arrest. In *United States v. Edwards*, 415 U.S. 218 (1973), the Court held that a warrantless search at the place of detention is valid even if a substantial period of time has lapsed between the arrest and the search. In *Maryland v. Buie*, 494 U.S. 325 (1990), the Court held that a limited protective sweep during an arrest in a home is allowed if justified. In *Illinois v. LaFayette* (462 U.S. 640 [1982]), the Court said that searching the personal effects of a person under lawful arrest is valid if it is part of the administrative procedure incident to the booking and jailing of the suspect.

Other principles set by the Court in searches after arrest indicate that there are limits to searches after arrest. For example, the warrantless search of a house after an arrest, when the arrest does not take place in a house, is justified only in a few cases (*Vale v. Louisiana*, 399 U.S. 30 [1970]). Although not addressed by the Supreme Court, lower courts have held that body cavity searches after an arrest are unconstitutional unless justified by considerations other than the arrest itself.

The leading cases briefed in this section on searches after arrest are *Chimel v. California* and *United States v. Robinson*.

Warden v. Hayden
387 U.S. 294 (1967)

CAPSULE: A warrantless seizure is valid if probable cause and exigent circumstances are present. "Mere evidence" may be searched, seized, and admitted in court.

FACTS: Police went to Hayden's house pursuant to a call from an individual who had followed a robbery suspect until the suspect entered a house. Hayden's wife consented to a search of the house. Hayden was arrested when it was determined that he was the only man in the house. An officer, attracted to an adjoining bathroom by the sound of running water, found a shotgun and pistol in a flush tank. Another officer, looking for "a man or the money," found clothes fitting the description of those worn by the robber in a washing machine. All items of evidence were admitted at the trial. Hayden was convicted of armed robbery.

ISSUES:
1. Was the search without a warrant valid? YES.
2. Are items considered "mere evidence" (the pistol, shotgun, and clothes), as distinguished from contraband and instrumentalities of crimes, seizable by the police for use as evidence? YES.

SUPREME COURT DECISIONS:
1. The warrantless seizure in this case was valid because probable cause and exigent circumstances were present.
2. There is no difference between "mere evidence" and contraband or instrumentalities of a crime under the provisions of the Fourth Amendment. "Mere evidence" may be searched for, seized, and admitted in court as evidence.

REASON: The search was valid because "[s]peed here was essential, and only a thorough search of the house for persons and weapons could have insured that Hayden was the only man present and that the police had control of all weapons which could be used against them or to effect an escape. . . . Nothing in the language of the Fourth Amendment supports the distinction between 'mere evidence' and instrumentalities, fruits of crime, or contraband."

CASE SIGNIFICANCE: This case establishes that a warrant is not needed if there is probable cause and "exigent" (emergency) circumstances. This justifies making warrantless searches and seizures. The Court also settled the issue of whether "mere evidence" (as opposed to contraband or illegal items) can be seized by the police. Earlier cases decided by lower courts were divided on the issue. Under this ruling, any evidence, not just contraband, that can help prove the case against the defendant can be seized by the police.

Chimel v. California
395 U.S. 752 (1969)

CAPSULE: After an arrest, police may search the area within a person's immediate control.

FACTS: Chimel was suspected of having robbed a coin shop. Armed with an arrest warrant (but without a search warrant), police officers went to Chimel's house and were admitted by his wife. Chimel was not at home, but was immediately arrested when he arrived. The police asked Chimel if they could "look around." Chimel denied the request, but the officers searched the entire house anyway and discovered some stolen coins. At the trial, the coins were introduced as evidence over Chimel's objection. Chimel was convicted of robbery.

ISSUE: In the course of making a lawful arrest, may officers search the immediate area where the person was arrested without a search warrant? YES.

SUPREME COURT DECISION: After making an arrest, the police may search the area within the person's immediate control. The purpose of such a search is to discover and remove weapons and to prevent the destruction of evidence.

REASON: "When an arrest is made, it is reasonable for the arresting officer to search the person arrested in order to remove any weapons that the latter might seek to use in order to resist arrest or effect his escape. Otherwise, the officer's safety might well be endangered, and the arrest itself frustrated. In addition, it is entirely reasonable for the arresting officer to search for and seize any evidence on the arrestee's person in order to prevent its concealment or destruction. And the area into which an arrestee might reach in order to grab a weapon or evidentiary items must, of course, be governed by a like rule. . . . There is ample justification, therefore, for a search of the arrestee's person and the area within his immediate control."

CASE SIGNIFICANCE: *Chimel* categorically states that the police may search the area in the arrestee's "immediate control" when making a valid arrest, whether the arrest takes place with or without a warrant. That area of "immediate control" is defined by the Court as "the area from within which he might gain possession of a weapon or destructible evidence." *Chimel* therefore authoritatively settled an issue over which lower courts had given inconsistent and diverse rulings. The current rule is that the police may search without a warrant after a lawful arrest, but the extent of that search is limited to the area of the arrestee's "immediate control." The safest, and most limited, interpretation of the term "area of immediate control" is a person's wingspan, where it might be possible to grab a weapon or destroy evidence. Some lower courts have given a more liberal interpretation to include such areas as the whole room in which the person is arrested. This interpretation appears to go beyond what the Court had in mind in *Chimel*.

Vale v. Louisiana
399 U.S. 30 (1970)

CAPSULE: The warrantless search of a house after an arrest with a warrant, when the arrest does not take place in a house, is justified only in "a few specifically established and well-delineated exceptions."

FACTS: After obtaining an arrest warrant, the police set up surveillance outside Vale's home. While watching the house, they observed what they suspected to be an exchange of drugs between Vale and a known addict. After the exchange of narcotics, the police blocked the path of the addict, arrested Vale on the front steps of his home, and searched the house without a search warrant. Narcotics were found in a bedroom. Vale was convicted of possession of heroin.

ISSUE: May the police make a warrantless search of a house incident to an arrest without exigent circumstances and when the person was not arrested in the house? NO.

SUPREME COURT DECISION: The warrantless search of a house incident to an arrest when the arrest does not take place in the house is justified only in "a few specifically established and well-delineated exceptions." The facts in this case did not come under one of those exceptions.

REASON: "If a search of a house is to be upheld as incident to an arrest, that arrest must take place inside the house . . . not somewhere outside— whether two blocks away, *James v. Louisiana*, 382 U.S. 36 (1965), 20 feet away, *Shipley v. California*, 395 U.S. 818 (1969), or on the sidewalk near the front steps."

CASE SIGNIFICANCE: The Court in this case gave a narrow interpretation to the phrase "area of immediate control," where a search incident to an arrest is valid. In this case, the arrest took place at the front steps of the house. The subsequent search of the house did not come under the area of allowable search and, therefore, the evidence obtained was not admissible in court.

United States v. Robinson
414 U.S. 218 (1973)

CAPSULE: A body search is valid when a full custody arrest occurs.

FACTS: Based on a previous investigation, a police officer stopped Robinson on the suspicion that he was operating a motor vehicle after his license had been revoked. After making a full-custody arrest with probable cause, the officer made a search of Robinson's person. He felt an unrecognizable object in Robinson's left breast pocket, but admitted in court that he knew it was not a weapon. The officer removed the object, which turned out to be a "crumpled-up cigarette package" that contained fourteen gelatin capsules of heroin. The capsules were admitted as evidence in Robinson's trial and he was convicted of possession of heroin.

ISSUE: Is it constitutional for a police officer to search (as opposed to merely frisking) a person's body after a lawful custodial arrest even though the officer does not fear for his or her personal safety or believe that evidence will be destroyed? YES.

SUPREME COURT DECISION: A body search is valid in any situation in which a full-custody arrest occurs. There is no requirement that officers fear for their safety or believe that they will find evidence of a crime before the body search can be made.

REASON: "A custodial arrest of a suspect based on probable cause is a reasonable intrusion under the Fourth Amendment; that intrusion being lawful, a search incident to the arrest requires no additional justification. It is the fact of the lawful arrest which establishes the authority to search, and we hold that in the case of a lawful custodial arrest a full search of the person is not only an exception to the warrant requirement of the Fourth Amendment, but is also a 'reasonable' search under that Amendment."

CASE SIGNIFICANCE: *Robinson* allows the search of a person's body after a lawful arrest. Prior to *Robinson*, courts allowed a full body search (as opposed to a frisk) only if the officer feared for his or her personal safety. In this case, the officer had probable cause to make the arrest (therefore the arrest was valid), but admitted that he could not tell what the object was and did not feel that there were reasons to fear for his safety. Under the then-prevailing standard, the search would have been invalid. *Robinson*, therefore, expands the scope of search incident to a valid arrest and does away with the "fear for personal safety" limitation. It differs from *Chimel* in that the *Chimel* case deals with the "area within the arrestee's immediate control," whereas *Robinson* specifically refers to body searches. The suspect's body is obviously within the area of immediate control, but the authority to search it was not necessarily included in *Chimel* because a person's body enjoys greater protection from governmental intrusion than the area around the person.

United States v. Edwards
415 U.S. 800 (1974)

CAPSULE: After a lawful arrest and detention, any search conducted at the place of detention, which would have been lawful at the time of the arrest, may be conducted without a warrant, even though a substantial period of time may have elapsed between the arrest and the search.

FACTS: Edwards was arrested shortly after 11:00 P.M., charged with attempting to break into a post office, and taken to jail. Subsequent investigation at the scene of the crime revealed that the attempted entry was made through a wooden window that had been forced open with a pry bar, leaving paint chips on the window sill. The next morning substitute clothes were purchased for Edwards and his clothes were seized and held as evidence. Examination of the clothes revealed paint chips matching those taken from the window. His motion to suppress the evidence seized from his clothes was denied and Edwards was convicted.

ISSUE: Is a warrantless seizure of clothes taken from a suspect several hours after being placed in custody valid under the Fourth Amendment? YES.

SUPREME COURT DECISION: After being lawfully arrested and placed in custody, any search conducted at the place of detention that would have been lawful at the time of the arrest may be conducted without a warrant, even though a substantial period of time may have elapsed between the arrest and the search.

REASON: "This [search and seizure] was and is a normal incident of a custodial arrest and a reasonable delay in effectuating it does not change the fact that Edwards was no more imposed upon than he could have been at the time and place of the arrest or immediately upon arrival at the place of detention."

CASE SIGNIFICANCE: A search incident to an arrest does not have to take place immediately after the arrest as long as such arrest is justified, as in this case. The key is whether the arrest was valid. If the arrest was valid and the suspect is in custody, the search may take place at a later time and the evidence will be admissible in court. There is reason to believe that the Court in this case would have considered the search valid even if substitute clothing was available at the time Edwards was placed in custody.

Illinois v. LaFayette
462 U.S. 640 (1982)

CAPSULE: Searching the personal effects of a person under lawful arrest is valid if it is part of the administrative procedure incident to the booking and jailing of the suspect.

FACTS: After Lafayette was arrested for disturbing the peace, he was taken to the booking room at the police station where an officer removed the contents of a shoulder bag he was carrying. The officer found amphetamine pills. Lafayette was charged with violating the Illinois Controlled Substances Act. At the pretrial hearing, the trial court ordered the evidence suppressed. The prosecutor argued that the search was valid under a previous court ruling and that it was standard procedure to inventory everything in the possession of an arrested person.

ISSUE: Was the warrantless search of defendant's shoulder bag valid? YES.

SUPREME COURT DECISION: It is not a violation of the Fourth Amendment for the police to search the personal effects of a person under lawful arrest if the search is part of the routine administrative procedure incident to the booking and jailing of the suspect.

REASON: "The governmental interests [of searching at the station house may be even greater] than those supporting a search immediately following arrest" because some necessary searches cannot be done in public, but all searches may be done in private at the station. Furthermore, "at the station house, it is entirely proper for police to remove and list . . . property found on the person or in the possession of an arrested person [about] to be jailed. A standardized procedure for making a list or inventory as soon as reasonable after reaching the station not only deters false claims but also inhibits theft or careless handling of articles taken from the arrested person" and protects everyone from dangerous weapons. Additionally, "[the] inspection of an arrestee's personal property may assist the police in ascertaining or verifying his identity."

CASE SIGNIFICANCE: In this case, the Court said that the warrantless search of the suspect's bag was justified because it was part of a valid inventory search. Lafayette had argued that the search was invalid either as a search incident to a lawful arrest or as part of the inventory search. The Court disagreed, saying that what the police did in this case was reasonable under the Fourth Amendment, hence giving broad authority to the police when making inventory searches. The Court approved of inventory searches for the following reasons: (1) protection of a suspect's property, (2) deterrence of false claims of theft against the police, (3) security, and (4) identification of the suspect. All these, said the Court, benefit both the police and the public.

Maryland v. Buie
494 U.S. 325 (1990)

CAPSULE: A limited protective sweep during arrest in a home is allowed if justified.

FACTS: After surveillance, six or seven police officers obtained and executed arrest warrants for Buie and an accomplice in connection with an armed robbery. Upon reaching Buie's house, the officers "fanned out through the first and second floors." One of the officers observed the basement so that no one would surprise the officers. This officer shouted into the basement and ordered anyone there to come out. A voice asked who was there. The officer ordered the person to come out three more times before Buie emerged from the basement. After placing Buie under arrest, another officer entered the basement to see whether there was anyone else there. Once in the basement, the officer noticed in plain view a red running suit similar to the one worn by one of the suspects in the robbery. The running suit was admitted as evidence at Buie's trial over his objection, and he was convicted of robbery with a deadly weapon and using a handgun in the commission of a felony.

ISSUE: May officers conduct a warrantless protective sweep of the area in which a suspect is arrested in order to determine whether another person might be there who would be a danger to the officers? YES.

SUPREME COURT DECISION: "The Fourth Amendment permits a properly limited protective sweep in conjunction with an in-home arrest when the searching officer possesses a reasonable belief based on specific and articulable facts that the area to be swept harbors an individual posing a danger to those on the arrest scene."

REASON: "We . . . hold that as an incident to the arrest the officers could, as a precautionary matter and without probable cause or reasonable suspicion, look in closets and other spaces immediately adjoining the place of arrest from which an attack could be immediately launched. Beyond that, however, we hold that there must be articulable facts which, taken together with the rational inferences from those facts, would warrant a reasonably prudent officer in believing that the area to be swept harbors an individual posing a danger to those on the scene. This no more and no less was required in *Terry* and *Long* and, as in those cases, we think this balance is the proper one."

"We should emphasize that such a protective sweep, aimed at protecting the arresting officers, if justified by the circumstances, is nevertheless not a full search of the premises, but may extend only to cursory inspection of those spaces where a person may be found. The sweep lasts no longer than is necessary to dispel the reasonable suspicion of danger and in any event no longer than it takes to complete the arrest and depart the premises."

CASE SIGNIFICANCE: This case is significant because it authorizes the practice in some police departments of conducting a "protective sweep" during an arrest. It is important for police officers to note, however, that *Buie* does not give the police unlimited authority, when making an arrest, to search the whole house. The protective sweep allowed by *Buie* is limited in scope. The following limitations (taken from the language of the court's decision) must be observed:

1. There must be articulate facts which . . . would warrant a reasonably prudent officer in believing that the area to be swept harbors an individual posing a danger;

2. Such a protective sweep is not a full search of the premises, but may extend only to a cursory inspection of the spaces where a person may be found; and

3. The sweep lasts no longer than is necessary to dispel the reasonable suspicion of danger and in any event no longer than it takes to complete the arrest and depart the premises.

The police must be careful to observe the above limitations, otherwise the search becomes invalid.

Buie does not indicate a broadening of the Court's ruling in *Chimel v. California*, in which the Court said that once a lawful arrest has been made, the police may search any area within the suspect's "immediate control." The Court itself distinguished *Chimel* from *Buie* as follows:

1. *Chimel* was concerned with a full-blown, top-to-bottom search of an entire house for evidence of the crime for which the arrest was made, not the more limited intrusion contemplated by a protective sweep; and

2. The justification for the search incident to arrest in *Chimel* was the threat posed by the arrestee, not the safety threat posed by the house or more properly by unseen third parties in the house.

Searches with Consent 8

Introduction

The general rule under the Fourth Amendment is that searches must be conducted with a warrant for the search to be valid. An exception is searches with consent. This exception is important because it is used every day by the police in a variety of situations. The requests, "May I search your car?" or "Would you mind if I come in and search your apartment?" or "May I look around?" are routinely heard by the public from the police.

To be valid, consent must be voluntary and intelligent, based on a totality of circumstances. "Voluntary" means that the consent was not forced or coerced; "intelligent" means that the person giving consent must know what he or she is doing. Mere silence or failure to object to a search does not necessarily indicate valid consent. Written consent is not constitutionally required, but it goes a long way toward proving the validity of the consent if later challenged in court.

Aside from the need for the consent to be voluntary and intelligent, there are other important principles in consent searches. First, consent to enter a dwelling does not necessarily mean consent to search. If a container or closet is to be opened after entry, for example, another consent must be sought by the police. Second, warning the occupant that he or she has the right to re-fuse permission is not necessary for the consent to be valid. Third, the scope of an allowable search depends on the type of consent given. For example, the consent to search a garage does mean consent to search an adjoining house or barn.

The following types of consent are valid, if voluntary and intelligent: consent given by a wife or husband, by a roommate (as to areas used in common), by the driver of a vehicle (even if he or she is not the owner of the vehicle), and by high school administrators. On the other hand, consent given by the following are not valid: consent given by a child, a landlord, a lessor, a hotel clerk, college and university administrators, and business employees.

The leading cases briefed in this chapter on searches with consent are *Bumper v. North Carolina* and *Schneckloth v. Bustamonte*.

Stoner v. California
376 U.S. 483 (1964)

CAPSULE: A hotel clerk cannot give consent to search the room of a hotel guest.

FACTS: Two men were described to the police by eyewitnesses after a robbery of a food market in California. Soon thereafter, a checkbook belonging to Stoner was found in an adjacent parking lot and turned over to the police. Checkbook stubs indicated that checks had been made out to a hotel in a nearby city. Upon checking the records in that city, the police learned that Stoner had a criminal record. The police then obtained a photograph of Stoner. Eyewitnesses identified the man in the photograph as one of the men involved in the robbery. Without an arrest or search warrant, the police went to the hotel where the suspect resided. The hotel clerk notified the police that the suspect was not in his room, but consented to open the room for them. After gaining entrance to the room, the police made an extensive search and discovered articles like those described by the eyewitnesses to the robbery. Stoner was arrested two days later in another state and extradited to California. He was charged with and convicted of armed robbery.

ISSUE: May a hotel clerk give valid consent to a warrantless search of the room of one of the occupants? NO.

SUPREME COURT DECISION: A hotel guest is entitled to protection against unreasonable searches and seizures. This cannot be waived by the consent of a hotel clerk.

REASON: "It is important to bear in mind that it was the petitioner's constitutional right which was at stake here, and not the night clerk's nor the hotel's. It was a right, therefore, which only the petitioner could waive by word or deed . . ."

CASE SIGNIFICANCE: A hotel guest has a reasonable expectation of privacy that cannot be waived by the hotel management simply because the management has the key. A wife can consent to the search of a house, parents can consent to the search of a child's room (with some exceptions), or a roommate to the search of a dormitory room; but a hotel clerk cannot consent to a search of the room of a guest. Note, however, that if the police want to *arrest* a suspect in a room, the fact that access to the room was made by borrowing a key from the hotel clerk does not invalidate the arrest. The rule on consent, therefore, differs in arrest and in search cases.

Bumper v. North Carolina
391 U.S. 543 (1968)

CAPSULE: Consent obtained by deception through a claim of lawful authority, which did not in fact exist, is not voluntary. A search conducted by virtue of a warrant cannot later be justified by consent if the warrant turns out to be invalid.

FACTS: During a rape investigation, and prior to his arrest, officers went to Bumper's home where he lived with his grandmother. One of the four officers went to the door and was met by the grandmother. When the officer announced that he had a warrant to search the house (although he did not), the grandmother responded "Go ahead" and opened the door. The officers found a rifle in the kitchen that was seized and entered as evidence. Bumper was subsequently charged with and convicted of rape.

ISSUE: Can a search be justified as lawful on the basis of consent when the alleged consent is given only after the official conducting the search asserts possession of a warrant? NO.

SUPREME COURT DECISION: The alleged consent in this case was not voluntary because it was obtained by deception through a claim of lawful authority that did not exist. A search conducted by virtue of a warrant cannot later be justified by consent if the warrant turns out to be invalid.

REASON: "When a prosecutor seeks to rely upon consent to justify the lawfulness of a search, he has the burden of proving that the consent was, in fact, freely and voluntarily given. This burden cannot be discharged by showing no more than acquiescence to a claim of lawful authority. A search conducted in reliance upon a warrant cannot later be justified on the basis of consent if it turns out that the warrant was invalid. . . . When a law officer claims authority to search a home under a warrant, he announces in effect that the occupant has no right to resist the search. The situation is [rife] with coercion—albeit colorably lawful coercion. Where there is coercion there cannot be consent."

CASE SIGNIFICANCE: Consent to search is not valid if permission is given as a result of police misrepresentation or deception. In this case, the police said they had a warrant when, in fact, they did not. Lower courts are divided on the related issue of whether consent is valid if the officer does not have a warrant but threatens to obtain one. That issue has not been resolved by the Supreme Court.

Schneckloth v. Bustamonte
412 U.S. 218 (1973)

CAPSULE: Voluntariness of consent to search is determined from the totality of circumstances, of which consent is only one element.

FACTS: An officer on routine patrol stopped an automobile containing Bustamonte and five others after observing that a headlight and the license plate light were burned out. When the driver could not produce a driver's license, the officer asked if any of the others had any type of identification. Only one, Joe Alcala, was able to produce a driver's license. He explained that the vehicle belonged to his brother. The men were ordered out of the car, and the officer asked Alcala if he could search the car. Alcala replied, "Sure, go ahead." Prior to the search, no one had been threatened with arrest or given the impression they were suspected of any wrongdoing. Alcala assisted in the search by opening the trunk and glove compartment. During the search, the officer found three checks under the left rear seat that had been stolen from a car wash. Using the checks as evidence, Bustamonte was convicted of possession of a check with intent to defraud.

ISSUE: Is knowledge by a suspect of the right to refuse consent required for consent to a search to be valid? NO.

SUPREME COURT DECISION: Voluntariness of consent to search is to be determined from the totality of the circumstances, of which consent is one element. Knowledge of the right to refuse consent is not a prerequisite for voluntary consent.

REASON: "Our decision today is a narrow one. We hold only that when the subject of a search is not in custody and the State attempts to justify a search on the basis of his consent, the Fourth and Fourteenth Amendments require that it demonstrate that the consent was in fact voluntarily given and not the result of duress or coercion, expressed or implied. Voluntariness is a question of fact to be determined from all the circumstances, and while the subject's knowledge of a right to refuse is a factor to be taken into account, the prosecution is not required to demonstrate such knowledge as a prerequisite to establishing voluntary consent."

CASE SIGNIFICANCE: In *Miranda v. Arizona*, 384 U.S. 436 (1966), the Court said that the suspect must be made aware of the right to remain silent during questioning if responses to questions are later to be admissible in court. *Schneckloth* says that there is no such requirement in consent search cases. The suspect does not have to be advised that he or she has the right to refuse consent for the search to be valid. All that is required is that the consent be voluntary. The Court also said that "voluntariness is a question of fact to be determined from all the circumstances; and, while the subject's knowledge of a right to refuse is a factor to be taken into account, the prosecution is not required to demonstrate such knowledge as a prerequisite to establishing voluntary consent." The police must prove that consent is voluntary; however, unlike *Miranda*, where the police must say "you have the right to remain silent," the police in consent searches do not have to say "you have the right to refuse consent."

Florida v. Royer
460 U.S. 491 (1983)

CAPSULE: More serious intrusion of personal liberty than is allowable on mere suspicion of criminal activity taints the consent and makes the search illegal.

FACTS: Police observed an individual in Miami International Airport who fit a so-called "drug courier profile" of being young, nervous, casually dressed, with heavy American Tourister luggage, and paying for a one-way ticket in cash under an assumed name. Based on this information, the officers approached the suspect. Upon request, but without oral consent, Royer produced his airline ticket and driver's license with his correct name. When questioned about the discrepancy in names, Royer responded that a friend had bought the ticket under that friend's name. Without returning Royer's airline ticket or license, the officers then informed him that he was suspected of trafficking in narcotics and requested that he follow them to a room 40 feet away. Without consent, Royer's luggage was brought to the room. Although he did not respond to the officer's request to consent to a search of the luggage, Royer produced a key and opened one of the suitcases. Marijuana was found in the suitcase. When the suspect said that he did not know the combination to the other suitcase but that he did not object to its being opened, the officers pried open the suitcase and found more marijuana. Royer was then informed he was under arrest. He pleaded *nolo contendere* and was convicted of felony possession of marijuana.

ISSUE: Is evidence obtained through a consent search admissible in court if the initial detention of the suspect was without probable cause, and in violation of the Fourth Amendment? NO.

SUPREME COURT DECISION: At the time the suspect consented to the search of his luggage, ". . . the detention to which he had been subjected was a more serious intrusion of his personal liberty than was allowable on mere suspicion of criminal activity . . ."; thus, the consent was tainted by illegality and could not justify the search.

REASON: "When the detectives identified themselves as narcotics agents, told respondent he was suspected of transporting narcotics, and asked him to accompany them to the police room, while retaining his airline ticket and driver's license and without indicating in any way that he was free to depart, respondent was effectively seized for purposes of the Fourth Amendment. At the time respondent produced the key to his suitcase, the detention to which he was then subjected was a more serious intrusion on his personal liberty than is allowable on mere suspicion of criminal activity. What had begun as a consensual inquiry in a public place escalated into an investigatory procedure in a police interrogation room, and respondent, as a practical matter, was under arrest at that time. Moreover, the detectives' conduct was more intrusive than necessary to effectuate an investigative detention otherwise authorized by the *Terry v. Ohio* line of cases."

CASE SIGNIFICANCE: Consent given after an illegal act by the police is not valid because such consent is tainted. For the consent to be valid, the police must be careful that no illegal act precedes it because once the illegal act is committed, consent cannot cure it. The only possible exception is if the taint has somehow been purged by an independent source, inevitable discovery, etc. In this case, however, consent did not purge the taint.

Illinois v. Rodriguez
497 U.S. 177 (1990)

CAPSULE: Searches in which the person giving consent has "apparent authority" are valid.

FACTS: After being summoned to a house, the police were met by Gail Fischer, who showed signs of a severe beating. She informed the officers that she had been assaulted by Rodriguez earlier that day in an apartment. Fischer and the police subsequently drove to the apartment of Rodriguez because she stated that Rodriguez would be asleep at that time and that she could let them into the apartment with her key so that they could arrest him. Several times she referred to the apartment as "our" apartment and stated that she had clothes and furniture there. She did not tell the police, however, that she was no longer living there. Upon entrance, without a warrant but with a key and permission provided by Fischer, the police saw in plain view drug paraphernalia and containers filled with cocaine. The officers seized these and other drug paraphernalia found in the apartment where Rodriguez was sleeping. Rodriguez was arrested and charged with possession of a controlled substance with intent to deliver. On appeal, the Circuit Court suppressed the evidence, holding that at the time Fischer consented to the entry of the apartment, she did not have common authority over it because she had actually moved out several weeks earlier.

ISSUE: Is a warrantless entry and subsequent search, based on the consent of a person whom the police believed to have possessed common authority over the premises, but who in fact did not have such authority, valid? YES.

SUPREME COURT DECISION: The warrantless entry of private premises by the police is valid if based on the consent of a third party whom the police reasonably believed to possess common authority over the premises, but who in fact did not have such authority.

REASON: The appellate court was correct in determining that Fischer had no common authority over the apartment; however, the State contended that even if she did not have the authority to consent, it should suffice to validate the entry that the law enforcement officers reasonably believed she did. Furthermore, the Fourth Amendment only protects against unreasonable searches, not searches performed without the owner's consent. The "reasonableness" clause of the Fourth Amendment ". . . does not demand that the government be factually correct in its assessment . . ." Furthermore, "[t]he Constitution is no more violated when officers enter without a warrant because they reasonably (though erroneously) believe that the person who has consented to their entry is a resident of the premises, than it is violated when they enter without a warrant because they reasonably (though erroneously) believe they are in pursuit of a violent felon who is about to escape."

CASE SIGNIFICANCE: This case reiterates the "apparent authority" rule in searches with consent. The rule says that consent given by a third party whom the police reasonably believe to possess common authority over the premises is valid even if it is later established that the person did not in fact have that authority. In this case, the girlfriend, who gave consent and provided the key, had moved out of the apartment. She led the police to the house and allowed them entry by using her key. She did not tell them that she no longer lived there. The officers reasonably believed that she had authority to give consent, hence the entry was valid, and the evidence subsequently obtained was admissible. It is important to note, however, that for the "apparent authority" rule to apply, the belief by the police must be reasonable, considering the circumstances.

Florida v. Jimeno
499 U.S. 934 (1991)

CAPSULE: Consent justifies the warrantless search of a container in a car if it is objectively reasonable for the police to believe that the scope of the suspect's consent permitted them to open that container.

FACTS: A Dade County police officer overheard Jimeno arranging what appeared to be a drug transaction over a public telephone. The officer followed Jimeno's car and saw him make an illegal right turn at a red light. The officer stopped Jimeno to issue a traffic citation. After informing Jimeno why he had been stopped, the officer stated that he had reason to believe that Jimeno was carrying narcotics in his car and asked permission to search the car. The officer explained that Jimeno did not have to grant permission, but Jimeno stated that he had nothing to hide and gave consent to the search. Pursuant to the search, the officer found a kilogram of cocaine in a brown paper bag located on the floorboard of the passenger compartment. Jimeno was convicted of possession with the intent to distribute cocaine.

ISSUE: Does consent for the police to search a vehicle extend to closed containers found inside the vehicle? YES.

SUPREME COURT DECISION: "A criminal suspect's Fourth Amendment right to be free from unreasonable searches is not violated when, after he gives police permission to search his automobile, they open a closed container found within the car that might reasonably hold the object of the search."

REASON: "The standard for measuring the scope of a suspect's consent under the Fourth Amendment is that of 'objective' reasonableness—what would the typical reasonable person have understood by the exchange between the officer and the suspect? The question before us, then, is whether it is reasonable for an officer to consider a suspect's general consent to a search of his car to include consent to examine a paper bag lying on the floor of the car. We think that it is."

"The scope of a search is generally defined by its expressed object. In this case, the terms of the search's authorization were simple. Respondent granted Officer Trujillo permission to search his car, and did not place any explicit limitation on the scope of the search. Trujillo had informed the respondent that he believed the respondent was carrying narcotics, and that he would be looking for narcotics in the car. We think that it was objectively reasonable for the police to conclude that the general consent to search the respondent's car included consent to search containers within that car which might bear drugs. A reasonable person may be expected to know that narcotics are generally carried in some form of a container. 'Contraband goods rarely are strewn across the trunk or floor of a car.' The authorization to search in this case, therefore, extended beyond the surfaces of the car's interior to the paper bag lying on the car's floor." [Citations omitted].

CASE SIGNIFICANCE: In an earlier case, *United States v. Ross*, 102 S. Ct. 2157 (1982), the Court held that when the police have probable cause to justify a warrantless search of a car, they may search the entire car and open the trunk and any packages or luggage found therein that could reasonably contain the items for which they have probable cause to search. This case reiterates that holding, although with a different twist.

The immediate issue in this case is whether it was "objectively reasonable for the police to believe that the scope of the suspect's consent permitted them to open the particular container." The issue was not one of probable cause, but the scope of the suspect's consent to search. The Court concluded that the authorization to search given by the suspect to the police "extended beyond the car's interior surfaces to the bag, since Jimeno did not place any explicit limitation on the scope of the search and was aware that Trujillo [the officer] would be looking for narcotics in the car, and since a reasonable person may be expected to know that narcotics are generally carried in some form of container." The Court added that there is "no basis for adding to the Fourth Amendment's basic test of objective reasonableness a requirement that, if the police wish to search closed containers within a car, they must separately request permission to search each container."

This case defines the extent of what the police can do in cases of searches based on consent. The police do not need specific consent to look at each container. The Court said that, in these cases, the Fourth Amendment is satisfied if, given the circumstances, "it is objectively reasonable for the police to believe that the scope of the suspect's consent permitted them to open the particular container." Conversely, this depends upon what the police are looking for and the possibility that the item or items can be found in that container.

Vehicle Stops
and Searches

9

Introduction

The Fourth Amendment imposes two requirements for searches and seizures, in general, to be valid: a search warrant and probable cause. The rule is different, however, in vehicular stops and searches, because motor vehicles are mobile and can be driven away at any time, making obtaining a warrant impractical. This rule was laid out in 1925 in *Carroll v. United States*, 267 U.S. 132 (1925), in which the Supreme Court said that the search, without a warrant, of an automobile is valid as long as probable cause is present.

Vehicle stops and vehicle searches must be distinguished because they are governed by different rules. Vehicular stops and searches are similar in that they do not need a warrant; they differ in that reasonable suspicion of involvement in unlawful activity justifies a stop, but probable cause must be present for a search to be valid. Vehicle stops do not need a warrant or probable cause. The only requirement for a valid stop is that the police have reasonable suspicion (less than probable cause) of unlawful activity. A vehicle search after a valid stop is governed by a different rule. Such searches do not need a warrant, but probable cause must be present or the search is invalid.

Court decisions have established that, after a vehicle is stopped, the officer may legally do the following:

1. Order the driver to exit the vehicle;
2. Order the passengers to exit the vehicle;
3. Ask the driver to produce a driver's license and other documents required by state law;
4. Ask questions of the driver and occupants;
5. Require drunk-driving suspects to take a Breathalyzer test;
6. Locate and examine the vehicle identification number;
7. Search the vehicle if probable cause develops.

The search of a vehicle is governed by rules that, over the years, have expanded the power of the police. The Supreme Court has held that police officers may do the following during vehicle searches (assuming the search is valid, and based on probable cause):

1. Conduct a search of the passenger compartment of a car and of the contents therein if it is incident to a lawful arrest;
2. Search the entire car and open the trunk and any packages or luggage found therein that could reasonably contain the items they are looking for;
3. Search a container in a car if there is probable cause to believe that it holds contraband or seizable items, even in the absence of probable cause to search the car.

Recent Supreme Court decisions have expanded the power of the police even further in motor vehicle cases. Some of the most recent decisions include the following:

1. The police may make a warrantless search of a vehicle even if there is time to obtain a warrant.

2. The officer does not have to tell a detained motorist that he or she is "free to go" before consent to search the vehicle will be voluntary and therefore valid.

3. If there is probable cause to search a vehicle, police officers may also inspect the belongings of passengers found in the vehicle as long as those belongings are capable of concealing the object of the search.

The decisions in vehicle searches may be summed up as follows: as long as probable cause is present, the Supreme Court has given the police extensive authority to search motor vehicles.

It is important to note that vehicle stops and searches also include passengers traveling on public transportation. Several cases in this chapter deal with the people traveling in the vehicle rather than a stop or search of the vehicle itself. This sets up a different set of issues in relation to stops and searches, but the basic rules governing vehicle stops and searches still apply.

Three more recent cases have further clarified the extent of police authority in motor vehicle cases. In *Bond v. United States*, 529 U.S. 334 (2000), the Court held that a traveler's luggage is an "effect" and is therefore under the protection of the Fourth Amendment. As such, officers may not physically manipulate (squeeze) the luggage to inspect it without a warrant or probable cause. In another case, the Court ruled that highway checkpoints whose primary purpose is to detect evidence of ordinary criminal wrongdoing violate the Fourth Amendment (*Indianapolis v. Edmond*, l531 U.S. 32 [2000]). The Court has also held that the Fourth Amendment permits police officers to approach bus passengers, ask questions, and request their consent to search, provided that a reasonable person would understand that he or she is free to refuse. There is no requirement in the Fourth Amendment for officers to advise people of their right to refuse to cooperate (*United States v. Drayton*, et al. [2002]).

The leading cases briefed in this chapter are *Carroll v. United States, New York v. Belton, United States v. Ross, Wyoming v. Houghton, Bond v. United States, Indianapolis v. Edmond*, and *United States v. Drayton*. Vehicle stops and searches is an area of police work that has recently drawn a significant amount of attention from the Supreme Court. Four cases were decided by the Court on this issue in 2004 and 2005. These cases are: *Illinois v. Lidster* (2004), *United States v. Flores-Montano* (2005), *Thornton v. United States* (2004), and *Illinois v. Caballes* (2005). These decisions add clarity to current law on what the police can and cannot do in vehicle stops and searches.

Carroll v. United States
267 U.S. 132 (1925)

CAPSULE: The warrantless search of an automobile is valid if probable cause is present.

FACTS: Officers observed the automobile of Carroll while on a regular patrol from Detroit to Grand Rapids. The same officers had been in contact with Carroll twice in the four months prior to this sighting. In September, the officers attempted to buy illegal liquor from Carroll, but he was alerted to their true identity and did not produce the contraband. In October, the officers recognized Carroll's automobile returning to Grand Rapids from Detroit (a city possessing an international boundary and that was known as a city from which illegal liquor was regularly imported). The officers gave chase but failed to apprehend Carroll. Carroll was later apprehended. He and his companion were ordered out of the car. No liquor was visible in the front seat of the automobile. Officers then opened the rumble seat and looked under the cushions, again finding no liquor. One of the officers then struck the "lazyback" of the seat, tore open the seat cushion, and discovered 68 bottles of gin and whiskey. Carroll was arrested and convicted of transporting intoxicating liquor.

ISSUE: May officers search an automobile without a search warrant but with probable cause that it contains illegal contraband? YES.

SUPREME COURT DECISION: The risk of the vehicle being moved from the jurisdiction, or the evidence being destroyed or carried off, justifies a warrantless search as long as such search is conducted with probable cause that the vehicle that is subject to seizure contains contraband.

REASON: ". . . [T]he guarantee of freedom from unreasonable searches and seizures by the Fourth Amendment has been construed, practically since the beginning of government, as recognizing a necessary difference between a search of a store, dwelling house, or other structure in respect of which a proper official warrant readily may be obtained and a search of a ship, motor boat, wagon, or automobile for contraband goods, where it is not practicable to secure a warrant, because the vehicle can be quickly moved out of the locality or jurisdiction in which the warrant must be sought."

CASE SIGNIFICANCE: The general rule is that searches may be conducted only if a warrant has been issued. There are several exceptions to this rule, however, searches of automobiles being one of them. This case, decided in 1925, created the so-called "automobile exception" to the warrant requirement by ruling that warrantless searches of motor vehicles are valid as long as there is probable cause to believe that there are seizable items in the vehicle. The justification for this exception is the mobile nature of the automobile.

Chambers v. Maroney
399 U.S. 42 (1969)

CAPSULE: An automobile may be searched without a warrant as long as probable cause is present.

FACTS: Shortly after a gas station attendant and two bystanders gave police a description of two men and the getaway car used in the robbery of a gas station, the police arrested Chambers and three other occupants of a station wagon who fit the description. After the arrest, the car was taken to the police station. The police searched the car and found two revolvers concealed under the dashboard, a glove with the money Chambers had obtained from the gas attendant, and credit cards with the name of another gas station attendant in a different town who had been robbed the previous week. During a warrant-authorized search of Chambers' home the following day, the police found and seized ammunition similar to that found in the guns taken from the station wagon. Chambers was indicted and subsequently convicted of both robberies.

ISSUE: Is the evidence seized by the police from an automobile, after the automobile has been taken to the police station and searched without a warrant, admissible in court? YES.

SUPREME COURT DECISION: A car may be searched without a warrant as long as probable cause is present. Under the Constitution, there is no difference between seizing and holding a car before presenting the probable cause issue to a magistrate and carrying out an immediate search without a warrant.

REASON: The search made at the police station, some time after the arrest, cannot be justified as a search incident to arrest. "There are, however, alternative grounds arguably justifying the search of the car . . ." Here, the officers had probable cause to arrest the occupants of the car and, therefore, had probable cause to search the car for guns and stolen money. As ruled in *Carroll v. United States* (1925), with probable cause, an automobile can be searched without a warrant in circumstances that would not justify a warrantless search of a house or office. "But the circumstances that furnish probable cause to search a particular auto for particular articles are most often unforeseeable. . . . Where an effective search is to be made at any time, either the search must be made immediately without a warrant or the car itself must be seized and held without a warrant for whatever period is necessary to obtain a warrant. . . . Only in exigent circumstances will the judgment of the police as to probable cause serve as a sufficient authorization for a search. . . . For constitutional purposes, we see no difference between . . . seizing and holding a car before presenting the probable cause issue to a magistrate and . . . carrying out an immediate search without a warrant. Given probable cause to search, either course is reasonable under the Fourth Amendment."

CASE SIGNIFICANCE: This case is significant because it does away with the previous requirement that the police must obtain a warrant to search a vehicle with probable cause if there is time to obtain a warrant. What the former rule said was that once the police take control of the vehicle and the danger of it being driven away by the suspect is gone because the vehicle is now under police control, a warrant must first be obtained if the vehicle is to be searched further. This case does away with that rule, saying instead that if the police had probable cause to search the vehicle when it was first stopped, then it can be searched without a warrant even if there is time to obtain a warrant. This case reiterates the rule that warrantless searches of vehicles are valid as long as there is probable cause, even if a warrant could have been obtained.

Delaware v. Prouse
440 U.S. 648 (1979)

CAPSULE: Stopping an automobile and detaining the driver to check the license and registration is unreasonable under the Fourth Amendment, unless there is probable cause.

FACTS: Without observing traffic or equipment violations or suspicious activity, a police officer stopped Prouse's vehicle to check the driver's license and registration. Upon approaching the vehicle, the officer smelled marijuana. He seized a quantity of marijuana in plain view on the floor of the automobile. The officer was not acting pursuant to any departmental regulations governing spot checks. Prouse was charged with and convicted of illegal possession of a controlled substance.

ISSUE: May a police officer make a random stop of an automobile simply to check the driving license of the operator and registration of the automobile in the absence of probable cause that its occupants are engaging in illegal activity? NO.

SUPREME COURT DECISION: Stopping an automobile and detaining the driver in order to check the license and registration is unreasonable under the Fourth Amendment unless there is probable cause to believe that the motorist is unlicensed or that the automobile is in violation of equipment laws, or that its occupants are exhibiting suspicious behavior.

REASON: "The Fourth and Fourteenth Amendments are implicated in this case because stopping an automobile and detaining its occupants constitutes a 'seizure' within the meaning of those Amendments, even though the purpose of the stop is limited and the resulting detention quite brief. The essential purpose of the proscriptions in the Fourth Amendment is to impose a standard of reasonableness upon the exercise of discretion by government officials, including law enforcement agents, in order to 'safeguard the privacy and security of individuals against invasions.' " [Citations omitted.]

CASE SIGNIFICANCE: This case holds that officers cannot arbitrarily stop motor vehicles without probable cause to believe that an illegality or violation has occurred or is occurring. Vehicles may be searched without a warrant, but probable cause must be present. Does this mean that vehicle spot checks are illegal? Not necessarily. The Court in this case said that this decision does not preclude a state from "developing methods for spot checks that involve less intrusion or that do not involve the unconstrained exercise of discretion." For example, questioning all oncoming traffic at roadblock-type stops is valid and may be used by the police.

New York v. Belton
453 U.S. 454 (1981)

CAPSULE: The police may conduct a warrantless search of the passenger compartment of a car and of the contents therein if it is incident to a lawful arrest.

FACTS: Police stopped an automobile in which Belton was an occupant. A check of driver's licenses and automobile registration revealed that none of the occupants owned the vehicle or were related to the owner. The officer smelled burnt marijuana and saw an envelope marked "Supergold" on the floor of the automobile, which the officer associated with marijuana. After administering *Miranda* warnings, the officer placed the occupants under arrest, picked up the envelope, and found marijuana. He then searched the passenger compartment of the automobile and, on the back seat, found a jacket belonging to Belton. He unzipped one of the pockets of the jacket and discovered cocaine. Belton was arrested for and convicted of possession of a controlled substance.

ISSUE: Is the warrantless seizure of evidence in the passenger compartment of a car, after a lawful arrest, valid? YES.

SUPREME COURT DECISION: The police may conduct a warrantless search of the passenger compartment of a car incident to a lawful arrest. The search may include containers found within the passenger compartment. The term "container" denotes any object capable of holding another object. It includes closed or open glove compartments, consoles, or other receptacles located anywhere within the passenger compartment, as well as luggage, boxes, bags, clothing, and similar items.

REASON: "[I]n *United States v. Robinson*, 414 U.S. 218, the Court hewed a straightforward rule . . . in the case of a lawful custodial arrest a full search of the person is not only an exception to the warrant requirement of the Fourth Amendment, but is also a 'reasonable' search under that Amendment. . . . Accordingly, we hold that when a policeman has made a lawful custodial arrest of the occupant of an automobile, he may, as a contemporaneous incident of that arrest, search the passenger compartment of that automobile. . . . It follows from this conclusion that the police may also examine the contents of any containers found within the passenger compartment, for if the passenger compartment is within the reach of the arrestee, so also will containers in it be within his reach."

CASE SIGNIFICANCE: This case defined the extent of allowable searches inside the automobile after a lawful arrest. Prior to this, there was confusion about whether the police may search parts of the automobile outside the driver's "wingspan." The Court expanded the area of allowable search to the whole passenger compartment, including the back seat; it also authorized the opening of containers found in the passenger compartment that might contain the object sought. In this case, Belton's jacket could contain prohibited drugs; its search was therefore valid. This case also authorizes the police to search the interior of the car even if the passenger has been removed from the car or no longer constitutes a danger to the police (such as when the passenger has been handcuffed). (Note, however, that the *Belton* case did not decide whether the trunk could also be searched. This case was decided later in *United States v. Ross*, 456 U.S. 798 [1982]).

United States v. Cortez
449 U.S. 411 (1981)

CAPSULE: In determining probable cause to make an investigatory stop, the totality of circumstances must be taken into account.

FACTS: Based on footprints found over a period of time, officers concluded that groups of illegal immigrants were walking over a well-defined path from the Mexican border to a highway where they would be picked up by a motor vehicle. A similar set of footprints were found in each group; therefore, officers further concluded that one person was acting as a guide to these groups. Based on the times the tracks were found, officers determined that the crossings occurred on nights during the weekend when the weather was clear. Because the tracks approached the highway then turned to the east, the officers finally concluded that the vehicle would approach from and return to the east. Based on these deductions, and the fact that a particular Sunday was the first clear night in three days, officers set up surveillance on the highway. Of the 15-20 vehicles that passed the officers during their surveillance, only two matched the type they were looking for. As one truck passed, the officers obtained a partial license plate number. When the same vehicle passed them again, heading east, they pursued and stopped it. Cortez was driving the truck and a man wearing shoes with soles matching those found in the desert was a passenger. The officers told Cortez they were conducting an immigration check. In the back of the truck were six illegal immigrants. Cortez and his companion were arrested, charged with, and convicted of transporting illegal aliens.

ISSUE: May objective facts and circumstantial evidence observed and collected by the police justify an investigative stop of a vehicle? YES.

SUPREME COURT DECISION: In determining probable cause to make an investigatory stop, the totality of the circumstances (meaning the whole picture) must be taken into account. The officers must, however, have a particularized, objective basis for suspecting that the individual stopped is engaged in criminal activity.

REASON: The totality of the circumstances must yield a particularized suspicion that contains two elements that must be present before the stop can occur. First, the assessment of the situation must be based on an analysis of all of the circumstances. Second, "the whole picture must yield a particularized suspicion" that the individual being stopped is engaged in criminal activity.

CASE SIGNIFICANCE: The decision to stop must be made with justification. This means that the police cannot arbitrarily stop anyone for investigative purposes. There must be a particularized and objective basis for suspecting that the person stopped has engaged in or will engage in criminal activity. Such suspicion must be based on "the whole picture," as observed by the police. In deciding to make an investigative stop, the experience and training of the law enforcement officer may be taken into account. What may look like innocent activity to an untrained person may look otherwise to a trained officer. Such observation gives an officer a legitimate basis for suspicion that can then justify an investigative stop.

United States v. Ross
456 U.S. 798 (1982)

CAPSULE: When making a valid search of a car, the police may search the entire car and open the trunk and any packages or luggage found therein that could reasonably contain the items for which they have probable cause to search.

FACTS: Police received a telephone tip from a reliable informant that Ross was selling drugs kept in the trunk of his car. The informant provided a detailed description of Ross, his automobile, and the location of the sale. The police drove to the location, spotted the person and car that matched the description given by the informant, and made a warrantless arrest. One of the officers found a bullet on the front seat of the automobile. Without a warrant, officers conducted a more thorough search of the interior of the automobile and discovered a pistol in the glove compartment. Ross was arrested. Officers then took Ross's keys and opened the trunk of his automobile, where they found a closed brown paper bag containing glassine bags of a substance that was later determined to be heroin. The officers then drove the car to police headquarters where another warrantless search of the trunk revealed a zippered leather pouch containing cash. Ross was charged with and convicted of possession of heroin with intent to distribute.

ISSUE: After a valid arrest, may the police open the trunk of a car and containers found therein without a warrant and in the absence of exigent circumstances? YES.

SUPREME COURT DECISION: When the police have probable cause to justify the warrantless search of a car, they may search the entire car, and open the trunk and any packages or luggage found therein that could reasonably contain the items for which they have probable cause to search.

REASON: "If probable cause justifies the search of a lawfully stopped vehicle, it justifies the search of every part of the vehicle and its contents that may conceal the object of the search. . . . The scope of a warrantless search of an automobile thus is not defined by the nature of the container in which the contraband is secreted. Rather, it is defined by the object of the search and the places in which there is probable cause to believe that it may be found."

CASE SIGNIFICANCE: The *Ross* case is important because it further defines the scope of police authority in vehicle searches. The *Belton* case specifically refused to address the issue of whether the police could open the trunk of a car in connection with a search incident to a valid arrest. *Ross* addressed that issue and authorized such action. *Ross* further stated that any packages or luggage found in the car that could reasonably contain the items for which they have probable cause to search could also be opened without a warrant. *Ross* has, therefore, greatly expanded the scope of allowable warrantless searches, limited only by what is reasonable. Note, however, that this authorization has limits. The police may not open large items taken from the car (such as a footlocker) without a warrant if there is time to obtain one. This is because those items have identities of their own, separate and apart from the car. Also, although the police may constitutionally open smaller items without a warrant, that action may be prohibited by state law or departmental policy, which prevails over a constitutional license.

Michigan v. Long
463 U.S. 1032 (1983)

CAPSULE: A limited search of an automobile, after a valid stop, is permissible if the officer has a reasonable belief that the suspect is dangerous and might gain immediate control of a weapon.

FACTS: Officers observed an automobile traveling erratically and at a high rate of speed. When the automobile swerved into a ditch, the officers stopped to investigate. They were met at the rear of the car by Long, who "appeared to be under the influence of something" and did not respond to a request to produce his license. Upon a second request, Long did produce his license. After a second request to see his registration, Long began walking toward the open door of the vehicle. The officers followed him and noticed a large hunting knife on the floorboard of the vehicle. They then stopped Long and frisked him. No other weapons were found. One of the officers shined his flashlight into the car and discovered marijuana. Long was then arrested. The officers then opened the unlocked trunk and discovered approximately 75 pounds of marijuana. Long was charged with and convicted of possession of marijuana.

ISSUE: May officers conduct a protective search (similar to a pat-down search authorized in *Terry v. Ohio*, 392 U.S. 1 [1968]) of the passenger compartment of a lawfully stopped vehicle to look for possible weapons? YES.

SUPREME COURT DECISION: The search of an automobile, after a valid stop and limited to the areas in which a weapon may be placed or hidden, is permissible if the officer has a reasonable belief that the suspect is dangerous and might gain immediate control of a weapon.

REASON: "[A]rticles inside the relatively narrow compass of the passenger compartment of an automobile are in fact generally, even if not inevitably, within the area into which an arrestee might reach in order to grab a weapon." [Footnote and quotes omitted.] . . . "If there is reasonable belief that the suspect is dangerous and might gain control of weapons, the officer is justified by self-protection to make search of the interior of the automobile. . . . If, while conducting a legitimate *Terry* search of the interior of the automobile, the officer should, as here, discover contraband other than weapons, he clearly cannot be required to ignore the contraband . . ."

CASE SIGNIFICANCE: This case gives the police authority to conduct a limited search (similar to a pat-down search of a person) of the passenger compartment of a car if the officers have reasonable belief that they may be in danger. In this case, the officer saw a hunting knife on the floorboard of the driver's side of the car, hence justifying the search of the passenger compartment. Such a search, however, must be limited to the areas in which a weapon may be placed or hidden. If, while conducting such a search, contraband or other illegal items are discovered, they can be seized and may be admitted as evidence into court. The Court added that the fact that the suspect is under the officers' control during the investigative stop does not render unreasonable their belief that the suspect could injure them. This implies that, as long as the officers have probable cause to believe that they are in danger, the search may continue even after the suspect has been placed under control, such as when the suspect has been handcuffed.

California v. Carney
471 U.S. 386 (1985)

CAPSULE: Motor homes used on public highways are automobiles for purposes of the Fourth Amendment and therefore a warrantless search is valid.

FACTS: A police agent had uncorroborated information that Carney's motor home was being used to exchange marijuana for sex. He then set up surveillance on the motor home. The agent observed Carney approach a youth who accompanied him to the motor home parked in a nearby lot. Agents followed the youth after he emerged from the motor home and stopped him. The youth said that Carney was exchanging marijuana for sex. At the request of the agents, the youth returned to the motor home and knocked on the door. When Carney stepped out, the agents identified themselves, entered the motor home, and made a search without consent or a warrant. Agents found a quantity of marijuana on a table in the motor home. Agents then arrested Carney and impounded the motor home. A subsequent search of the motor home at the police station revealed additional marijuana. Carney was charged with and convicted of possession of marijuana for sale.

ISSUE: May police officers make a warrantless search, based on probable cause, of a motor home located in a public place under the automobile exception? YES.

SUPREME COURT DECISION: If a vehicle is being used on public highways or is capable of such use and it is found in a place not regularly used for residential purposes, it may be considered an automobile under the warrantless search doctrine; thus, a warrantless search based on probable cause is justified.

REASON: "When a vehicle is being used on the highways or is capable of such use and is found stationary in a place not regularly used for residential purposes, the two justifications for the vehicle exception come into play. First, the vehicle is readily mobile, and, second, there is a reduced expectation of privacy stemming from the pervasive regulation of vehicles capable of traveling on highways. Here, while respondent's vehicle possessed some attributes of a home, it clearly falls within the vehicle exception. To distinguish between respondent's motor home and an ordinary sedan for purposes of the vehicle exception would require that the exception be applied depending on the size of the vehicle and the quality of its appointments. Moreover, to fail to apply the exception to a vehicle such as a motor home would ignore the fact that a motor home lends itself easily to use as an instrument of illicit drug traffic or other illegal activity."

CASE SIGNIFICANCE: The Court in this case held that motor homes are automobiles for the purposes of the Fourth Amendment and therefore fall under the automobile exception, meaning that they can be searched without a warrant. It is important to note, however, that this decision is limited to a motor home that is capable of being used on the road and is located in a place that is not regularly used for residential purposes. The decision specifically states that this case does not resolve whether the automobile exception would apply to a motor home "situated in a way or place that objectively indicates that it is being used as a residence." The police are advised to treat those places as residences that generally need a search warrant.

Colorado v. Bertine
479 U.S. 367 (1987)

CAPSULE: Warrantless inventory searches of the person and possessions of arrested individuals are permissible under the Fourth Amendment.

FACTS: Bertine was arrested for driving under the influence of alcohol. After he was taken into custody, and prior to the arrival of a tow truck to impound the van, another officer inventoried the van in accordance with departmental procedures. During the inventory search, the officer opened a backpack in which he found various containers containing controlled substances, drug paraphernalia, and money. Bertine was charged with and convicted of driving under the influence of alcohol, unlawful possession of cocaine with intent to distribute, and unlawful possession of methaqualone.

ISSUE: Is evidence seized by opening a closed container without a warrant during an inventory search incident to a lawful arrest admissible? YES.

SUPREME COURT DECISION: Inventory searches without a warrant of the person and possessions of arrested individuals are permissible under the Fourth Amendment:
1. to protect an owner's property while it is under police control;
2. to ensure against claims of lost, stolen, or vandalized property; and
3. to protect the police from danger.

Evidence found in the course of the inventory search, even if found by opening a closed backpack, is admissible.

REASON: "The policies behind the warrant requirement, and the related concept of probable cause, are not implicated in an inventory search, which serves the strong governmental interests in protecting an owner's property while it is in police custody, insuring against claims of lost, stolen or vandalized property, and guarding the police from danger. There was no showing here that the police, who were following standardized caretaking procedures, acted in bad faith or for the sole purpose of investigation. Police, before inventorying a container, are not required to weigh the strength of the individual's privacy interest in the container against the possibility that the container might serve as a repository for dangerous or valuable items."

CASE SIGNIFICANCE: This case allows inventory searches without a warrant even in situations in which containers must be opened. This is significant because prior to this decision it was not clear whether the police, in the course of an inventory search, could open a closed container. The current rule is to allow this type of inventory, as long as the police follow standardized caretaking procedures and they do not act in bad faith or for the sole purposes of an investigation. It is questionable whether the opening of a closed container in the absence of departmental rules authorizing the police to do so is valid. This case synthesized *South Dakota v. Opperman*, 428 U.S. 364 (1976) (inventory search of an impounded vehicle) and *Illinois v. Lafayette*, 462 U.S. 640 (1983) (inventory search of individual possessions while person is in custody).

Florida v. Wells
495 U.S. 1 (1989)

CAPSULE: Evidence obtained from closed containers during inventory searches is not admissible in court unless authorized by departmental policy.

FACTS: Suspect Wells was stopped by the police for speeding and was subsequently arrested for drunk driving. At the station, Wells gave permission for the police to open the trunk after he was told that his car would be impounded. During an inventory search, the police found two marijuana cigarette butts in an ashtray and a locked suitcase in the trunk. The police forced open the suitcase, whereupon a garbage bag full of marijuana was found. Wells was charged with possession of a controlled substance. The trial court denied his motion to suppress the marijuana based on a violation of the Fourth Amendment.

ISSUE: Was the seizure of the marijuana by the police valid? NO.

SUPREME COURT DECISION: A police department's lack of policy regarding the opening of closed containers found during inventory searches requires the suppression of the marijuana found in a locked suitcase that was removed from the trunk of an impounded vehicle and pried open by the police.

REASON: "The individual police officer must not be allowed so much latitude that inventory searches are turned into 'purposeful and general means of discovering evidence of crime.' . . . But in forbidding uncanalized discretion to police officers conducting inventory searches, there is no reason to insist they be conducted in a total . . . 'all or nothing' fashion" as ruled in *Colorado v. Bertine* (1987). Policies for ". . . opening all containers or for opening no containers are unquestionably permissible . . ." It is, however, ". . . equally permissible . . . to allow the opening of closed containers whose contents [the] officers determine they [cannot] ascertain from examining the [exterior of the containers.]" To allow ". . . the exercise of judgment based on concerns related to the purposes of an inventory search does not violate the Fourth Amendment."

CASE SIGNIFICANCE: This case stresses the importance of a carefully crafted departmental policy governing the opening of closed containers after vehicle impoundment. The evidence seized in this case was suppressed because there was no departmental policy authorizing the officer's actions. Had the act been authorized by agency policy, the evidence would have been admissible. The main problem in this case was not the opening of the container itself but the absence of a policy authorizing that opening. Courts have held that the absence of a departmental policy, either authorizing the opening of containers or prohibiting such opening, leaves too much discretion to officers such that it has the potential of turning inventory searches into a "general rummaging in order to discover incriminating evidence." It is therefore important that law enforcement departments have a policy governing impoundment inventories. Note that the Court is not concerned with whether that policy allows the opening of the container or not; what the Court is concerned with instead is that there be a policy so that "fishing expeditions" by the police in the process of impoundment inventory are avoided. The Court also said: "While an 'all or nothing' policy is permissible, one that allows a police officer sufficient latitude to determine whether a particular container should be opened in light of the nature of the search and characteristics of the container itself does not violate the Fourth Amendment." This implies that some latitude to open or not to open a container may be given to the officer by departmental policy; what the court disapproves of is the total absence of a policy.

Michigan Department of State Police v. Sitz
496 U.S. 444 (1990)

CAPSULE: Sobriety checkpoints are constitutional.

FACTS: The Michigan State Police established a highway checkpoint program pursuant to guidelines established by a Checkpoint Advisory Committee that governed checkpoint operations, site selection, and publicity. Under these guidelines, checkpoints would be set up at selected sites along state roads and all vehicles passing through the checkpoints would be stopped and the drivers checked for signs of intoxication. If intoxication was noted, the vehicle would be pulled to the side of the road for further tests; all other drivers would be permitted to resume their journey.

During the only operation of the checkpoint, which lasted approximately one hour and 15 minutes, 126 vehicles were checked, with an average delay of 25 seconds per vehicle. Two individuals were arrested for driving under the influence of alcohol.

ISSUE: Is the use of a sobriety checkpoint that stops all vehicles a violation of the Fourth and Fourteenth Amendments? NO.

SUPREME COURT DECISION: Sobriety checkpoints, in which the police stop every vehicle, do not violate the Fourth and Fourteenth Amendment protections against unreasonable searches and seizures and are therefore constitutional.

REASON: The Court said that sobriety checkpoints are a form of seizure, but such a seizure is reasonable because the "measure of intrusion on motorists stopped briefly at sobriety checkpoints—is slight." In *United States v. Martinez-Fuerte*, 428 U.S. 543 (1976), the Court used a balancing test to uphold checkpoints for detecting illegal aliens. The Court held that the state has a substantial interest in preventing illegal aliens from entering the United States. This substantial interest, when balanced against the degree of intrusion placed on motorists passing through the checkpoint, supported the constitutionality of the procedure under the Fourth Amendment. In this case, the Court decided that "[t]he intrusion resulting from the brief stop at the sobriety checkpoint is for constitutional purposes indistinguishable from the checkpoint stops we upheld in *Martinez-Fuerte*," hence the two cases were decided similarly by the Court.

CASE SIGNIFICANCE: For a long time, lower courts had conflicting opinions about the constitutionality of sobriety checkpoints. Courts in 21 states had upheld sobriety checkpoints, while courts in 12 states had declared them unconstitutional. By a 6-to-3 vote, the Court declared that the police may establish highway checkpoints in an effort to catch drunk drivers.

Although the Court admitted that sobriety checkpoints constitute a form of seizure and therefore come under the Fourth Amendment, the intrusion on the driver is minimal and therefore considered reasonable, particularly in light of the state interest involved. The Court quoted media accounts of the seriousness of drunk drivers, saying "drunk drivers cause an annual death toll of over 25,000 and in the same span cause nearly one million personal injuries and more than five billion dollars in property damage." Balancing the state interest involved and the individual constitutional rights invoked, the Court came down on the side of the state, thus giving the police an added weapon in the fight against drunk driving.

In an earlier decision, the Court said that police officers were not authorized to stop a single vehicle for the sole purpose of checking the driver's license and vehicle registration (*Delaware v. Prouse*, 440 U.S. 648 [1979]). In *Prouse*, the Court disapproved of random stops made by Delaware Highway Patrol officers in an effort to apprehend unlicensed drivers and unsafe vehicles because there was no empirical evidence to indicate that such stops would be an effective means of promoting road safety. In the *Sitz* case, however, the Court said that the detention of each of the 126 vehicles resulted in the arrest of two drunk drivers, or approximately 1.5 percent of the drivers. This is a much higher percentage than the number of aliens (.12 percent) found in the *Martinez-Fuerte* case. The Court in *Sitz* decided in favor of the state for three reasons: (1) the balance of the state's interest in preventing drunk driving; (2) the extent to which sobriety checkpoints can reasonably be said to advance that state interest; and (3) the minimal degree of intrusion upon individual motorists who are stopped briefly.

Police departments should note that the sobriety checkpoint procedures declared constitutional by the Court in *Sitz* were a product of careful study and thinking. According to the Court, the following were the main features of the Michigan procedure:

> . . . checkpoints would be set up at selected sites along state roads. All vehicles passing through a checkpoint would be stopped and their drivers briefly examined for signs of intoxication. In cases where a checkpoint officer detected signs of intoxication, the motorist would be directed to a location out of the traffic flow where an officer would check the motorist's driver's license and car registration and, if warranted, conduct further sobriety tests. Should the field tests and the officer's observations suggest that the driver was intoxicated, an arrest would be made. All other drivers would be permitted to resume their journey immediately.

The *Sitz* case does not allow police to make random stops; what it does authorize are well-conceived and carefully structured sobriety checkpoints such as that of Michigan. Although sobriety checkpoints are constitutional, they may be prohibited by departmental policy or state law.

California v. Acevedo
500 U.S. 565 (1991)

CAPSULE: Probable cause to believe that a container in an automobile holds contraband or seizable evidence justifies a warrantless search of that container even in the absence of probable cause to search the vehicle.

FACTS: A Santa Ana, California police officer received a telephone call from a federal drug enforcement agent in Hawaii who stated that he had intercepted a package containing marijuana that was to have been delivered to the Federal Express Office in Santa Ana and that was addressed to J.R. Daza. The agent arranged to have the package sent to the police officer, who verified the contents as marijuana and took it to the Federal Express Office for a controlled delivery.

A man claiming to be Daza picked up the package and took it to an apartment. A short time later, Daza left the apartment and dropped the Federal Express box and the paper that had contained the marijuana into a trash bin. At that point, one police officer left the scene of the apartment to obtain a search warrant.

A short time later, other officers observed another man leave the apartment carrying a knapsack, which appeared to be half-full. The officers stopped the man as he was driving off, searched the knapsack and found one and one-half pounds of marijuana.

Later, Acevedo arrived at the apartment, stayed about 10 minutes, and left carrying a brown paper bag that appeared to be the size of the one that contained the marijuana packages sent from Hawaii. Acevedo placed the bag in the trunk of his car and started to drive away. At that time, the police stopped him, opened the trunk and the bag, and found marijuana. Acevedo pleaded guilty to possession of marijuana for sale.

ISSUE: Does the Fourth Amendment require the police to obtain a warrant to open a closed container in a vehicle if they lack probable cause to search the car but have probable cause to believe that the container itself holds contraband? NO.

SUPREME COURT DECISION: Probable cause to believe that a container in a car holds contraband or seizable evidence justifies a warrantless search of that container even in the absence of probable cause to search the vehicle.

REASON: "Until today, this Court has drawn a curious line between the search of an automobile that coincidentally turns up a container and the search of a container that coincidentally turns up in an automobile. The protections of the Fourth Amendment must not turn on such coincidences. We therefore interpret *Carroll* [*v. United States,* 267 U.S. 132 (1925)] as providing one rule to govern all automobile searches. The police may search an automobile and the containers within it where they have probable cause to believe contraband or evidence is contained."

CASE SIGNIFICANCE: This case, in effect, reverses two earlier Supreme Court rulings. In *United States v. Chadwick*, 433 U.S. 1 (1977) the Court held that the police could seize movable luggage or other closed containers but could not open them without a warrant because a person has a heightened privacy expectation in such containers. In *Arkansas v. Sanders*, 442 U.S. 753 (1979), the Court prohibited the warrantless search of a closed container located in a vehicle when there was probable cause to search only the container but not the vehicle. The Court clarifies the confusion by rejecting these two cases and reiterating instead the Court's ruling in two other cases. The first is *Carroll v. United States*, 267 U.S. 132 (1925), in which the Court held that a warrantless search of an automobile based upon probable cause to believe that the vehicle contained evidence of crime, and in the light of the vehicle's likely disappearance, did not contravene the Fourth Amendment's Warrant Clause. The second is *United States v. Ross*, 456 U.S. 789 (1982), in which the Court said that the warrantless search of an automobile includes a search of closed containers found inside the car when there is probable cause to search the vehicle. *Acevedo* goes one step further than *Ross* in that, while *Ross* allows the warrantless search of a container found in a car if there is probable cause to search the car (as long as the opening of the container is reasonable, given the object of the search), *Acevedo* allows the warrantless search of a container as long as there is probable cause to do so—even if there is no probable cause to search the car.

Florida v. Bostick
501 U.S. 429 (1991)

CAPSULE: The test to determine whether a police/citizen encounter on a bus is a seizure is whether, taking into account all the circumstances, a reasonable passenger would feel free to decline the officers' requests or otherwise terminate the encounter.

FACTS: Without any suspicion and with the intention of catching drug smugglers, two uniformed law enforcement officers boarded a bus in Fort Lauderdale, Florida that was en route from Miami to Atlanta. The officers approached Bostick and asked for identification and his bus ticket. The officers asked Bostick for consent to search his bag and told Bostick he could refuse consent. Bostick consented to the search of his luggage and cocaine was found. He later sought to suppress the evidence in court, alleging that it was improperly seized.

ISSUE: Did the police conduct in this case constitute a seizure of Bostick under the Fourth Amendment, such that he felt compelled to consent to the officer's request? NO.

SUPREME COURT DECISION: "The Florida Supreme Court erred in adopting a *per se* rule that every encounter on a bus is a seizure. The appropriate test is whether, taking into account all of the circumstances surrounding the encounter, a reasonable passenger would feel free to decline the officers' requests or otherwise terminate the encounter."

REASON: "Our cases make it clear that a seizure does not occur simply because a police officer approaches an individual and asks a few questions. So long as a reasonable person would feel free 'to disregard the police and go about his business,' the encounter is consensual and no reasonable suspicion is required. The encounter will not trigger Fourth Amendment scrutiny unless it loses its consensual nature."

"Since *Terry*, we have held repeatedly that mere police questioning does not constitute a seizure. In *Florida v. Royer*, 460 U.S. 491 (1983) (plurality opinion), for example, we explained that 'law enforcement officers do not violate the Fourth Amendment by merely approaching an individual on the street or in another public place, by asking him if he is willing to answer some questions, by putting questions to him if the person is willing to listen, or by offering in evidence in a criminal prosecution his voluntary answers to such questions.' "

"There is no doubt that if this same encounter had taken place before Bostick boarded the bus or in the lobby of the bus terminal, it would not rise to the level of a seizure. The Court has dealt with similar encounters in airports and has found them to be 'the sort of consensual encounters that implicate no Fourth Amendment interests.' We have stated that even when officers have no basis for suspecting a particular individual, they may generally ask questions of that individual and request consent to search his or her luggage—as long as the police do not convey a message that compliance with their requests is required."

CASE SIGNIFICANCE: This case is significant because it clarifies what test is to be used when determining whether a bus encounter constitutes a seizure. The Florida Supreme Court had adopted an inflexible rule stating that the Broward County Sheriff's practice of "working the buses" was *per se* unconstitutional. The U.S. Supreme Court said that the "result of this decision is that police in Florida, as elsewhere, may approach persons at random in most public places, ask them questions and seek consent to a search, but they may not engage in the same behavior on a bus." The Court rejected this rule, saying that "the appropriate test is whether, taking into account all of the circumstances surrounding the encounter, a reasonable passenger would feel free to decline the officers' requests or otherwise terminate the encounter." The case was therefore remanded for the Florida courts "to evaluate the seizure question under the correct legal standard." This was because Florida's Supreme Court based its decision on a single fact—that the encounter took place on a bus and was therefore unconstitutional. The Court remanded the case so Florida courts could use the "totality of circumstances" standard instead.

Whren v. United States
517 U.S. 806 (1996)

CAPSULE: The temporary detention of a motorist upon probable cause to believe that he has violated the traffic laws does not violate the Fourth Amendment's prohibition against unreasonable seizures, even if a reasonable officer would not have stopped the motorist absent some additional law enforcement objective.

FACTS: Plainclothes vice officers were patrolling a high drug activity area in an unmarked car when they noticed a vehicle with temporary license plates and youthful occupants waiting at a stop sign. The truck remained stopped at the intersection for what appeared to be an unusually long time while the driver stared into the lap of the passenger. When the officers made a U-turn and headed toward the vehicle, it made a sudden right turn without signaling and sped off at an "unreasonable" speed. The officers overtook the vehicle when it stopped at a red light. When one of the officers approached the vehicle, he observed two large plastic bags of what appeared to be crack cocaine in Whren's hands. At trial, Whren sought to suppress the evidence, saying that the plainclothes officer would not normally stop traffic violators and that there was no probable cause to make a stop on drug charges; therefore, the stop on the traffic violation was merely a pretext to determine whether Whren had drugs. This motion to suppress was denied and Whren and his accomplice were convicted of drug charges.

ISSUE: Is the temporary detention of a motorist who the police have probable cause to believe has committed a civil traffic violation constitutional under the Fourth Amendment if the officer in fact had some other law enforcement objective? YES.

SUPREME COURT DECISION: "The temporary detention of a motorist upon probable cause to believe that he has violated the traffic laws does not violate the Fourth Amendment's prohibition against unreasonable seizures, even if a reasonable officer would not have stopped the motorist absent some additional law enforcement objective."

REASON: "We think these cases [discussed in the preceding paragraphs] foreclose any argument that the constitutional reasonableness of traffic stops depends on the actual motivations of the individual officers involved. We of course agree with petitioners that the Constitution prohibits selective enforcement of the law based on considerations such as race. But the constitutional basis for objecting to intentionally discriminatory application of laws is the equal protection clause, not the Fourth Amendment. Subjective intentions play no role in ordinary, probable-cause Fourth Amendment analysis."

CASE SIGNIFICANCE: This case is important because it gives law enforcement officers an additional tool to make valid searches and seizures. In this case, the defendant alleged that what the police did was illegal because they did not have probable cause to search him for drugs. Although it was true that they had probable cause to believe that he committed a civil traffic violation (waiting at a stop sign at an intersection for an unusually long time, then turning suddenly without signaling, and speeding off at an unreasonable speed), but that alone would not ordinarily have caused the police to make a stop. He claimed that the stop was merely a pretext for the officers to be able to search for drugs, which they in fact found. The Court disagreed, saying that the officers' probable cause to believe that the motorist had committed a traffic violation made the stop valid even if the actual purpose was to look for drugs, making the stop for a traffic violation merely a pretext for another law enforcement objective. The Court in effect said that whether ordinarily the police officers "would have" made the stop is not the test for validity; instead, the test is whether the officers "could have" made the stop. The fact that they "could have" made a valid stop because there was a traffic violation made the stop valid even if the actual purpose for making the stop was to look for drugs. The message for the police from this case is this: the real purpose of the stop does not render the stop and subsequent search invalid if there was in fact a valid reason for the stop.

Maryland v. Wilson
519 U.S. 408 (1997)

CAPSULE: ". . . an officer making a traffic stop may order passengers to get out of the car pending completion of the stop."

FACTS: A state trooper attempted to stop a car, in which Wilson was a passenger, for speeding and an irregular license plate. After activating his blue lights, the trooper followed the car for more than a mile before it stopped. During this time, two of the three passengers in the car kept looking back at the trooper, ducking below the line of sight and then reappearing. As the trooper approached the car after it stopped, the driver got out and met him halfway. The trooper reported that the driver was trembling and appeared very nervous, but did produce a valid driver's license. When the driver returned to the car to retrieve the rental papers, the trooper noticed that Wilson was sweating and appeared very nervous. When the trooper ordered Wilson out of the car, a quantity of crack cocaine fell to the ground. Wilson was arrested and charged with possession of cocaine with intent to distribute.

ISSUE: After stopping a car, may an officer order the passengers to exit the vehicle? YES.

SUPREME COURT DECISION: After a traffic stop, the officer may also order the passengers, not just the driver, to exit the car.

REASON: In *Pennsylvania v. Mimms*, 434 U.S. 106 (1977), the Supreme Court ruled that "[t]he touchstone of our analysis under the Fourth Amendment is always 'the reasonableness in all the circumstances of the particular governmental intrusions on a citizen's personal security' . . . and . . . that reasonableness depends on 'a balance between the public's interest and the individual's right to personal security. . . .'" (*Pennsylvania v. Mimms*, 434 U.S. at 108-109). Here, the Court ruled that "[o]n the public interest side of the balance, the same weighty interest in officer safety is present regardless of whether the occupant of the stopped car is a driver or passenger. Regrettably, traffic stops may be dangerous encounters. . . . On the personal liberty side of the balance, the case for the passengers is in one sense stronger than that for the driver. There is probable cause to believe that the driver has committed a minor vehicular offense, but there is no such reason to stop or detain the passengers. But as a practical matter, the passengers are already stopped by virtue of the stop of the vehicle. The only change in their circumstances which will result from ordering them out of the car is that they will be outside of, rather than inside of, the stopped car." "While there is [therefore] not the same basis for ordering the passengers out of the car as there is for ordering the driver out, the additional intrusion on the passenger is minimal. We therefore hold that an officer making a traffic stop may order passengers to get out of the car pending completion of the stop."

CASE SIGNIFICANCE: In *Mimms,* the Supreme Court ruled that a law enforcement officer may, as a matter of course, order the driver to exit the car. It was not clear from *Mimms*, however, whether that rule also extended to passengers. The Court in *Wilson* clarified this issue and said that it did, hence both the driver and passenger can now be ordered by the police to exit the car after a stop. The reason for this rule is simple: officer safety. The Court said that the government's "legitimate and weighty" interest in protecting officers prevails against the minimal infringement on the liberties of both the car driver and the passengers. Although a passenger has a stronger claim of liberty than the driver (who is suspected to have committed a traffic offense), the passenger nonetheless "has the same motivation as a driver to use a weapon concealed in the car to prevent the officer from finding evidence of more serious crime." Given this danger, the Court said that the car driver and the passengers can be made to exit the car. The Court stopped short, however, of ruling that officers could forcibly detain the passenger for the entire duration of the stop absent exigent circumstances.

Pennsylvania v. Labron
518 U.S. 938 (1996)

CAPSULE: There is no need for a warrant in vehicle searches if the vehicle is readily mobile, even if there is time to obtain a warrant.

FACTS: Police observed Labron and others engaging in a series of drug transactions on the street. After arresting the suspects, the police searched the trunk of the car where they had observed the suspects retrieving the drugs. The search revealed bags of cocaine. The search was made without a warrant, although the police had time to obtain one.

ISSUE: Are warrantless searches of vehicles valid even if there is time for the police to obtain a warrant? YES.

SUPREME COURT DECISION: "If a car is readily mobile and probable cause exists to believe it contains contraband, the Fourth Amendment thus permits police to search the vehicle without more." Thus, warrantless searches of vehicles are valid even if there is time to obtain a warrant as long as probable cause is present.

REASON: "Our first cases establishing the automobile exception to the Fourth Amendment's warrant requirement were based on the automobile's 'ready mobility,' an exigency sufficient to excuse failure to obtain a search warrant once probable cause to conduct the search is clear. More recent cases provide a further justification: the individual's reduced expectation of privacy in an automobile, owing to its pervasive regulation" (citations omitted).

CASE SIGNIFICANCE: This case again extends the authority of the police to make warrantless searches of automobiles. Beginning with *Carroll v. United States*, the Court has continually allowed greater freedom to search automobiles without a warrant. This case removed another roadblock to automobile searches: that of the requirement to obtain a warrant to search if there is time to do so. In this holding, the Court seems to have overturned the language in *Coolidge v. New Hampshire*, which stated: "Since the police knew of the presence of the automobile and planned all along to seize it, there was no 'exigent circumstance' to justify their failure to obtain a warrant." The difference between this case and *Coolidge* is that, in this case, the car was on the street rather than at the suspect's house. This case makes clear that law enforcement officers may conduct a warrantless search if there is probable cause, even if there is time to obtain a warrant.

Ohio v. Robinette
519 U.S. 33 (1996)

CAPSULE: The Fourth Amendment does not require police officers to inform motorists who are lawfully stopped for traffic violations that the legal detention has concluded before any subsequent interrogation or search will be found to be consensual.

FACTS: After a deputy stopped Robinette for speeding, he asked Robinette to step out of the car, where he was issued a verbal warning. After the deputy returned Robinette's license, he asked "One question before you get gone: are you carrying any illegal contraband in your car?" When Robinette replied "no," the deputy asked if he could search the car. Robinette consented and the deputy searched the car, where he found a small amount of marijuana and a pill that turned out to be methylenedioxymethamphetamine. The evidence was admitted over Robinette's objection and he was convicted of possession of a controlled substance. Robinette later claimed that he should have been informed that he was "free to go" for the consent to search the car to be valid.

ISSUE: Does the Fourth Amendment require "that a lawfully seized defendant must be advised that he is 'free to go' before his consent to search will be recognized as voluntary"? NO.

SUPREME COURT DECISION: The Fourth Amendment does not require ". . . police officers to inform motorists lawfully stopped for traffic violations that the legal detention has concluded before any subsequent interrogation or search will be found to be consensual."

REASON: The Court ruled in *Pennsylvania v. Mimms,* 434 U.S. 106 (1977) ". . . that once a motor vehicle has been lawfully detained for a traffic violation, the police officers may order the driver to get out of the vehicle without violating the Fourth Amendment's proscription of unreasonable searches and seizures." The Court then found that "there is no question that, in light of the admitted probable cause to stop Robinette for speeding, [the deputy] was objectively justified in asking Robinette to get out of the car . . . ." Using the standard of the totality of the circumstances, the Court ruled that: (1) "voluntariness is a question of fact to be determined from all the circumstances"; (2) while "knowledge of the right to refuse consent is one factor to be taken into account, the government need not establish such knowledge as the *sine qua non* of an effective consent"; and (3) it would "be unrealistic to require police officers to always inform detainees that they are free to go before a consent to search may be deemed voluntary."

CASE SIGNIFICANCE: There is no requirement under the Fourth Amendment for the officer to first inform the detained motorist that "you are free to go" before consent to search the car will be held voluntary and therefore valid. The Court added that "the voluntariness of a consent to search is a question of fact to be determined from all the circumstances," and not on a *per se* rule that requires an officer to inform the motorist that he or she is "free to go." This case confirms and extends the Court's ruling that the totality of circumstances applies in search and seizure cases. Here, the Court ruled that officers may obtain consent to search a vehicle from stopped motorists without the requirement to first inform them that they are free to go.

Knowles v. Iowa
525 U.S. 113 (1998)

CAPSULE: Officers may search a vehicle incident to an arrest, but a search incident to the issuance of a traffic citation, absent consent or probable cause, violates the Fourth Amendment.

FACTS: Knowles was stopped for speeding and issued a citation (although the officer had the authority to arrest him). The officer then conducted a full search of Knowles' car, where he found marijuana and drug paraphernalia. At trial, the officer conceded that he had neither consent nor probable cause for the search and that he relied on state law that permitted "searches incident to citation." The evidence was admitted over Knowles' objection and he was convicted of possession of drug paraphernalia.

ISSUE: May an officer search a vehicle incident to a traffic stop without consent or probable cause? NO.

SUPREME COURT DECISION: While officers may search a vehicle incident to an arrest, a search incident to the issuance of a traffic citation, absent consent or probable cause, violates the Fourth Amendment, even if authorized by state law.

REASON: "We have recognized that the first rationale—officer safety—is ' "both legitimate and weighty," ' *Maryland v. Wilson*, 519 U.S. 408, 412 (1997) (quoting *Pennsylvania v. Mimms*, 434 U.S. 106, 110 (1977) *(per curiam)*. The threat to officer safety from issuing a traffic citation, however, is a good deal less than in the case of a custodial arrest. In *Robinson*, we stated that a custodial arrest involves 'danger to an officer' because of 'the extended exposure which follows the taking of a suspect into custody and transporting him to the police station.' 414 U.S., at 234-235. . . . A routine traffic stop, on the other hand, is a relatively brief encounter and 'is more analogous to a so-called "*Terry* stop" . . . than to a formal arrest.' *Berkemer v. McCarty*, 468 U.S. 420, 437 (1984)." ". . . while the concern for officer safety in this context may justify the 'minimal' additional intrusion of ordering a driver and passengers out of the car, it does not by itself justify the often considerably greater intrusion attending a full field-type search."

CASE SIGNIFICANCE: This case reaffirms the rule that, to be valid, vehicle searches must have either probable cause or consent. There was none in this case, but the officer justified the search because of an Iowa law which stated that a search incident to citation "is justified because a suspect may try to hide evidence of his identity or of other crimes." The Court found this unpersuasive and reaffirmed the ruling that, to conduct a search during a traffic stop, officers must have demonstrable probable cause or the consent of the driver.

Wyoming v. Houghton
526 U.S. 295 (1999)

CAPSULE: Police officers with probable cause to search a car may inspect passengers' belongings found in the car that are capable of concealing the object of the search.

FACTS: During a routine traffic stop, an officer stopped an automobile in which Houghton was riding. While questioning the driver, the officer noticed a hypodermic needle in his shirt pocket. When the driver admitted using the needle to use drugs, the passengers in the vehicle were ordered out of the car. Pursuant to the driver's admission, officers searched the passenger compartment of the vehicle. On the back seat, officers found a purse that Houghton claimed as hers. Methamphetamine and drug paraphernalia were found in the purse and Houghton was arrested. After the trial court denied Houghton's motion to suppress the evidence, she was convicted of felony possession of drugs.

ISSUE: Do law enforcement officers "violate the Fourth Amendment when they search a passenger's personal belongings inside an automobile that they have probable cause to believe contains contraband?" NO.

SUPREME COURT DECISION: Police officers with probable cause to search a car may inspect passengers' belongings found in the car that are capable of concealing the object of the search.

REASON: "The critical element in a reasonable search is not that the owner of the property is suspected of crime but that there is reasonable cause to believe that the specific 'things' to be search for and seized are located on the property to which entry is sought" (citing *Zurcher v. Stanford Daily*, 436 U.S. 547 [1978]). ". . . [N]either [*U.S. v.*] *Ross* [456 U.S. 798] itself nor the historical evidence it relied upon admits of a distinction among packages or containers based on ownership." "Passengers, no less than drivers, possess a reduced expectation of privacy with regard to the property that they transport in cars, which 'travel public thoroughfares'. "

CASE SIGNIFICANCE: This is an important decision because it settles an issue that is often raised in vehicle searches, but which the Court had not addressed previously: whether the police may inspect the belongings of passengers in a car. In this case, the arrest of the driver and the search of the driver's property was valid because probable cause was present after the driver admitted that a hypodermic needle in his shirt pocket was used in taking drugs. The officer, however, went beyond that and also searched a purse that the officer knew belonged to a passenger. The passenger was not suspected of any criminal activity, although contraband was later found during the search. The Court held that the search of the passenger's purse was valid under these circumstances based on two reasons: (1) the passenger's reduced expectation of privacy; and (2) "the governmental interest in effective law enforcement would be appreciably impaired without the ability to search the passenger's belongings, since an automobile's ready mobility creates the risk that evidence or contraband will be permanently lost while a warrant is obtained . . ."

Bond v. United States
529 U.S. 334 (2000)

CAPSULE: A traveler's luggage is an "effect" and is under the protection of the Fourth Amendment. Officers may not physically manipulate (squeeze) the luggage to inspect it without a warrant or probable cause.

FACTS: Bond was riding on a Greyhound bus when a Border Patrol Agent boarded the bus to check the immigration status of passengers. After satisfying himself that the passengers were lawfully in the U.S., the agent began to walk to the front of the bus. Along the way, he squeezed the soft luggage passengers had placed in overhead storage space. The agent squeezed a canvas bag above Bond's seat and felt that it contained "a brick-like object". Bond admitted owning the bag and agreed to allow the agent to open it, whereupon the agent found a brick of methamphetamine.

ISSUE: Does the physical manipulation of a bus passenger's carry-on luggage by a law enforcement officer violate the Fourth Amendment prohibition against unreasonable searches? YES.

SUPREME COURT DECISION: A traveler's luggage is an "effect" and is under the protection of the Fourth Amendment. Officers may not physically manipulate (squeeze) the luggage to inspect it without a warrant or probable cause.

REASON: A Fourth Amendment analysis involves two issues. First is whether an individual has exhibited an expectation of privacy for an effect protected by the Fourth Amendment. A traveler's luggage is clearly an effect within the Fourth Amendment. Here, Bond sought to preserve privacy by using an opaque bag and placing it directly above his seat. The second issue is whether the individual's expectation of privacy is "one that society is prepared to recognize as reasonable". Although there is an expectation that the luggage will be handled by other passengers or bus employees, there is no expectation that the luggage will be physically manipulated in an exploratory manner. Visual inspection of items in public view has been ruled not to be protected by the Fourth Amendment, but a physically invasive inspection is more intrusive than a visual inspection; therefore, the law enforcement officer's physical manipulation of the luggage violated the Fourth Amendment.

CASE SIGNIFICANCE: The Government argued that by "exposing the bag to the public, Bond lost a reasonable expectation of privacy that his bag would not be physically manipulated." Bond admitted that "by placing his bag in the overhead compartment, he could expect that it would be exposed to certain kinds of touching and handling." He maintained, however, that the officer's physical manipulation of the luggage "far exceeded the casual contact" that Bond could have expected from other passengers. The Court agreed with Bond, holding: "When a bus passenger places a bag in an overhead bin, he expects that other passengers or bus employees may move it for one reason or another. Thus, a bus passenger clearly expects that his bag may be handled. He does not expect that other passengers or bus employees will, as a matter of course, feel the bag in an exploratory manner. But this is exactly what the agent did here. We therefore hold that the agent's physical manipulation of petitioner's bag violated the Fourth Amendment."

The Court in this case reiterated two questions that must be asked when analyzing Fourth Amendment cases: (1) whether the individual, by his or her conduct, exhibited an actual, expectation of privacy, and (2) whether that individual's expectation of privacy "one that society is prepared to recognize as reasonable." The Court concluded that the answer to both questions in this case was yes; therefore the conduct of the agent was unconstitutional. This case defines the limit of what police officers can do to pieces of luggage and belongings of passengers. It holds that passengers have a reasonable expectation of privacy as to their belongings while traveling in public transportation and in public places. Officers need probable cause to search.

Indianapolis v. Edmond
531 U.S. 32 (2000)

CAPSULE: Highway checkpoints whose primary purpose is to detect evidence of ordinary criminal wrongdoing violate the Fourth Amendment.

FACTS: Indianapolis police began a program of vehicle checkpoints in an effort to detect illegal drugs. The roadblocks were to operate during daylight hours and be clearly marked by signs. The locations of the roadblocks were planned well in advance, and a predetermined number of vehicles was to be stopped. At the stop, an officer required the driver to produce a driver's license and registration. The officer would check for signs of impairment in the driver and conduct a plain view observation of the vehicle from the outside while a narcotics detecting dog was walked around the outside of the vehicle. Only if the officer developed particularized suspicion of illegality was the driver detained and further investigation conducted; and officers had no discretion to stop any vehicle out of sequence. The total time of the stop was to be less than five minutes. Edmond and others were stopped at the checkpoints.

ISSUE: Do roadblocks that have the primary purpose of crime control violate the Fourth Amendment? YES.

SUPREME COURT DECISION: Highway checkpoints whose primary purpose is to detect evidence of ordinary criminal wrongdoing violate the Fourth Amendment.

REASON: "We have never approved a checkpoint program whose primary purpose was to detect evidence of ordinary criminal wrongdoing. Rather our checkpoint cases [*Michigan v. Sitz, U.S. v. Martinez-Fuerte*, and *Delaware v. Prouse* in this text] have recognized only limited exceptions to the general rule that a seizure must be accompanied by some measure of individualized suspicion. We suggested in *Prouse* that we would not credit the 'general interest in crime control' as justification for a regime of suspicionless stops, 440 U.S. at 659, n 18. Consistent with this suggestion, each of the checkpoint programs that we have approved was designed primarily to serve purposes closely related to the problems of policing the border or the necessity of ensuring roadway safety. Because the primary purpose of the Indianapolis narcotics checkpoint program is to uncover evidence of ordinary criminal wrongdoing, the program contravenes the Fourth Amendment."

CASE SIGNIFICANCE: The general rule in Fourth Amendment cases is that searches and seizures are unreasonable unless there is individualized suspicion of criminal wrongdoing. In roadblocks, there is no individualized suspicion of wrongdoing. There are exceptions to this need for individualized suspicion, however, which are: (1) when the purpose of the roadblock is securing the border, (2) when the purpose is apprehending drunken drivers, and (3) when the purpose is verifying drivers' licenses and registrations. Setting up checkpoints to control the flow of drugs was sought by the City of Indianapolis as another exception. The Court rejected this contention, concluding that the purpose of the checkpoint was general law enforcement, which could not be allowed because it was too general. The Court argued that "if this case were to rest at such a high level of generality, there would be little check on the authorities' ability to construct roadblocks for almost any conceivable law enforcement purpose." The drug problem is severe, but the Court did not think it justified setting up roadblocks. The Court concluded, "We have never approved a checkpoint program whose primary purpose was to detect evidence of ordinary criminal wrongdoing. Rather, our checkpoint cases have recognized only limited exceptions to the general rule that a seizure must be accompanied by some measure of individualized suspicion. We suggested in *Prouse* that we would not credit the 'general interest in crime control' as justification for a regime of suspicionless stops." The lesson for law enforcement from this case is this: Properly designed roadblocks for traffic and immigration purposes are valid, but roadblocks for general crime control are unconstitutional. If the purpose is crime control, there must be individualized suspicion before the officer can stop motor vehicles.

United States v. Drayton
536 U.S. 194 (2002)

CAPSULE: The Fourth Amendment permits police officers to approach bus passengers, to ask questions, and to request their consent to search, provided that a reasonable person would understand that he or she is free to refuse. There is no requirement in the Fourth Amendment for officers to advise the persons of their right to refuse to cooperate.

FACTS: Drayton and Clifton Brown were traveling on a Greyhound bus from Ft. Lauderdale, Florida, to Detroit, Michigan, when it made a scheduled stop in Tallahassee, Florida. While the bus driver left to complete paperwork, three police officers boarded the bus as a part of a drug interdiction program. One of the officers knelt in the driver's seat and watched the passengers. The other two officers went to the back of the bus. One officer stayed at the back to watch passengers while the other began to move forward, speaking with individual passengers as he went. He asked passengers about their travel and attempted to match passengers with luggage. To avoid blocking the aisle, the officer stood behind the passenger's seat while speaking. Passengers who declined to speak to the officer or who left the bus were allowed to do so. As the officer approached Drayton and Brown, he leaned forward from the rear and spoke in a tone just loud enough for them to hear. When asked if they had any bags, they both pointed to a single bag overhead. The officer examined the bag and found nothing. Both Drayton and Brown were wearing heavy coats and baggy pants despite the warm weather. Based on the officer's experience that this was typical for persons trafficking narcotics, he asked Brown if he could check his person. Brown agreed, leaned forward in his seat, and opened his jacket. The officer patted down Brown and felt objects on his legs consistent with drug packages he had detected on other occasions. The officer then arrested and handcuffed Brown. The officer then asked Drayton if he could check him, to which Drayton agreed. A pat-down of Drayton's thighs produced evidence of similar objects. Drayton was also arrested and both were found to have drugs taped to their thighs.

ISSUE: Does the Fourth Amendment require police officers to advise bus passengers of their right not to cooperate when asked questions and to refuse consent to a search? NO.

SUPREME COURT DECISION: The Fourth Amendment permits police officers to approach bus passengers, ask questions, and request their consent to search, provided a reasonable person under the same circumstances would understand that he or she is free to refuse to cooperate. The Fourth Amendment does not require officers to advise persons of their right to refuse to cooperate when asked questions and to refuse consent to a search.

REASON: "Law enforcement officers to not violate the Fourth Amendment prohibition of unreasonable seizures merely by approaching individuals on the street or in other public places and putting questions to them if they are willing to listen. Even when law enforcement officers have no basis for suspecting a particular individual, they may pose questions, ask for identification, and request consent to search luggage provided they do not induce cooperation by coercive means. If a reasonable person would feel free to terminate the encounter, then he or she has not been seized." [Citations omitted]. "Applying the *Bostick* framework to the facts of this particular case, we conclude that the police did not seize respondents when they boarded the bus and began questioning passengers. The officers gave the passengers no reason to believe that they were required to answer the officers' questions."

CASE SIGNIFICANCE: The Court in this case held the police are not required to inform bus passengers of their right to refuse to cooperate when asked questions or when seeking consent to search, as long as a reasonable individual under the same circumstances would have felt that he or she did not have to cooperate. The Court stressed that "law enforcement officers do not violate the Fourth Amendment's prohibition of unreasonable seizures merely by approaching individuals on the street or in other public places and putting questions to them if they are willing to listen." This is true even if they do not have any basis for suspecting that an individual is involved in a criminal act. Officers are free to "pose questions, ask for identification, and request consent to search luggage—provided they do not induce cooperation by coercive means." There is no seizure under the Fourth Amendment if a reasonable person would feel free to terminate the encounter.

As in most cases involving the Fourth Amendment, the decision in this case was based on a totality of the circumstances. The Court further said: " 'While knowledge of the right to refuse consent is one factor to be taken into account, the government need not establish such knowledge as the sine qua non of an effective consent.' Nor do this Court's decisions suggest that even though there are no per se rules, a presumption of invalidity attaches if a citizen consented without explicit notification that he or she was free to refuse to cooperate. Instead, the Court has repeated that the totality of the circumstances must control, without giving extra weight to the absence of this type of warning."

This decision informs law enforcement officers that no specific information about an individual's right to refuse to cooperate need be given, but that the confrontation itself should not be coercive and the officer must be prepared to establish, if the legality of the act is later challenged, that the totality of the circumstances was such that a reasonable person would have felt free to refuse to cooperate. It should be noted that the reality is that most suspects answer questions by the police and give permission to search even if they have something to hide. What makes suspects do that despite awareness that the police will find something incriminating is hard to tell. Encounter with the police may be deemed by some to be inherently coercive such that they do not feel free to refuse. Or they may think that refusal to search in itself creates added suspicion and that the police can then go ahead and search anyway. Whatever the reason, suspects giving consent to the police to search even if they have something to hide, which will likely be discovered, is an interesting topic to study.

Illinois v. Lidster
540 U.S. 419 (2004)

CAPSULE: Police checkpoints set up for the purpose of obtaining information from motorists about a hit-and-run accident are valid under the Fourth Amendment.

FACTS: Police set up a highway checkpoint to obtain information from motorists about a hit-and-run accident. The checkpoint was established at about the same time of night and at the same location as the hit-and-run. Officers stopped each vehicle for 10 to 15 seconds, asked the occupants if they saw anything related to the accident, and handed them a flyer asking for their assistance. As Lidster approached the checkpoint, his van swerved, almost hitting an officer. When the officer smelled alcohol on Lidster's breath, he directed him to a side street where another officer administered a sobriety test and then arrested Lidster.

ISSUE: Does a checkpoint designed to obtain information from motorists about a hit-and-run accident violate the Fourth Amendment? NO.

SUPREME COURT DECISION: Police checkpoints set up to obtain information from motorists about a hit-and-run accident are valid under the Fourth Amendment. When officers have probable cause that a stopped person is engaged in illegal activity, they may take appropriate action.

REASON: This case is another in the line of cases related to police checkpoints (included in this chapter). In *Michigan v. Sitz*, the Court ruled that checkpoints established to control drunk driving were constitutional if based on certain standards of reasonableness. The Court ruled unconstitutional, however, the police use of roadblocks for general crime control purposes (see *Indianapolis v. Edmond*). Lidster argued here that the *Edmond* rule should apply, making this checkpoint unconstitutional also. The Court disagreed. The Court held that *Edmond* did not govern the outcome of this case because it dealt with crime control stops without individualized suspicion. In this case, the purpose was not to determine whether a vehicle's occupants were engaged in crime, but to request the assistance of motorists related to a crime for which they were likely not involved. The Court rejected a rule of automatic unconstitutionality for such stops, arguing that they will normally lack individualized suspicion, but that does not automatically make it unconstitutional. The Court relied on previous cases to support its argument that sometimes special law enforcement concerns justify highway stops without individualized suspicion.

CASE SIGNIFICANCE: This case is significant because it adds more information concerning the validity of roadblocks set up by the police. Not all police roadblocks are constitutional under the Fourth Amendment. In previous cases, the Court held that the following types of roadblocks are valid: (1) roadblocks in which the police stop every vehicle for the purpose of controlling drunk driving (*Michigan Department of State Police v. Sitz*, 496 U.S. 444 [1990]); (2) roadblocks established to check drivers' licenses and vehicle registrations (*Delaware v. Prouse*, 440 U.S. 648 [1979]); and (3) roadblocks to control the flow of illegal aliens (*United States v. Martinez-Fuerte*, 428 U.S. 543 [1976]). But the Court has also held that checkpoints set up to detect evidence of general criminal wrongdoing are unconstitutional (*Indianapolis v. Edmond*, 531 U.S. 32 [2000]). In this case, the Court held that whether a roadblock is constitutional (given the absence of individualized suspicion that the person stopped committed a crime) are these: (1) "the gravity of the public concerns served by the seizure"; (2) "the degree to which the seizure advances the public interest"; and (3) "the severity of the interference with individual liberty." The roadblock here was valid because the purpose was not for general "crime control," but had a much more specific purpose—to seek information about a hit-and-run incident that took place about a week earlier. Moreover, "each stop required only a brief wait in line and contact with police for only a few seconds." In sum, police checkpoints set up for a specific purpose are valid, but checkpoints whose purpose is to obtain information for general crime control are unconstitutional.

United States v. Flores-Montano
541 U.S. 149 (2004)

CAPSULE: "The Government's authority to conduct suspicionless inspections at the border includes the authority to remove, disassemble, and reassemble a vehicle's fuel tank."

FACTS: Flores-Montano attempted to enter the United States at a border crossing. A customs inspector examined the vehicle and asked Flores-Montano to leave the vehicle for secondary inspection. At the secondary station, another customs inspector tapped on the gas tank and noted that it sounded solid. The inspector then asked a mechanic to help remove the gas tank. The mechanic arrived approximately 20 minutes later. The mechanic removed the gas thank, then the inspector hammered off the putty used to seal the top of the gas tank. When the inspector opened an access plate underneath the putty, he found 37 kilograms of marijuana. Flores-Montano sought suppression of the evidence, saying the inspectors did not have reasonable suspicion that he was engaged in criminal activity and reasonable suspicion is required to remove a gas tank.

ISSUE: Must officers have reasonable suspicion of criminal activity to remove the gas tank of a vehicle at an international border crossing? NO.

SUPREME COURT DECISION: "The Government's authority to conduct suspicionless inspections at the border includes the authority to remove, disassemble, and reassemble a vehicle's fuel tank."

REASON: "The Government's interest in preventing the entry of unwanted persons and effects is at its zenith at the international border. Time and again, we have stated that 'searches made at the border, pursuant to the longstanding right of the sovereign to protect itself by stopping and examining persons and property crossing into this country, are reasonable simply by virtue of the fact that they occur at the border.' Congress, since the beginning of our Government, 'has granted the executive plenary authority to conduct routine searches and seizures at the border, without probable cause or a warrant, in order to regulate the collection of duties and to prevent the introduction of contraband into this country.' " [internal citations omitted]. "That interest in protecting the borders is illustrated in this case by the evidence that smugglers frequently attempt to penetrate our borders with contraband secreted in their automobiles' fuel tanks. Over the past 5½ fiscal years, there have been 18,788 vehicle drug seizures at the southern California ports of entry. Of those 18,788, gas tank drug seizures have accounted for 4,619 of the vehicle drug seizures, or approximately 25%."

CASE SIGNIFICANCE: This case involves one type of search—border searches. The rule here, therefore, does not apply to searches and seizures other than border searches. Border searches may be conducted without probable cause or reasonable suspicion because they are a special kind of search done in a different kind of place—a border. The Court noted in this case that ". . . on many occasions, we have noted that the expectation of privacy is less at the border than it is in the interior" and "We have long recognized that automobiles seeking entry into this country may be searched."

Flores-Montano argued that reasonable suspicion (a lower degree of certainty than probable cause) was required for the type of search conducted by the officers, claiming that: (1) he "has a privacy interest in his fuel tank, and that the suspicionless disassembly of his tank is an invasion of his privacy," and that (2) because the Fourth Amendment "protects property as well as privacy," the "disassembly and reassembly of his gas tank was a significant deprivation of his property interest because it could damage the vehicle." Despite the intrusiveness of the search, the Court rejected both arguments, saying Flores-Montano "cites not a single accident involving the vehicle or motorist in the many thousands of gas tank disassemblies that have occurred at the border,". The Court concluded that "while it may be true that some searches of property are so destructive as to require a different result, this is not one of them."

Thornton v. United States
541 U.S. 615 (2004)

CAPSULE: Officers may search the passenger compartment of a vehicle after a lawful arrest even if the suspect was not in the vehicle when arrested.

FACTS: An officer became suspicious of Thornton when he slowed down to avoid driving next to the officer (who was in uniform but in an unmarked car). The officer pulled over so he could get behind Thornton and check his license plate. The check revealed that the tags were not registered to the car

Thornton was driving. Before the officer could pull him over, Thornton pulled into a parking lot, parked, and got out of his vehicle. The officer saw Thornton leave the vehicle. The officer then stopped Thornton and asked about the tags on his vehicle. When Thornton began to act nervous and suspicious, the officer, concerned for his safety, asked Thornton if he had any illegal narcotics or weapons on him or in his vehicle. Thornton replied no and consented to a pat-down search. The officer felt a bulge in Thornton's left front pocket and again asked about illegal narcotics. This time, Thornton stated he had drugs, and reached into his pocket and retrieved two bags, one containing marijuana and one containing crack cocaine. The officer handcuffed Thornton, told him he was under arrest, and placed him in the backseat of the patrol car. The officer then searched Thornton's vehicle and discovered a handgun under the driver's seat.

ISSUE: Does a search of the passenger compartment of a vehicle incident to an arrest violate the Fourth Amendment if the suspect was not in the vehicle when arrested? NO.

SUPREME COURT DECISION: Officers may search the passenger compartment of a motor vehicle after a lawful arrest even if the suspect was not in the vehicle when arrested.

REASON: In this case, Thornton sought to differentiate the circumstances of this case from *New York v. Belton* based on Belton being inside the vehicle when first encountered by police and Thornton having exited his vehicle. The Court, however, found congruence between the two cases. The Court restated their holding in *Belton* that "when a policeman has made a lawful custodial arrest of the occupant of an automobile, he may, as a contemporaneous incident of that arrest, search the passenger compartment of that automobile." The Court reasoned that "in all relevant aspects, the arrest of a suspect who is next to a vehicle presents identical concerns regarding officer safety and the destruction of evidence as the arrest of one who is inside the vehicle." In fact, the Court noted, "in some circumstances, it may be safer and more effective for the officers to conceal their presence from a suspect until he has left his vehicle." The Court concluded with the statement that: "So long as an arrestee is the sort of 'recent occupant' of a vehicle such as petitioner was here, officers may search that vehicle incident to the arrest."

CASE SIGNIFICANCE: The Court in *Chimel v. California*, 395 U.S. 752 (1969), held that an officer could search the "area of immediate control" of an arrested person for weapons or evidence. The exact extent of the term "area of immediate control" has been debated in many cases for years. In *New York v. Belton*, 453 U.S. 454 (1981), the Court held that the area of immediate control included the passenger compartment of a vehicle when officers encountered the suspect in the vehicle. In *Thornton*, the Court extended that ruling to those who are connected with the vehicle (here the officer observed Thornton leaving the vehicle) but who were not in the vehicle when first approached by the officer. The Court in this case did not set specific boundaries for the "area of immediate control" from the vehicle, stating instead that "while an arrestee's status as a 'recent occupant' may turn on his temporal or spatial relationship to the car at the time of the arrest and search, it certainly does not turn on whether he was inside or outside the car at the moment that the officer first initiated contact with him." Similarly, the Court conceded that "To be sure, not all contraband in the passenger compartment is likely to be readily accessible to a 'recent occupant'." These statements leave unresolved the issue of whether a situation could arise where the occupant of a vehicle could be far enough removed from the vehicle, either temporally or spatially, such that the police can no longer search the passenger compartment incident to a lawful arrest.

Illinois v. Caballes
543 U.S. 405, 125 S. Ct. 834 (2005)

CAPSULE: A dog examination conducted during a lawful traffic stop that reveals no information other than the location of an illegal substance that no individual has any right to possess does not violate the Fourth Amendment.

FACTS: An officer stopped Caballes for speeding and radioed the dispatcher. Hearing the radio transmission, another officer drove to the scene with his drug detection dog. While the first officer wrote Caballes a warning ticket, the K-9 officer walked his dog around Caballes's car. The dog alerted on the trunk. Based on that alert, the officers searched the trunk and found marijuana. Caballes sought suppression of the evidence, arguing that because there was no suspicion of him being involved in drug activity, use of the dog violated the Fourth Amendment.

ISSUE: Does "the Fourth Amendment require reasonable, articulable suspicion to justify using a drug detection dog to sniff a vehicle during a legitimate traffic stop?" NO.

SUPREME COURT DECISION: "A dog sniff conducted during a . . . lawful traffic stop that reveals no information other than the location of [an illegal] substance that no individual has any right to possess does not violate the Fourth Amendment.

REASON: "In our view, conducting a dog sniff would not change the character of a traffic stop that is lawful at its inception and otherwise executed in a reasonable manner, unless the dog sniff itself infringed respondent's con-

stitutionally protected interest in privacy. Our cases hold that it did not. . . .
We have held that any interest in possessing contraband cannot be deemed
'legitimate,' and thus, governmental conduct that *only* reveals the possession
of contraband 'compromises no legitimate privacy interest' [emphasis in orig-
inal]. . . . Accordingly, the use of a well-trained narcotics-detection dog—
one that 'does not expose non-contraband items that otherwise would
remain hidden from public view,' *Place*, 462 U.S. at 707—during a lawful
traffic stop, generally does not implicate a legitimate privacy interests. In
this case, the dog sniff was performed on the exterior of respondent's car
while he was lawfully seized for a traffic violation. Any intrusion on respondent's privacy expectations does not rise to the level of a constitutionally cognizable infringement."

CASE SIGNIFICANCE: This case ruled that the use of dogs to sniff cars
during a lawful stop is valid. The defendant here was validly stopped for
speeding, but not for drug possession. While the first officer wrote a warning ticket, another officer, who had driven to the scene, walked the dog around
Caballes's car. The dog indicated the presence of drugs in the car trunk, so
the officers opened the trunk, found marijuana, and then arrested Caballes.
On appeal, Caballes argued that the use of the dog to sniff for drugs in the
absence of any "specific and articulable facts to suggest drug activity"
extended the routine traffic stop and converted it into a drug investigation.
The Court disagreed and held the seizure valid, saying, "in our view, conducting a dog sniff would not change the character of a traffic stop that is
lawful at its inception and otherwise executed in a reasonable manner . . ."
The Court added that no privacy interest was violated because "the dog sniff
was performed on the exterior of respondent's car while he was lawfully
seized for a traffic violation. Any intrusion on respondent's privacy expectation does not rise to the level of a constitutionally cognizable infringement."
In sum, if the stop of a motor vehicle is valid, the use of dogs to sniff the car
for drugs is also valid even if the reason for the stop was not drug-related.

Electronic Surveillance   10

Introduction

The law on electronic surveillance has changed drastically over the years. In *Olmstead v. United States*, the Supreme Court said that wiretapping does not violate the Fourth Amendment if there is no trespass into a constitutionally protected area. This enabled the police to conduct legal wiretaps as long as they did not illegally intrude into a person's dwelling.

This rule was changed in *Katz v. United States*, when the Court expressly overruled *Olmstead* and held that any form of electronic surveillance (including wiretapping) that violates a reasonable expectation of privacy constitutes a search under the Fourth Amendment. This means that electronic surveillance is unconstitutional anywhere if it violates a person's reasonable expectation of privacy. Trespass into a dwelling was no longer a requirement; thus electronic surveillance could be illegal, even if done in a public place, if a person has a reasonable expectation of privacy. This change was inevitable because technology had become so sophisticated that surveillance could be conducted without entering a person's dwelling.

The other cases in this section hold that evidence obtained as a result of permission given to the police to listen in on a conversation by a "friend" is admissible as evidence in court. The Court has also held that the use of electronic devices to record or listen to a conversation constitutes a search under the Fourth Amendment; therefore, safeguards are needed in order for the search to be valid. The warrantless use of a homing device in a public place does not constitute a search, but becomes a search if it involves a private residence.

At present, the rules on electronic surveillance are governed strictly by federal and state laws. The main federal law governing electronic surveillance is Title III of the Omnibus Crime Control and Safe Streets Act of 1968. This law is long and complex, but it basically states that law enforcement officers (federal, state, and local) cannot tap or intercept wire communications or use electronic devices to intercept private conversations, except: (1) if there is a court order authorizing the wiretap; or (2) if consent is given by one of the parties. In addition, a court order authorizing the wiretap can be issued only if state law authorizes it, subject to the provisions of Title III of the Omnibus Crime Control and Safe Streets Act. On the other hand, consent given by one of the parties to the conversation may be prohibited by state law. In sum, the police must comply with state and federal laws if they wish to obtain a warrant. Reliance on the cases briefed here can be misleading because these cases do not take into account state law that may further limit, but cannot expand, what the police can do.

The leading cases on electronic surveillance briefed in this chapter are *Berger v. New York* and *Katz v. United States*.

Olmstead v. United States
277 U.S. 438 (1928)

CAPSULE: Wiretapping does not violate the Fourth Amendment unless there is a trespass into a "constitutionally protected area." (This case was overruled by *Katz v. United States*, 389 U.S. 347 [1967].)

FACTS: Olmstead and co-conspirators of a huge conglomerate involved in importing and distributing illegal liquor were convicted of conspiracy to violate the National Prohibition Act. Information leading to the arrests was gathered primarily by intercepting messages from the telephones of the conspirators. The information was obtained by placing wiretaps on the telephone lines outside the conspirators' office and homes. The wiretaps were installed without trespass on any property of the conspirators.

ISSUE: Do telephone wiretaps violate the Fourth Amendment protection from illegal searches and seizures? NO.

SUPREME COURT DECISION: Wiretapping does not violate the Fourth Amendment unless there is a trespass into a "constitutionally protected area." (Note: This doctrine was expressly overruled by the Supreme Court in *Katz v. United States,* 389 U.S. 347 [1967].)

REASON: "The [Fourth] Amendment does not forbid what was done here. There was no searching. There was no seizure. The evidence was secured by the use of the sense of hearing and that only. There was no entry of the houses or offices of the defendants . . ."

CASE SIGNIFICANCE: The *Olmstead* case is significant because it represents the old rule on wiretaps. This was the first major case decided by the Court on electronic surveillance and reflects the old concept that evidence obtained through a bugging device placed against a wall to overhear conversation in an adjoining office was admissible because there was no actual trespass. The rule lasted from 1928 to 1967. In 1967, the Court decided *Katz v. United States*, 389 U.S. 347, which held that any form of electronic surveillance (including wiretapping) that violates a reasonable expectation of privacy constitutes a search. Under the new rule, the search may be unreasonable even though no physical trespass occurred.

On Lee v. United States
343 U.S. 747 (1952)

CAPSULE: Evidence obtained as a result of permission given by a "friend" who allowed the police to listen in on a conversation is admissible in court.

FACTS: A federal "undercover agent" who was an old acquaintance and former employee of On Lee entered his laundry wearing a radio transmitter and engaged On Lee in a conversation. Self-incriminating statements made by On Lee at that time and later in another conversation were listened to on a radio receiver by another federal agent located outside the laundry. The conversations were submitted as evidence at On Lee's trial over his objection. He was convicted of conspiring to sell and selling opium.

ISSUE: Is electronic eavesdropping a violation of the Fourth Amendment's protection from unreasonable searches and seizures? NO.

SUPREME COURT DECISION: There is no violation of a suspect's Fourth Amendment right if a "friend" allows the police to listen in on a conversation; hence, the evidence obtained is admissible in court.

REASON: The conduct of the officers in this case did not constitute the kind of search and seizure that is prohibited by the Fourth Amendment. There was no trespass when the undercover agent entered the suspect's place of business, and his subsequent conduct did not render his entry a trespass *ab initio* (from the beginning). The suspect here claimed that the undercover officer's entrance constituted a trespass because consent was obtained by fraud, and that the other agent was a trespasser because, by means of the radio receiver outside the laundry, the agent overheard what went on inside. The Court, however, rejected these allegations.

CASE SIGNIFICANCE: This case allows the police to obtain evidence against a suspect by bugging or listening to a conversation as long as the police have the permission of one of the parties to the conversation and such practice is not prohibited by state law. The Supreme Court in this case said that the Fourth Amendment does not protect persons against supposed friends who turn out to be police informers. Thus, a person assumes the risk that whatever is said to another person may be reported by that person to the police; there being no police "search" in such cases. It follows that if the supposed "friend" allows the police to listen in on a telephone conversation with a suspect, there is no violation of the suspect's constitutional right. The evidence can be used in court.

Berger v. New York
388 U.S. 41 (1967)

CAPSULE: The use of electronic devices to capture a conversation constitutes a search under the Fourth Amendment, and therefore safeguards are needed in order for the search to be valid.

FACTS: Berger was indicted and convicted of conspiracy to bribe the chairperson of the New York State Liquor Authority. The conviction was based on evidence obtained by eavesdropping. The orders authorizing the placement of the bugs were pursuant to a New York statute on electronic eavesdropping. This statute allowed the Attorney General, a District Attorney, or any police officer above the rank of Sergeant to issue the order. The order must have described who was to be bugged and the general information sought, but it did not require the particular conversation or information to be described. Finally, the order was valid for up to a two-month period with no provisions for halting the search once the specific information was found, and it had no provisions for the return of information gathered.

ISSUE: Did the New York state statute authorizing electronic eavesdropping violate the Fourth Amendment guarantee against unreasonable searches and seizures? YES.

SUPREME COURT DECISION: Electronic devices used to capture a conversation constitute a search under the Fourth Amendment. The New York statute authorizing eavesdropping without describing the particular conversation sought was too broad and did not contain sufficient safeguards against unwarranted invasions of constitutional rights.

REASON: "The Fourth Amendment commands that a warrant issue not only upon probable cause supported by oath or affirmation, but also 'particularly describing the place to be searched, and the person or things to be seized.' New York's statute lacks particularization. It merely says that a warrant may issue on reasonable grounds to believe that evidence of crime may be obtained. It lays down no requirement for particularity in the warrant as to what specific crime has been or is being committed, nor 'the place to be searched,' or 'the person or things to be seized' as specifically required by the Fourth Amendment. The need for particularity and evidence of reliability in the showing required when judicial authorization of a search is sought is especially great in the case of eavesdropping. By its very nature eavesdropping involves an intrusion on privacy that is broad in scope. As was said in *Osborn v. United States*, 385 U.S. 323 (1966), the indiscriminate use of such devices in law enforcement raises grave constitutional questions under the Fourth and Fifth Amendments, and imposes a heavier responsibility on the Court in its supervision of the fairness procedures . . ."

CASE SIGNIFICANCE: The *Berger* case was decided in 1967, one year prior to the enactment of Title III of the Omnibus Crime Control and Safe Streets Act. The Court in this case spelled out the six requirements for a state law authorizing electronic surveillance to be constitutionally valid. These are:

1. The warrant must describe with particularity the conversations that are to be overheard;

2. There must be a showing of probable cause to believe that a specific crime has been or is being committed;

3. The wiretap must be for a limited period, although extensions may be obtained by adequate showing;

4. The suspects whose conversations are to be overheard must be named in the judicial order;

5. A return must be made to the court, showing what conversations were intercepted; and

6. The wiretapping must terminate when the desired information has been obtained.

These six requirements have since, in effect, been enacted into law by Title III, along with many other provisions. The *Berger* case is important in that:

1. It tells us that overly broad eavesdropping statutes are unconstitutional; and

2. It laid out the requirements that state statutes need in order to be valid.

The *Berger* case has since lost some of its value as precedent because of the passage of Title III.

Katz v. United States
389 U.S. 347 (1967)

CAPSULE: Any form of electronic surveillance, including wiretapping, that violates a reasonable expectation of privacy, constitutes a search under the Fourth Amendment. No physical trespass is required. (This case expressly overruled *Olmstead v. United States*, 277 U.S. 438 [1928].)

FACTS: Katz was convicted of transmitting wagering information across state lines. The evidence against Katz consisted of a conversation overheard by FBI agents who had attached an electronic listening device to the outside of a public telephone booth from which the calls were made.

ISSUE: Is a public telephone booth a constitutionally protected area such that evidence collected by an electronic listening or recording device is obtained in violation of the right to privacy of the user of the booth? YES.

SUPREME COURT DECISION: Any form of electronic surveillance, including wiretapping, that violates a reasonable expectation of privacy, constitutes a search. No physical trespass is required.

REASON: "The government stresses the fact that the telephone booth from which the petitioner made his call was constructed partly of glass, so that he was as visible after he entered it as he would have been if he had remained outside. But what he sought to exclude when he entered the booth was not the intruding eye, it was the uninvited ear. He did not shed his right to do so simply because he made his calls from a place where he might be seen. No less than an individual in a business office, in a friend's apartment, or in a taxicab, a person in a telephone booth may rely upon the protection of the Fourth Amendment. One who occupies it, shuts the door behind him, and pays the toll that permits him to place a call is surely entitled to assume that the words he utters into the mouthpiece will not be broadcast to the world. To read the Constitution more narrowly is to ignore the vital role that the public telephone has come to play in private communication."

CASE SIGNIFICANCE: The *Katz* decision expressly overruled the decision 39 years earlier in *Olmstead v. United States,* 277 U.S. 348 (1928), which held that wiretapping did not violate the Fourth Amendment unless there was some trespass into a "constitutionally protected area." In *Katz,* the Court said that the coverage of the Fourth Amendment does not depend on the presence or absence of a physical intrusion into a given enclosure. The current test is that a search exists, and therefore comes under the Fourth Amendment protection, whenever there is a "reasonable expectation of privacy." The concept that the Constitution "protects people rather than places" is very significant because it makes the protection of the Fourth Amendment "portable," meaning that it is carried by persons wherever they go as long as their behavior and circumstances are such that they are entitled to a reasonable expectation of privacy. This was made clear by the Court when it said that "No less than an individual in a business office, in a friend's apartment, or in a taxicab, a person in a telephone booth may rely upon the protection of the Fourth Amendment. One who occupies it, shuts the door behind him, and pays the toll that permits him to place a call is surely entitled to assume that the words he utters into the mouthpiece will not be broadcast to the world." *Katz,* therefore, has made a significant change in the concept of the right to privacy and has greatly expanded the coverage of that right, particularly as applied to Fourth Amendment cases. It is the current standard by which the legality of search and seizure cases are tested.

United States v. Karo
468 U.S. 705 (1984)

CAPSULE: The warrantless monitoring of a beeper (homing device) in a private residence violates the Fourth Amendment.

FACTS: Upon learning that Karo and co-conspirators had ordered ether from a government informant, to be used in extracting cocaine from clothing imported into the United States, government agents obtained a court order authorizing the installation of a beeper (a homing device) in one of the cans. With the informant's consent, Drug Enforcement Administration agents substituted one of their cans containing a beeper for one of the cans to be delivered to respondent. Over several months, the beeper enabled the agents to monitor the can's movement to a variety of locations, including several private residences and two commercial storage facilities. Agents obtained a search warrant for one of the homes, relying in part on information derived through the use of the beeper. Based on the evidence obtained during the search, Karo and co-conspirators were arrested and charged with various drug offenses.

ISSUE: Did the monitoring of a beeper without a warrant violate the defendant's Fourth Amendment rights? YES.

SUPREME COURT DECISION: The warrantless monitoring of a beeper in a private residence violates the Fourth Amendment rights of individuals to privacy in their own homes and therefore cannot be conducted without a warrant. (The Court, however, reversed the decision on other grounds.)

REASON: "The monitoring of a beeper in a private residence, a location not opened to visual surveillance, violates the Fourth Amendment rights of those who have a justifiable interest in the privacy of the residence. Here, if a DEA agent had entered the house in question without a warrant to verify that the ether was in the house, he would have engaged in an unreasonable search within the meaning of the Fourth Amendment. The result is the same where, without a warrant, the government surreptitiously uses a beeper to obtain information that it could not have obtained from outside the curtilage of the house. There is no reason in this case to deviate from the general rule that a search of a house should be conducted pursuant to a warrant."

CASE SIGNIFICANCE: A year earlier, in *United States v. Knotts*, 459 U.S. 817 (1983), the Court held that the use of beepers in a car on a public road by the police does not constitute a search because there is no reasonable expectation of privacy. Moreover, the Court added that the Fourth Amendment does not prohibit the police from supplementing their sensory faculties with technological aids to help police identify a car's location. The

Karo and *Knotts* cases were decided differently because their facts were different. In *Knotts*, the agents learned nothing from the beeper that they could not have visually observed, hence there was no Fourth Amendment violation. Moreover, the monitoring in *Knotts* occurred in a public place, whereas the beeper in *Karo* intruded on the privacy of a home. The two cases are, therefore, complementary, not inconsistent, in legal principles.

The Court held in dicta that a warrant for the monitoring of a beeper should contain the:

1. object into which the beeper would be installed,

2. circumstances leading to the request for the beeper, and

3. length of time for which beeper surveillance is requested.

Kyllo v. United States
533 U.S. 27 (2001)

CAPSULE: Using a technological device to explore details of a home that would previously have been unknowable without physical intrusion is a search and is presumptively unreasonable without a warrant.

FACTS: Officers who suspected Kyllo of growing marijuana in his home used a thermal imaging device to examine the heat radiating from his house. The thermal imaging device was used from across the street and took only a few minutes. The scan showed that the roof over the garage and a side wall of Kyllo's house were relatively hot compared to the rest of his house and substantially hotter than neighboring homes. Based on this information, utility bills, and tips from informants, officers obtained a search warrant for Kyllo's home. The search revealed more than 100 marijuana plants.

ISSUE: "Whether the use of a thermal imaging device aimed at a private home from a public street to detect relative amounts of heat within the home constitutes a search within the meaning of the Fourth Amendment." YES.

SUPREME COURT DECISION: Where the Government uses a device that is not in general public use to explore details of the home that would have been unknowable without physical intrusion, the surveillance is a search and is presumptively unreasonable without a warrant.

REASON: "At the very core of the Fourth Amendment stands the right of a man to retreat into his own home and there be free from unreasonable governmental intrusions. With few exceptions, the question whether a warrantless search of a home is reasonable and hence constitutional must be answered no" [Citations omitted]. "We think that obtaining by sense-enhancing technology any information regarding the interior of the home that could not otherwise have been obtained without physical intrusion into a constitutionally protected area constitutes a search, at least where (as here) the technology in question is not in general public use." "On the basis of this criterion, the information obtained by the thermal imager in this case was the product of a search."

CASE SIGNIFICANCE: This case addresses the use of thermal imaging devices in law enforcement, an issue of concern in many jurisdictions because of technological advances. The Court describes what thermal imagers do as follows: "Thermal imagers detect infrared radiation, which virtually all objects emit but which is not visible to the naked eye. The imager converts radiation into images based on relative warmth—black is cool, white is hot, shades of gray connote relative differences; in that respect, it operates somewhat like a video camera showing heat images."

The Government argued that thermal imaging does not constitute a search because: (1) it detects "only heat radiating from the external surface of the house" and therefore there is no entry; and (2) it did not "detect private activities occurring in private areas" because everything that was detected was on the outside. The Court disagreed, concluding that the Fourth Amendment draws "a firm line at the entrance of the house." It conceded that while no significant compromise of the homeowner's privacy occurred in this case, "we must take the long view, from the original meaning of the Fourth Amendment forward." Acknowledging that "it would be foolish to contend that the degree of privacy secured to citizens by the Fourth Amendment has been entirely unaffected by the advance of technology," it nonetheless concluded that "the Fourth Amendment is to be construed in the light of what was deemed an unreasonable search and seizure when it was adopted, and in a manner that will conserve public interest as well as the interest and rights of individual citizens." In sum, there is a limit to electronic surveillance even if it does not directly intrude into individual privacy. The limit here was drawn "when the Government uses a device that was not in general public use, to explore details of a private home that would previously have been unknowable without physical intrusion."

Plain View and
Open Fields Searches 11

Introduction

The plain view doctrine states that items within the sight of an officer who is legally in a place from which the view is made may be seized without a warrant as long as such items are immediately recognizable as subject to seizure. Items in plain view are not protected by the Fourth Amendment guarantee against unreasonable searches and seizures, thus no warrant or probable cause is necessary for a valid seizure. There are, however, three requirements for the plain view doctrine to apply:

1. The item must be within the officer's sight;

2. The officer must legally be in the place from which the item is seen; and

3. It must be immediately apparent to the officer that the item is subject to seizure.

The requirement that the item be within the officer's sight means that the item must be noted through the sense of sight and not through the use of the other four senses. If the officer is not legally in the place from which the item is seen, the seizure of the item is illegal and therefore cannot be used as evidence. It must also be immediately clear to the officer that the item seen is subject to seizure. If the officer does not immediately know the item is seizable (such as if the item is identified as seizable only after touching or looking at it more closely), the plain view doctrine does not apply because other senses were used to determine seizability.

"Inadvertence," meaning the accidental finding by the officer of the item rather than prior knowledge that the item is in a particular place, used to be a fourth requirement for plain view. In *Horton v. California* (496 U.S. 128 [1990]), however, the Court said: "The Fourth Amendment does not prohibit the warrantless seizure of evidence in plain view even though the discovery of the evidence was not inadvertent," thus doing away with the inadvertence requirement. In reality, most items seized under plain view are discovered by the officers inadvertently and not because they know beforehand that seizable items can be found in a location.

The open fields doctrine states that items in open fields are not protected by the Fourth Amendment and may be properly seized by an officer without a warrant or probable cause. Plain view and open fields are similar in that, in both situations, there is no need for a search warrant or probable cause for the police to be able to seize the items. They are different, however, in two ways:

1. Under the plain view doctrine, the seizable property is usually in a house or another enclosed place (such as a car), whereas under open fields the item is found in a non-enclosed area such as in a parking lot, a public street, or a park that is accessible to the public;

2. Under plain view, the item seized is limited to what is in the officer's sight. By contrast, items known or observed through the use of the officer's other senses (smell, hearing, touching, and tasting) also fall under open fields.

In *United States v. Dunn*, 480 U.S. 294 (1987), the Supreme Court held that the warrantless search of a barn that is not part of the curtilage of a house is valid. In that case, the Court listed four factors that determine whether an area is considered part of the curtilage and therefore not considered an open field. The *Dunn* case, briefed in this chapter, provides a list of four factors that determine whether an area is protected by the Fourth Amendment. These four factors are so vague, however, that they are of little practical help to law enforcement officers and judges in determining where the curtilage ends and where open fields begin.

The leading cases briefed in this chapter on plain view and open fields are *Oliver v. United States*, *United States v. Dunn*, and *Horton v. California*.

Texas v. Brown
460 U.S. 730 (1983)

CAPSULE: "Certain knowledge" that evidence seen is incriminating is not necessary under the plain view doctrine. Probable cause suffices.

FACTS: An officer stopped Brown's vehicle at night at a routine driver's license checkpoint. The officer asked Brown for his driver's license and shined his flashlight into the automobile. When Brown withdrew his hand from his pocket, the officer observed an opaque, green party balloon, which was knotted one-half inch from the tip, fall from Brown's hand onto the seat. Based on his experience, the officer knew that such balloons were frequently used to transport drugs. Responding to the officer's second request to produce a driver's license, Brown reached across and opened the glove compartment. The officer shifted his position to get a better view of the glove compartment and observed several small plastic vials, a quantity of a white powdery substance, and an open package of party balloons. After rummaging through the glove compartment, Brown informed the officer that he did not have a driver's license. The officer picked up the balloon, which had a white powdery substance in the tied-off portion, and showed it to another officer who also recognized the balloon as one possibly containing narcotics. The officers placed Brown under arrest. A search of Brown's vehicle incident to the arrest revealed several plastic bags containing a green leafy substance and a bottle of milk sugar (often mixed with heroin before selling). Brown was charged with and convicted of possession of heroin.

ISSUE: Must an officer have certain knowledge that an object in plain view is contraband or evidence of criminal activity before it may be seized under the "plain view doctrine?" NO.

SUPREME COURT DECISION: Items must be "immediately recognizable" as subject to seizure if they are to fall under the "plain view" doctrine, but "certain knowledge" that incriminating evidence is involved is not necessary. Probable cause is sufficient to justify a seizure. The use of a flashlight by an officer during the evening to look into the inside of a car does not constitute a search under the Fourth Amendment. The items discovered still fall under plain view.

REASON: "In the *Coolidge* [*v. New Hampshire*, 403 U.S. 443 (1970)] plurality's view, the 'plain view' doctrine permits the warrantless seizure by police of private possessions where three requirements are satisfied. First, the police officer must lawfully make an 'initial intrusion' or otherwise properly be in a position from which he or she can view a particular area. Second, the officer must discover incriminating evidence 'inadvertently,' which is to say, he or she may not 'know in advance the location of [certain] evidence and intend to seize it,' relying on the plain-view doctrine only as a pretext. Finally, it must be 'immediately apparent' to the police that the items they observe may be evidence of a crime, contraband, or otherwise subject to seizure." [Citations omitted.] The "immediately apparent" language in *Coolidge*, however, does not require an officer to "know" that items are contraband or evidence of criminal activity; probable cause is sufficient.

CASE SIGNIFICANCE: There are four basic elements of the "plain view" doctrine. They are:

1. Awareness of the item must be gained solely through the sense of sight;

2. The officer must be legally present in the place from which he or she sees the items;

3. Discovery of the items must be inadvertent; and

4. The items must be immediately recognizable as subject to seizure.

This case clarifies the fourth requirement, saying that "immediate recognizability" does not mean "certain knowledge." All that is needed is probable cause. In this case, the officer shined his flashlight into the car's interior and saw the driver holding an opaque green party balloon, knotted about one-half inch from the tip. The officer also saw white powder in the open glove compartment. In court, the officer testified that he had learned from experience that inflated, tied-off balloons are often used to transport narcotics. The Supreme Court concluded that the officer had probable cause to believe that the balloon contained narcotics and that a warrantless seizure was, therefore, justified under the plain view doctrine. Significantly, the Court said that "plain view is perhaps better understood . . . not as an independent exception to the warrant clause, but simply as an extension of whatever the prior justification for an officer's access to an object may be."

Oliver v. United States
466 U.S. 170 (1984)

CAPSULE: "No Trespassing" signs do not effectively bar the public from viewing open fields, therefore the expectation of privacy by the owner of an open field does not exist. The police may enter and search unoccupied or undeveloped areas outside the curtilage without either a warrant or probable cause.

FACTS: Acting on reports that marijuana was being grown on petitioner's farm, but without a search warrant, probable cause, or exigent circumstances, police officers went to the farm to investigate. They drove past Oliver's house to a locked gate with a "No Trespassing" sign, and with a footpath around one side. Officers followed the footpath around the gate and found a field of marijuana more than one mile from the petitioner's house. Oliver was charged with and convicted of manufacturing a controlled substance.

ISSUE: Does the "open fields" doctrine apply when the property owner attempts to establish a reasonable expectation of privacy by posting a "No Trespassing" sign, using a locked gate, and when marijuana is located more than one mile from the house? YES.

SUPREME COURT DECISION: Because open fields are accessible to the public and the police in ways that a home, office, or commercial structure would not be, and because fences or "No Trespassing" signs do not effectively bar the public from viewing open fields, the expectation of privacy by an owner of an open field does not exist. Consequently, the police may enter and search unoccupied or underdeveloped areas outside the curtilage without either a warrant or probable cause.

REASON: "The test of a reasonable expectation of privacy is not whether the individual attempts to conceal criminal activity, but whether the government's intrusion infringes upon the personal and societal values protected by the Fourth Amendment. Because open fields are accessible to the public and because fences or 'No Trespassing' signs, etc. are not effective bars to public view of open fields, the expectation of privacy does not exist and police are justified in searching these areas without a warrant."

CASE SIGNIFICANCE: This case makes clear that the "reasonable expectation of privacy" doctrine under the Fourth Amendment, as established in *Katz v. United States*, 389 U.S. 347 (1967), does not apply when the property involved is an open field. The Court stressed that steps taken to protect privacy, such as planting the marijuana on secluded land and erecting a locked gate (but with a footpath along one side) and posting "No Trespassing" signs around the property, do not establish any reasonable expectation of privacy. This case allows law enforcement officers to make warrantless entries and searches without probable cause in open fields, thus affording them greater access to remote places where prohibited plants or drugs might be concealed.

California v. Ciraolo
476 U.S. 207 (1986)

CAPSULE: The naked-eye observation by the police of a suspect's backyard, which is part of the curtilage, does not violate the Fourth Amendment.

FACTS: After receiving an anonymous telephone tip that Ciraolo was growing marijuana in his backyard, police went to his residence to investigate. Realizing that the area in question could not be viewed from ground level, officers used a private plane and flew over the home at an altitude prescribed by law. Officers trained in the detection of marijuana readily identified marijuana plants growing in Ciraolo's yard. Based on that information and an aerial photograph of the area, officers obtained a search warrant for the premises. A search was made pursuant to the warrant and numerous marijuana plants were seized. Ciraolo was charged with and convicted of cultivation of marijuana.

ISSUE: May officers make an aerial observation of an area within the curtilage of a home without a search warrant? YES.

SUPREME COURT DECISION: The Constitutional protection against unreasonable searches and seizures is not violated by the naked-eye aerial observation of a suspect's backyard, which is a part of the curtilage, by the police.

REASON: "That the area is within the curtilage does not itself bar all police observation. The Fourth Amendment protection of the home has never been extended to require law enforcement officers to shield their eyes when passing by a home on public thoroughfares. Nor does the mere fact that an individual has taken measures to restrict some views of his activities preclude an officer's observations from a public vantage point where he has a right to be and which renders the activities clearly visible."

CASE SIGNIFICANCE: The term "curtilage" refers to the grounds and buildings immediately surrounding a dwelling. Ordinarily, the curtilage is not considered an open field and hence is protected against unreasonable searches and seizures. This means that searching a curtilage requires a warrant. In this case, however, the Court said that there was no need for a warrant because the search was in the form of a naked-eye aerial observation of a suspect's backyard and is, therefore, less intrusive. The Court said that the fact that the area is with the curtilage does not in itself prohibit all police observation. This case, therefore, expands police power to search the curtilage without a warrant, but only if the search is aerial in nature.

United States v. Dunn
480 U.S. 294 (1987)

CAPSULE: The warrantless search of a barn that is not part of the curtilage is valid. Four factors determine whether an area is considered part of the curtilage.

FACTS: After learning that a co-defendant purchased large quantities of chemicals and equipment used in the manufacture of controlled substances, drug agents obtained a warrant to place an electronic tracking beeper in some of the equipment. The beeper ultimately led agents to Dunn's farm. The farm was encircled by a perimeter fence with several interior fences of the type used to hold livestock. Without a warrant, officers entered the premises over the perimeter fence, interior fences, and a wooden fence that encircled a barn, approximately 50 yards from respondent's home. The officers were led to the barn by the odor of chemicals and the sound of a running motor. Without entering the barn, officers stood at a locked gate and shined a flashlight into the barn where they observed what appeared to be a drug laboratory. Officers returned twice the next day to confirm the presence of the laboratory, each time without entering the barn. Based on information obtained from these observations, officers obtained a search warrant and seized the drug lab from the barn and a quantity of controlled substances from the house. Dunn was charged with and convicted of conspiracy to manufacture controlled substances.

ISSUE: Is a barn located approximately 50 yards from a house and surrounded by a fence different from that of the house, part of the curtilage that cannot be searched without a warrant? NO.

SUPREME COURT DECISION: The barn that was searched by the police was not a part of the curtilage and, therefore, the warrantless search by the police was valid. Whether an area is considered a part of the curtilage of a home rests on four factors:

1. The proximity of the area to the home;

2. Whether the area is in an enclosure surrounding the home;

3. The nature and uses of the area; and

4. The steps taken to conceal the area from public view.

Applying these factors, the barn in this case could not be considered a part of the curtilage.

REASON: "Under *Oliver* [*v. United States*, 466 U.S. 170 (1984)] and *Hester* [*v. United States*, 265 U.S. 57 (1924)], there is no constitutional difference between police observations conducted while in a public place and while standing in an open field."

CASE SIGNIFICANCE: This case is important because, for the first time, the Court laid out the standards for determining whether a particular building falls within the curtilage of the main house. Applying the four factors enumerated above, the Court concluded that the barn searched by the police did not fall within the curtilage of the main building and therefore did not need a warrant in order to be searched. These four factors take into account such elements of reason as proximity, enclosure, uses, and steps taken to protect the area. The problem with these factors is that they are necessarily subjective and therefore lend themselves to imprecise application. Nonetheless, they are an improvement over the complete lack of guidelines under which the lower courts decided prior cases.

Arizona v. Hicks
480 U.S. 321 (1987)

CAPSULE: Probable cause to believe that items seen are contraband or evidence of criminal activity is required for the items to be seized under the "plain view" doctrine.

FACTS: A bullet fired through the floor of Hicks' apartment, injuring a man below, prompted the police to enter Hicks' apartment to search for the shooter, weapons, and other victims. The police discovered three weapons and a stocking cap mask. An officer noticed several pieces of stereo equipment that seemed to be out of place in the ill-appointed apartment. Based on this suspicion, he read and recorded the serial numbers of the equipment, moving some of the pieces in the process. A call to police headquarters verified that one of the pieces of equipment was stolen. A subsequent check of the serial numbers of the other pieces of equipment revealed that they were also stolen. A search warrant was then obtained and the other equipment was seized. Hicks was charged with and convicted of robbery.

ISSUE: May an officer make a "plain view" search with less than probable cause to believe the items being searched are contraband or evidence of criminal activity? NO.

SUPREME COURT DECISION: Probable cause to believe that items being searched are, in fact, contraband or evidence of criminal activity is required for the items to be searched under the "plain view" doctrine.

REASON: ". . . [M]oving the equipment . . . did constitute a 'search' separate and apart from the search for the shooter, victims, and weapons that was the lawful objective of [the officer's] entry into the apartment. Merely inspecting those parts of the turntable that came into view during the latter search would not have constituted an independent search, because it would have produced no additional invasion of respondent's privacy interest. But taking action, unrelated to the objectives of the authorized intrusion, which exposed to view concealed portions of the apartment or its contents, did produce a new invasion of respondent's privacy unjustified by the exigent circumstance that validated the entry."

CASE SIGNIFICANCE: The "plain view" doctrine states that items within the sight of an officer who is legally in the place from which the view is made, and who had no prior knowledge that the items were present, may properly be seized without a warrant as long as the items are immediately recognizable as subject to seizure. This case holds that even after the officer has seen an object in plain view, he or she may not search or seize it unless there is probable cause to believe that the object is contraband or stolen property, or that it is useful as evidence in court. Therefore, if, at the moment the object is picked up, the officer did not have probable cause but only "reasonable suspicion" (as was the case here), the seizure is illegal. The "plain view" doctrine as the basis for warrantless seizure may be invoked by the police only if there is probable cause to believe that the item is contraband or useful evidence; it may not be invoked based on "reasonable suspicion" or any other level of certainty that is less than probable cause.

Horton v. California
496 U.S. 128 (1990)

CAPSULE: "Inadvertent discovery" of evidence is no longer a necessary element of the plain view doctrine.

FACTS: A police officer determined that there was probable cause to search Horton's home for the evidence of a robbery and weapons used in the robbery. The affidavit filed by the officer referred to police reports that described both the weapons and the stolen property, but the warrant that was issued only authorized a search for the stolen property. When the officer went to Horton's home to execute the warrant, he did not find the stolen property, but found weapons in plain view and seized them. At the trial, the officer testified that while he was searching Horton's home for the stolen property, he was also interested in finding other evidence related to the robbery. Horton argued on appeal that the weapons should have been suppressed during the trial because their discovery was not "inadvertent."

ISSUE: Is inadvertence a necessary element of the "plain view" doctrine? NO.

SUPREME COURT DECISION: "The Fourth Amendment does not prohibit the warrantless seizure of evidence in plain view even though the discovery of the evidence was not inadvertent. Although inadvertence is a characteristic of most legitimate plain view seizures, it is not a necessary condition."

REASON: Justice Stewart [in *Coolidge v. New Hampshire*, 403 U.S. 443 (1979)] concluded that the inadvertence requirement was necessary to avoid a violation of the express constitutional requirement that a valid warrant must particularly describe the things to be seized. He explained:

> The rationale of the exception to the warrant requirement, as just stated, is that a plain view seizure will not turn an initially valid (and therefore limited) search into a "general" one, while the inconvenience of procuring a warrant to cover an inadvertent discovery is great. But where the discovery is anticipated, where the police know in advance the location of the evidence and intend to seize it, the situation is altogether different. The requirement of a warrant to seize imposes no inconvenience whatever, or at least none which is constitutionally cognizable in a legal system that regards warrantless searches as "*per se* unreasonable" in the absence of "exigent circumstances."

In *Horton*, the Court stated: "We find two flaws in this reasoning. First, evenhanded law enforcement is best achieved by the application of objective standards of conduct, rather than standards that depend upon the subjective state of mind of the officer. The fact that an officer is interested in an item of evidence and fully expects to find it in the course of a search should not invalidate its seizure if the search is confined in area and duration by the terms of a warrant or a valid exception to the warrant requirement. If the officer has knowledge approaching certainty that the item will be found, we see no reason why he or she would deliberately omit a particular description of the items to be seized from the application of a search warrant. Specification of the additional item could only permit the officer to expand the scope of the search. On the other hand, if he or she has a valid warrant to search for one item and merely a suspicion concerning the second, whether or not it amounts to probable cause, we fail to see why that suspicion should immunize the second item from seizure if it is found during a lawful search for the first.

"Second, the suggestion that the inadvertence requirement is necessary to prevent the police from conducting general searches, or from converting specific warrants into general warrants, is not persuasive because that interest is already served by the requirements that no warrant issue unless it "particularly describes the place to be searched and the persons or things to be seized," and that a warrantless search be circumscribed by the exigencies that justify its initiation."

CASE SIGNIFICANCE: This case does away with the requirement that for plain view to apply, the discovery of the evidence must be purely accidental. The police officer in this case knew that the evidence was there because it was in fact described in the officer's affidavit, but for some reason the warrant issued by the magistrate only authorized a search for the stolen property. Nonetheless, the officer saw the weapons in plain view during the search and seized them. Expressly rejecting the inadvertence requirement, the Court said that the seizure was valid because:

1. The items seized from petitioner's home were discovered during a lawful search authorized by a valid warrant.

2. When they were discovered, it was immediately apparent to the officer that they constituted incriminating evidence.

3. The officer had probable cause, not only to obtain a warrant to search for the stolen property, but also to believe that the weapons and handguns had been used in the crime he was investigating.

4. The search was authorized by the warrant.

Note that most seizures by the police under plain view are likely to be inadvertent, meaning that the police had no prior knowledge that the item was there. What *Horton* simply says is that even if the police know an item is to be found in a place, the item can be seized under plain view as long as the three elements mentioned above are present.

Lineups and Other Pretrial Identification Procedures 12

Introduction

The police generally use three methods in witness identification of suspects: lineups, showups, and photographic identifications. In a lineup, a victim or a witness to a crime is shown several possible suspects at the police station for identification. In a showup, only one suspect is shown to the witness or victim. This usually takes place at the scene of the crime and immediately following the arrest of the suspect. In photographic identification, the police show photographs of possible suspects to the victim or witnesses.

These three methods raise questions concerning the constitutional rights of suspects involved in identification proceedings. Do they have any rights at all? The answer is yes, but they are limited. The four constitutional rights usually invoked by suspects in identification proceedings are: the privilege against self-incrimination, the right to a lawyer, the right to due process, and the protection against unreasonable searches and seizures. Of these constitutional rights, only two have been held by the Supreme Court to apply in pretrial identification procedures. These are the right to counsel and the right to due process.

In the cases briefed in this chapter, the Court defines the rights of suspects in these proceedings. In sum, the Court holds that an accused who has been formally charged with a crime has the right to have a lawyer present during a lineup. In contrast, there is no right to counsel if the suspect has not been formally charged with a crime. As for due process rights, the Court has held that lineups are so suggestive that the resulting identification inevitably violates a suspect's constitutional rights. In a subsequent case, the Court concluded that the admission of testimony concerning a suggestive and unnecessary identification procedure does not violate due process as long as the identification is reliable.

Lineups, showups, and photographic identification procedures are helpful police practices for suspect identification. The police must be careful, however, not to violate the suspect's rights to counsel and due process. The cases in this chapter help determine (in addition to department rules and regulations) what the police can and cannot do.

The leading cases briefed in this chapter on lineups and other pretrial identification procedures are *United States v. Wade* and *Kirby v. Illinois*.

United States v. Wade
388 U.S. 218 (1967)

CAPSULE: An accused who has been formally charged with a crime has the right to have a lawyer present during a police lineup.

FACTS: A man with a small piece of tape on each side of his face entered a bank, pointed a pistol at a cashier and the vice president of the bank, and forced them to fill a pillow case with the bank's money. The man then drove away with an accomplice. An indictment was returned against Wade and others involved in the robbery. Wade was arrested and counsel was appointed. Fifteen days later, without notice to his counsel, Wade was placed in a lineup to be viewed by the bank personnel. Both employees identified Wade as the robber, but in court they admitted seeing Wade in the custody of officials prior to the lineup. At trial, the bank personnel re-identified Wade as the robber and the prior lineup identifications were admitted as evidence. Wade was convicted of bank robbery.

ISSUE: Should the courtroom identification of an accused be excluded as evidence because the accused was exhibited to the witness before trial at a post-indictment lineup conducted for identification purposes and without notice to and in the absence of the accused's appointed lawyer? YES.

SUPREME COURT DECISION: A police lineup or other "face-to-face" confrontation after the accused has been formally charged with a crime is considered a "critical stage of the proceedings"; therefore, the accused has the right to have counsel present. The absence of counsel during such proceedings renders the evidence obtained inadmissible.

REASON: "Since it appears that there is grave potential for prejudice, intentional or not, in the pretrial lineup, which may not be capable of reconstruction at trial, and since presence of counsel itself can often avert prejudice and assure a meaningful confrontation at trial, there can be little doubt that for Wade the post-indictment lineup was a critical stage of the prosecution at which he was 'as much entitled to such aid [of counsel] . . . as at the trial itself.' Thus both Wade and his counsel should have been notified of the impending lineup, and counsel's presence should have been requisite to conduct of the lineup, absent an 'intelligent waiver.'"

CASE SIGNIFICANCE: The *Wade* case settled the issue of whether an accused has a right to counsel after the filing of a formal charge. The standard used by the Court was whether identification was part of the "critical stage of the proceedings." The Court, however, did not say exactly what this phrase meant; hence, lower courts did not know where to draw the line. In a subsequent case, *Kirby v. Illinois* (see brief on page 183), the Court said that any pretrial identification prior to the filing of a formal charge was not part of a "critical stage of the proceedings," and therefore no counsel was required. The *Wade* case did not authoritatively state what is meant by "formal charge" either, so that phrase has also been subject to varying interpretations, depending on state law or practice.

Foster v. California
394 U.S. 440 (1969)

CAPSULE: Lineups that are so suggestive as to make the resulting identification virtually inevitable violate a suspect's constitutional right to due process.

FACTS: The day after a robbery, one of the robbers, Foster, surrendered to the police and implicated the other two people involved. Foster was placed in a lineup with two other men and was viewed by the only witness to the robbery. Foster was wearing a jacket similar to the one worn by the robber and was several inches taller than either of the two men. The witness could not positively identify Foster as the robber and asked to speak with him. Foster was brought into an office alone and was seated at a table with the witness; still the witness could not positively identify Foster as the robber. A week to ten days later, the witness viewed a second lineup of Foster and four completely different men. This time the witness positively identified Foster as the robber. The witness testified to the identification of Foster in the lineups and repeated the identification in court. Foster was convicted of robbery.

ISSUE: Do lineups conducted by the police that may bias a witness' identification of a suspect violate his or her constitutional rights? YES.

SUPREME COURT DECISION: Lineups that are so suggestive as to make the resulting identifications virtually inevitable violate a suspect's constitutional right to due process.

REASON: "This case presents a compelling example of unfair lineup procedures. In the first lineup arranged by the police, petitioner stood out from the other two men by the contrast of his height and by the fact that he was wearing a leather jacket similar to that worn by the robber. When this did not lead to positive identification, the police permitted a one-to-one confrontation between petitioner and the witness. . . . Even after this the witness' identification of petitioner was tentative. So some days later another lineup was arranged. Petitioner was the only person in this lineup who had also participated in the first lineup. . . . This finally produced a definitive identification. . . . The suggestive elements in this identification procedure made it all but inevitable that [the witness] would identify petitioner whether or not he was in fact 'the man.' In effect, the police repeatedly said to the witness, 'This is the man.' This procedure so undermined the reliability of the eyewitness identification as to violate due process."

CASE SIGNIFICANCE: This case tells the police how *not* to conduct a lineup. Lineups are important to the accused as well as to the police and, therefore, must be conducted properly. Any lineup that practically identifies the suspect for the witness is unfair to the suspect and violates due process. The procedure followed by the police in this case practically ensured the suspect's identification by the witness. Lineups must be fair to the suspect; otherwise, the due process rights of the suspect are violated. A fair lineup is one that guarantees no bias against the suspect.

Kirby v. Illinois
406 U.S. 682 (1972)

CAPSULE: There is no right to counsel at police lineups or identification procedures if the suspect has not been formally charged with a crime.

FACTS: A man reported that two men robbed him of a wallet containing traveler's checks and a social security card. The following day, police officers stopped Kirby and a companion. When asked for identification, Kirby produced a wallet that contained three traveler's checks and the social security card bearing the name of the robbery victim. The officers took Kirby and his companion to the police station. Only after arriving at the police station and checking police records did the arresting officers learn of the robbery. The victim was then brought to the police station. Immediately upon entering the room in the police station where Kirby and his companion were seated, the man positively identified them as the men who had robbed him. No lawyer was present in the room and neither Kirby nor his companion asked for legal assistance, nor were they advised by the police of any right to the presence of counsel. Kirby was convicted of robbery.

ISSUE: Is a suspect entitled to the presence and advice of a lawyer during pretrial identification? NO.

SUPREME COURT DECISION: There is no right to counsel at police lineups or identification procedures prior to the time the suspect is formally charged with the crime.

REASON: "The initiation of judicial criminal proceedings is far from mere formalism. It is the starting point of our whole adversarial system of criminal justice. For it is only then that the government has committed itself to prosecute, and only then that the adverse positions of government and defendant have solidified. It is then that a defendant finds himself faced with the prosecutorial forces of organized society, and immersed in the intricacies of substantive and procedural criminal law. It is this point, therefore, that marks the commencement of the 'criminal prosecutions' to which alone the explicit guarantees of the Sixth Amendment are applicable."

CASE SIGNIFICANCE: *Kirby* was decided five years after *United States v. Wade*. It clarified an issue that was not directly resolved in *Wade*: whether the ruling in *Wade* applied to cases in which the lineup or pretrial identification takes place prior to the filing of a formal charge. The court answered this question in the negative, saying that what happened in *Kirby* was a matter of routine police investigation, hence not considered a "critical stage of the proceedings." The Court reasoned that a post-indictment lineup is a "critical stage" whereas a pre-indictment lineup is not.

United States v. Dionisio
410 U.S. 1 (1973)

CAPSULE: Any person may be required against his or her will to appear before a grand jury or to give a voice exemplar without violating the Fourth or Fifth Amendments.

FACTS: In the course of its investigation into illegal gambling, a grand jury received voice recordings obtained pursuant to court orders. The grand jury subpoenaed 20 people, including Dionisio, and compelled them to provide voice exemplars for comparison with the intercepted messages. Each witness was advised that he was a potential defendant in the investigation and was given the right to have an attorney present during the taping. Each witness was provided a copy of the transcript of the messages and was compelled to read the transcript into a recording device. Dionisio and others refused to provide the voice exemplars. The government filed petitions in the District Court to compel the witnesses to make the voice recordings, which the court did. Dionisio maintained his refusal to provide the voice exemplars and was found in civil contempt and was incarcerated until he complied with the order or for 18 months.

ISSUE: May a person be required to appear before a grand jury? Is the providing of voice exemplars compelled by a grand jury for the purpose of comparison with intercepted messages a violation of the Fourth Amendment protection from unreasonable searches and seizures and the Fifth Amendment privilege against self-incrimination? NO.

SUPREME COURT DECISIONS:
1. Any person may be required against his or her will to appear before a grand jury. This is not a form of seizure protected by the Fourth Amendment.
2. Suspects may be required by the police to give voice exemplars. This requirement does not violate the Fifth Amendment privilege against self-incrimination.

REASONS:
1. "It is clear that a subpoena to appear before a grand jury is not a 'seizure' in the Fourth Amendment sense, even though that summons may be inconvenient or burdensome. . . . [W]e again acknowledge what has long been recognized, that 'citizens generally are not constitutionally immune from grand jury subpoenas. . . . These are recent reaffirmations of the historically grounded obligation of every person to appear and give his evidence before the grand jury. The personal sacrifice involved is a part of the necessary contribution of the individual to the welfare of the public.' "
2. "The physical characteristics of a person's voice, its tone and manner, as opposed to the context of a specific conversation, are constantly exposed to the public. Like a man's facial characteristics, or handwriting, his voice is repeatedly produced for others to hear. No person can have a reasonable expectation that others will not know the sound of his voice, any more than he can reasonably expect that his face will be a mystery to the world."

CASE SIGNIFICANCE: A suspect may be required to appear before a grand jury and can be forced to give a voice exemplar for the purposes of comparison with an actual voice recording. Neither the appearance before the grand jury nor the giving of a voice exemplar is a form of seizure that is protected by the Fourth Amendment. Appearance before a grand jury is a duty; therefore, non-appearance cannot be a constitutional right. In the case of a person's voice, there is no reasonable expectation of privacy to it because a voice is constantly exposed and available to the public. Although not discussed directly in this case, the Court considers voice exemplars to be a form of physical (as opposed to testimonial) evidence and, therefore, not protected by the Fifth Amendment prohibition against self-incrimination. It is important for police officers to know that the prohibition against self-incrimination applies only to testimonial and not to physical evidence. Physical self-incrimination would, therefore, compel a person to appear in a police lineup against his or her will.

Manson v. Brathwaite
432 U.S. 98 (1977)

CAPSULE: The admission of testimony concerning a suggestive and unnecessary identification procedure does not violate due process as long as the identification possesses sufficient aspects of reliability.

FACTS: Glover (an undercover police officer) and an informant (Brown) went to an apartment building to buy narcotics from a known drug dealer (it was later determined that the officers did not make the drug purchase from the intended person). As they stood at the door, the area was illuminated by natural light from a window in the hallway. Glover knocked on the door, and a man opened the door 12 to 18 inches. Brown identified himself, and Glover asked for "two things" of narcotics and then gave the man $20. The man closed the door and later returned and gave Glover two glassine bags. While the door was open, Glover stood within two feet of the man and observed his face. At headquarters, immediately after the sale, Glover described the seller to two other officers; however, at that time, Glover did not know the identity of the seller. He described the seller as "a colored man, approximately five feet eleven inches tall, dark complexion, black hair, short Afro style, and having high cheekbones, and of heavy build. He was wearing at the time blue pants and a plaid shirt." One of the officers suspected who the seller was, obtained a picture of Brathwaite from the Records Division, and left it in Glover's office. Glover identified the person as the man who sold him narcotics two days before. Brathwaite was arrested in the same apartment building where the narcotics sale had occurred. Brathwaite was charged with possession and sale of heroin. At his trial, the photograph from which Glover had identified Brathwaite was admitted into evidence. Although Glover had not seen Brathwaite in eight months, "there [was] no doubt whatsoever" in his mind that the person shown in the picture was Brathwaite. Glover also made a positive in-court identification of Brathwaite. Brathwaite testified that, on the day of the alleged sale, he had been ill at his apartment, and at no time on that particular day had he been at the place of the drug deal. His wife, after Brathwaite had refreshed her memory, also testified that he was home all day. Brathwaite was found guilty of possession and sale of heroin.

ISSUE: Should pretrial identification evidence obtained by a police examination of a single photograph be excluded as evidence under the due process clause if it was thought to be suggestive and unnecessary, regardless of whether it was reliable? NO.

SUPREME COURT DECISION: "The admission of testimony concerning a suggestive and unnecessary identification procedure does not violate due process so long as the identification possesses sufficient aspects of reliability."

REASON: Using a previous case, *Stovall v. Denno*, the Supreme Court concluded that reliability is the "... linchpin in determining the admissibility of identification testimony ..." The factors for the court to consider for reliability were stated in *Neil v. Biggers*. The factors are: (1) the opportunity for the witness to view the criminal at the time of the crime, (2) the witness' degree of attention, (3) the accuracy of his prior description of the criminal, (4) the level of certainty demonstrated at the confrontation, and (5) the time between the crime and the confrontation. The Court then took the facts of the case and applied the five-factor analysis. Glover had a substantial opportunity to view Brathwaite as he stood within two feet of Brathwaite for two to three minutes while the man twice stood with the door open. Also, there was natural light entering a window in the hallway aiding the view. Furthermore, Glover was not a casual observer; and, being of the same race as respondent, it was unlikely he would perceive only general features. Glover then provided a very detailed description of respondent to the other officer immediately after the sale and identified him from a picture two days later. Glover was also very positive in his identification of Brathwaite as he testified: "there is no question whatsoever." The time between the crime and the confrontation was very short, as Glover gave his description to the officer immediately after the crime and positively identified Brathwaite only two days later by the photograph. The Court concluded: "[t]hese indicators of Glover's ability to make an accurate identification are hardly outweighed by the corrupting effect of the challenged identification itself."

CASE SIGNIFICANCE: The Supreme Court concluded that the five factors set forth in *Biggers* should be used to test the reliability of the identification. The opportunity to view asks whether the officer was at a distance adequate enough to examine the suspect and whether the officer had a sufficient amount of time to examine him or her, while also considering the environmental factors, such as daylight. The degree of attention refers to the amount of attention the officer placed on examining the suspect. This could be revealed in the accuracy of the description: did the officer provide a very detailed description of the suspect, such as Glover's, or an undetailed description? The witness' level of certainty describes how certain the officer was of his identification of the suspect after the alleged incident or crime occurred. Finally, the time between the crime and the confrontation or identification of the suspect is important because long periods of time between the crime and identification produce a greater likelihood of the officer forgetting the exact details that he first saw in the suspect, thus making the officer's identification less reliable.

Use of Force 13

Introduction

The use of force is often necessary in police work, particularly when making an arrest. Force used in policing is categorized into two types: deadly force and non-deadly force. Deadly force is force that is likely to produce death or serious bodily injury. All other kinds of force are non-deadly force.

A crucial question is: When is the use of force by the police legal and when is it illegal? This is a difficult question to answer, because situations involving the use of force are never alike. In use of deadly force cases, the safest rule is: follow department policy strictly. Almost all law enforcement agencies presently have clear policies on the use of deadly force. These policies may be more restrictive than those allowed by the Constitution or state law. The more limiting department policies should be followed by the police.

In non-deadly force cases, the rule is: the police should use only reasonable force, meaning only as much force as is needed to accomplish a legitimate goal, such as subduing a resisting suspect or dispersing an illegal demonstration. The difficulty lies in determining what force is reasonable under the circumstances. Regardless of circumstances, the rule is that the police must never use punitive force, referring to force that aims to punish rather than to accomplish a legitimate goal.

The Supreme Court has decided only two cases on police use of force, both of which are briefed in this section. In *Tennessee v. Garner*, 471 U.S. 1 (1985), the Court held that the police may not use deadly force to prevent the escape of a suspect unless it is necessary and the officer has probable cause to believe that the suspect poses a significant threat of death or serious physical injury to the officer or to others. *Garner* limited the use of deadly force by police and declared unconstitutional rules allowing the use of deadly force to prevent escape of any suspect.

The other case, *Graham v. Connor*, 490 U.S. 396 (1989), sets the test for liability in police use of excessive force cases. The Court said that the test for liability under Section 1983 (as opposed to state tort) cases is "objective reasonableness," rather than "substantive due process." The Court said that if the officer's conduct is objectively reasonable (judged from the perspective of a reasonable officer on the scene, rather than with the 20/20 vision of hindsight), there is no excessive use of force even if the officer had bad motives or evil intent. In contrast, if the officer's conduct is objectively unreasonable, there is a violation against unreasonable searches and seizures, even if the officer's motives were good. Under *Graham*, then, the motivation for the use of force is irrelevant in police use of force cases; all that is relevant is whether such use was objectively reasonable.

Tennessee v. Garner
471 U.S. 1 (1985)

CAPSULE: The police may not use deadly force to prevent the escape of a suspect unless it is necessary and the officer has probable cause to believe that the suspect poses a significant threat of death or serious physical injury to the officer or to others.

FACTS: Memphis police officers were dispatched to answer a "prowler inside" call. At the scene, they saw a woman standing on her porch and gesturing toward the adjacent house. She told them she had heard glass breaking and that someone was breaking in next door. While one officer radioed the dispatcher, the other went behind the adjacent house. He heard a door slam and saw someone run across the backyard. The fleeing suspect, Edward Garner, stopped at a six-foot-high chain-link fence at the edge of the yard. With the aid of a flashlight, the officer was able to see Garner's face and hands. He saw no sign of a weapon, and, although not certain, was "reasonably sure" that Garner was unarmed. While Garner was crouched at the base of the fence, the officer called out "Police, halt" and took a few steps toward him. Garner then began to climb over the fence. Believing that if Garner made it over the fence he would elude capture, the officer shot him. Garner was taken by ambulance to a hospital, where he died. Ten dollars and a purse taken from the house were found on his body.

ISSUE: Is the use of deadly force to prevent the escape of an individual suspected of a non-violent felony constitutional? NO.

SUPREME COURT DECISION: "Deadly force may not be used unless it is necessary to prevent escape and the officer has probable cause to believe that the suspect poses a significant threat of death or serious physical injury to the officer or others."

REASON: "The use of deadly force to prevent the escape of all felony suspects, whatever the circumstances, is constitutionally unreasonable. It is not better that all felony suspects die than that they escape. Where the suspect poses no immediate threat to the officer and no threat to others, the harm resulting from failing to apprehend him does not justify the use of deadly force to do so. It is no doubt unfortunate when a suspect who is in sight escapes, but the fact that the police arrive a little late or are a little slower of foot does not always justify killing the suspect. A police officer may not seize an unarmed, nondangerous suspect by shooting him dead. The Tennessee statute is unconstitutional insofar as it authorizes the use of deadly force against such fleeing suspect."

CASE SIGNIFICANCE: This case clarifies the extent to which the police may use deadly force to prevent the escape of an unarmed felon. The Court made it clear that deadly force may be used only if the officer has probable cause to believe that the suspect poses a threat of serious physical harm to the officer or others. In addition, when feasible, the suspect must first be warned. The decision rendered unconstitutional existing laws in more than one-half of the states that imposed no restrictions on the use of force by police officers to prevent the escape of an individual suspected of a felony.

State laws and departmental rules can set narrower limits on the use of force (as in rules stating that use of deadly force may only be used in instances of self-defense), but broader limits are unconstitutional. The court based the decision on the Fourth Amendment, saying that "there can be no question that apprehension by the use of force is a seizure subject to the reasonableness requirement of the Fourth Amendment."

Graham v. Connor
490 U.S. 396 (1989)

CAPSULE: Police officers may be held liable under the Constitution for using excessive force. The test for liability is "objective reasonableness" rather than "substantive due process."

FACTS: Graham, a diabetic, asked a friend, Berry, to drive him to a convenience store to buy orange juice, which he needed to counteract the onset of an insulin reaction. They went to the store, but Graham saw many people ahead of him in line so he hurried out and asked Berry to drive him, instead, to a friend's house. Officer Connor became suspicious after he saw Graham hastily enter and leave the store. He followed Berry's car, made an investigative stop, and ordered Graham and Berry to wait while he determined what happened at the store. Other officers arrived, handcuffed Graham, and ignored Graham's attempt to explain his condition. An encounter ensued in which Graham sustained multiple injuries. Graham was later released when officer Connor learned that nothing had happened at the store. Graham brought a Section 1983 lawsuit against the police alleging a violation of his Fourth Amendment constitutional protection from excessive force.

ISSUE: May police officers be held liable under § 1983 for using excessive force? YES. What should be the standard for liability?

SUPREME COURT DECISION: Police officers may be held liable under the Constitution for using excessive force. Such liability must be judged under the Fourth Amendment's "objective reasonableness" standard, rather than under a "substantive due process" standard.

REASON: "The 'reasonableness' of a particular use of force must be judged from the perspective of a reasonable officer on the scene, rather than with the 20/20 vision of hindsight. The Fourth Amendment is not violated by an arrest based on probable cause, even though the wrong person is arrested, nor by the mistaken execution of a valid search warrant on the wrong premises. With respect to a claim of excessive force, the same standard of reasonableness at the moment applies: 'Not every push or shove, even if it may later seem unnecessary in the peace of a judge's chamber,' violates the Fourth Amendment. The calculus of reasonableness must embody allowance for the fact that police officers are often forced to make split-second judgments—in circumstances that are tense, uncertain, and rapidly evolving—about the amount of force that is necessary in a particular situation." [Citations omitted.]

CASE SIGNIFICANCE: This case gives police officers a "break" in civil liability cases involving the use of force. The old "substantive due process" test used by many lower courts prior to the *Graham* case required the courts to consider whether the officer acted in "good faith" or "maliciously and sadistically for the very purpose of causing harm." This meant that the officer's "subjective motivations" were of central importance in deciding whether the force used was unconstitutional. The *Graham* case requires a new test: that of "objective reasonableness" under the Fourth Amendment. This means that the reasonableness of an officer's use of force must be judged "from the perspective of a reasonable officer on the scene, rather than with the 20/20 vision of hindsight." This makes a big difference in determining whether such use of force was reasonable. This new test recognizes that police officers often make split-second judgments in situations that involve their own lives and must, therefore, be judged in the context of "a reasonable officer at the scene."

Confessions
and Admissions:
Cases Affirming *Miranda*   14

Introduction

By any standard, *Miranda* is a landmark case in policing. It has had a lasting and pervasive influence on police investigations and is the best-known case in law enforcement. The *Miranda* rule holds that evidence obtained by the police during custodial interrogation of a suspect is not admissible in court to prove guilt unless the suspect was given the "*Miranda* warnings" and there was a valid waiver by the suspect.

Miranda is important because it changed the way courts determine the admissibility of an admission or confession obtained from a suspect. Prior to *Miranda*, the test for admissibility was whether the admission or confession was voluntary or involuntary, done on a case-by-case basis. In contrast, under *Miranda*, the test consists of three questions: (1) Were the *Miranda* warnings given by the police? (2) Was there a waiver by the suspect? and (3) If there was a waiver, was the waiver voluntary and intelligent? If the answer to all three questions is "yes," the admission or confession is admissible. Conversely, if the answer to any of the questions is "no," the evidence is not admissible.

Miranda warnings must be given whenever there is a custodial interrogation. That phrase is best understood if discussed as two separate requirements. *Custodial* means the suspect is under arrest or is deprived of his or her freedom in a significant way. *Interrogation* denotes that the suspect is asked questions by the police that tend to link the suspect to a crime.

As the cases briefed in this chapter indicate, subsequent cases have affirmed the *Miranda* rule. Arguably, the most significant of these cases is *Edwards v. Arizona*, 451 U.S. 477 (1981), in which the Supreme Court held that an accused who, after having been given the *Miranda* warnings, invokes the right to remain silent and to have a lawyer present, cannot be interrogated further for the same crime until a lawyer is made available. In *Berkemer v. McCarty*, 468 U.S. 420 (1984), the Court ruled that the *Miranda* rule applies to felony and misdemeanor offenses. The only type of interrogation in which the *Miranda* warnings are not required is the roadside questioning of a motorist detained pursuant to a routine traffic stop.

If the trial judge errs in admitting evidence during trial that, on appeal, is determined by the appellate court not to be admissible, the former rule was that the conviction was automatically reversed. That rule was changed when the Supreme Court decided in *Arizona v. Fulminante*, 499 U.S. 279 (1991) that the "harmless error" doctrine applies to the admissibility of confessions. This means that the conviction is not automatically reversed; instead, the harmless error doctrine is used. If the wrongful admission by the trial court judge of the confession amounts to harmless error, the conviction is affirmed, but if the error is harmful, the conviction is reversed. The appellate court, based on the record, determines whether the error by the trial judge was harmless or harmful.

The most recent Court decision on *Miranda* is important because it holds that *Miranda* governs the admissibility in federal and state courts of confessions and admissions and that any law passed by Congress that seeks to overturn the *Miranda* decision is unconstitutional (*Dickerson v. United States*, 530 U.S. 428 [2000]). This is a significant decision because it affirms that the *Miranda* warnings are required by the Constitution and are not simply judge-made rules. Therefore, unless the Supreme Court changes its mind, the *Miranda* warnings are here to stay.

Aside from *Miranda*, the other important cases in this section are *Edwards v. Arizona, Berkemer v. McCarty, Arizona v. Fulminante*, and *Dickerson v. United States*. Further clarifications to *Miranda* were made by the Court in three more recent cases: *Kaupp v. Texas* (2003), *Fellers v. United States* (2004), and *Missouri v. Seibert* (2004).

Brown v. Mississippi
297 U.S. 278 (1936)

CAPSULE: Confessions obtained as a result of coercion and brutality are not admissible in court.

FACTS: A deputy sheriff and others went to Brown's home and asked him to accompany them to the house of a deceased person. While there, Brown was accused of the murder. When he denied the accusation, he was hanged from a tree limb, let down, and hanged again. Persisting in his claim of innocence, he was tied to a tree and whipped, but was later released. Several days later, the same deputy returned to Brown's home and arrested him. On the way to the jail, Brown was again beaten by the deputy, who said he would continue beating Brown until Brown confessed. Brown did confess and was held in jail.

Two other suspects were taken to the same jail. There they were forced to strip by the same deputy and others and were laid over chairs where they were whipped with a leather strap with a buckle on it. When they finally confessed, the officers left, saying that if they changed their story they would be whipped again.

The next day the three were brought before the sheriff and others, at which time they confessed to the crimes. Trial began the next day. The suspects testified that the confessions were false and were obtained by torture. The rope marks on the suspects were clearly visible and none of the participants in the beatings denied they had taken place. The suspects were convicted of murder and sentenced to death.

ISSUE: Are confessions obtained by brutality and torture by law enforcement officers a violation of the due process rights guaranteed by the Fourteenth Amendment? YES.

SUPREME COURT DECISION: Confessions obtained as a result of coercion and brutality by law enforcement officers violate the due process clause of the Fourteenth Amendment and are therefore inadmissible in court.

REASON: "The State is free to regulate the procedure of its courts in accordance with its own conceptions of policy, unless in so doing it 'offends some principle of justice so rooted in the traditions and conscience of our people as to be ranked fundamental.' . . . [T]he freedom of the State in establishing its policy is the freedom of constitutional government and is limited by the requirement of due process of law. Because a State may dispense with a jury trial, it does not follow that it may substitute trial by ordeal. The rack and torture chamber may not be substituted for the witness stand. The State may not permit an accused to be hurried to conviction under mob domination—where the whole proceeding is but a mask—without supplying corrective process."

CASE SIGNIFICANCE: This case was decided by the Court in 1936, before the Fifth Amendment right against self-incrimination was made applicable to the states. Instead of using the Fifth Amendment, the Court used the due process clause of the Fourteenth Amendment because the Fourteenth Amendment has always applied to state criminal proceedings.

This case renders inadmissible in court any evidence obtained as a result of physical torture. The methods used by the law enforcement officers in *Brown* were extreme, hence it was easy to prohibit their use. Subsequently, the Court said that any type of physical coercion (not necessarily hanging, as here) was also prohibited. Still later, even psychological coercion was prohibited. All these culminated in *Miranda v. Arizona* (see brief below), in which the test for admissibility shifted from voluntariness to one of "were *Miranda* warnings given?" *Brown* represents the first case in which evidence obtained as a result of physical torture in a state court criminal proceeding was held inadmissible by the Supreme Court. If a case similar to *Brown* were decided today, the evidence would be excluded based on the exclusionary rule and not on the Fourteenth Amendment due process clause.

Miranda v. Arizona
384 U.S. 436 (1966)

CAPSULE: Evidence obtained by the police during custodial interrogation of a suspect is not admissible in court to prove guilt unless the suspect was given the *Miranda* warnings and there is a valid waiver.

FACTS: Miranda was arrested at his home and taken to a police station for questioning in connection with a rape and kidnapping. Miranda was 23 years old, poor, and had completed only one-half of the ninth grade. The officers interrogated him for two hours, in which time they obtained a written confession. Miranda was convicted of rape and kidnapping.

ISSUE: Must the police inform a suspect who is subject to a custodial interrogation of his or her constitutional rights involving self-incrimination and right to counsel prior to questioning? YES.

SUPREME COURT DECISION: Evidence obtained by the police during a custodial interrogation of a suspect cannot be used in court unless the suspect was informed of the following rights prior to the interrogation:

1. The right to remain silent;

2. That any statement made may be used in a court of law;

3. The right to have an attorney present during questioning; and

4. If the suspect cannot afford an attorney, one will be appointed for him or her prior to questioning.

REASON: "The Fifth Amendment privilege is so fundamental to our system of constitutional rule and the expedient of giving an adequate warning as to the availability of the privilege so simple, we will not pause to inquire in individual cases whether the defendant was aware of his rights without a warning being given. Assessments of the knowledge the defendant possessed, based on information as to his age, education, intelligence, or prior contact with authorities, can never be more than speculation; a warning is a clearcut fact. More important, whatever the background of the person interrogated, a warning at the time of the interrogation is indispensable to overcome its pressures and to insure that the individual knows he is free to exercise the privilege at that point in time. . . . The warning of the right to remain silent must be accompanied by the explanation that anything said can and will be used against the individual in court. This warning is needed in order to make him aware not only of the privilege, but also of the consequences of forgoing it. It is only through an awareness of these consequences that there can be any assurance of real understanding and intelligent exercise of the privilege. Moreover, this warning may serve to make the individual more acutely aware that he is faced with a phase of the adversary system—that he is not in the presence of persons acting solely in his interest."

"The circumstances surrounding in-custody interrogation can operate very quickly to overbear the will of one merely made aware of his privilege by his interrogators. Therefore, the right to have counsel present at interrogation is indispensable to the protection of the Fifth Amendment privilege under the system we delineate today. Our aim is to assure the individual's right to choose between silence and speech remains unfettered throughout the interrogation process . . ."

"The presence of counsel at the interrogation may serve several significant subsidiary functions as well. If the accused decides to talk to his interrogators, the assistance of counsel can mitigate the dangers of untrustworthiness. With a lawyer present the likelihood that the police will practice coercion is reduced, and if coercion is nevertheless exercised the lawyer can testify to it in court. The presence of a lawyer can also help to guarantee that the accused gives a fully accurate statement to the police and that the statement is rightly reported by the prosecution at trial."

"We have concluded that without proper safeguards the process of in-custody interrogation of persons suspected or accused of crime contains inherently compelling pressures which work to undermine the individual's will to resist and to compel him to speak where he would not otherwise do so freely. In order to combat these pressures and to permit a full opportunity to exercise the privilege against self-incrimination, the accused must be adequately and effectively apprised of his rights and the exercise of those rights must be fully honored."

CASE SIGNIFICANCE: *Miranda v. Arizona* is, arguably, the most widely known case ever to be decided by the U.S. Supreme Court. It also has had the deepest impact on the day-to-day crime investigation phase of police work and has led to changes that have since become an accepted part of routine police procedure. No other law enforcement case has generated more controversy inside and outside police circles. Supporters of the *Miranda* decision hail it as properly protective of individual rights, whereas critics have accused the Supreme Court of being soft on crime and coddling criminals. The 5-4 split among the justices served to fan the flames of the controversy in its early stages, with opponents of the ruling hoping that a change in Court composition would hasten its demise. That has not happened, and neither is it likely to happen in the immediate future. *Miranda* has survived the test of time and, although the process of erosion has begun in recent years, a complete overruling of *Miranda*, even by a conservative Court, appears remote.

Miranda is unique in that seldom does the Court tell the police exactly what ought to be done. In this case, the court literally told police what warnings should be given if the evidence obtained from the interrogation is to be admitted in court. *Miranda* also clarified some of the ambiguous terms used in *Escobedo v. Illinois*, 378 U.S. 428 (1964). "By custodial interrogation," said the Court, "we mean questioning initiated by law enforcement officers after a person has been taken into custody or otherwise deprived of his freedom of action in any significant way." It then added in a footnote: "This is what we meant in *Escobedo* when we spoke of an investigation which had focused on an accused." Yet the "focus" test was abandoned by the Court in later cases, preferring to use the "custodial interrogation" test to determine whether the *Miranda* warnings needed to be given. The *Escobedo* case brought the right to counsel to the police station prior to trial; the *Miranda* case went beyond the police station and brought the right to counsel out into the street if an interrogation is to take place.

Edwards v. Arizona
451 U.S. 477 (1981)

CAPSULE: An accused who, after having been given the *Miranda* warnings, invokes the right to remain silent and to have a lawyer present, cannot be interrogated further by the police until a lawyer is made available.

FACTS: Edwards was arrested pursuant to a warrant. At the police station, he was read his *Miranda* warnings and indicated that he understood them and would answer questions. After being informed that an accomplice had made a sworn statement implicating him, Edwards sought to "make a deal," but later changed his mind and said that he wanted to speak to an attorney before making a deal. At that point questioning ceased. The next morning, two other officers went to the jail and asked to see Edwards. Edwards told the detention officer that he did not wish to speak to the officers; but was told that he had no choice in the matter. Edwards was again informed of his *Miranda* rights. He indicated that he would talk but first wanted to hear the taped statement of the accomplice. After listening to the statement, Edwards made a statement implicating himself in the crime. Edwards was charged with and convicted of several state criminal offenses.

ISSUE: If a suspect has been given the *Miranda* warnings and invokes the right to remain silent or to have counsel, may that suspect be later interrogated by the police if the *Miranda* warnings are given again? NO.

SUPREME COURT DECISION: An accused who, after having been given the *Miranda* warnings, invokes the right to silence and to have a lawyer, cannot be interrogated further by the police until a lawyer has been made available. An exception to this rule is if the accused initiates further communication, exchanges, or conversations with the police.

REASON: "When an accused asks for counsel, a valid waiver of that right cannot be established by showing only that he responded to further police-initiated custodial interrogation, even if he has been advised of his rights. We further hold that an accused, such as Edwards, having expressed his desire to deal with the police only through counsel, is not subject to further interrogation by the authorities until counsel has been made available to him, unless the accused himself initiates further communication, exchanges, or conversations with the police."

"We think it clear that Edwards was subjected to custodial interrogation on January 20 within the meaning of *Innis* and that this occurred at the insistence of the authorities. His statement, made without having access to counsel, did not amount to a valid waiver and hence was inadmissible."

CASE SIGNIFICANCE: The principle is clear: once a suspect invokes his or her rights after having been given the *Miranda* warnings, interrogation must cease. Further, the police cannot later interrogate the suspect again, even with another reading of the *Miranda* warnings, until the suspect has been provided with a lawyer. If the suspect, however, on his or her own, initiates further communication or conversation with the police, the confession will be admissible. In such instances, there is a need for the suspect to be given the *Miranda* warnings again.

Berkemer v. McCarty
468 U.S. 420 (1984)

CAPSULE: The *Miranda* rule applies to all types of offenses, except the roadside questioning of a motorist detained pursuant to a routine traffic stop.

FACTS: After following McCarty's car for two miles and observing it weave in and out of a lane, an officer stopped the car and asked McCarty to get out of the vehicle. McCarty had difficulty standing while getting out of the car. The officer decided that McCarty would be charged with a traffic offense, thus terminating his freedom to leave the scene. McCarty was not told he would be taken into custody, but was required to take a field sobriety test, which he failed. While still at the scene of the stop, McCarty was asked whether he had been using any intoxicants, to which he replied that he had consumed two beers and several marijuana cigarettes. McCarty was then formally arrested and taken to jail. A test given to McCarty to determine his blood-alcohol level did not detect any alcohol. The officer resumed the questioning, in which McCarty admitted to consuming alcohol. At no point was McCarty given *Miranda* warnings. McCarty pled no contest and was found guilty of operating a motor vehicle while under the influence of alcohol and/or drugs.

ISSUES:
1. Must *Miranda* warnings be given when interrogating suspects charged with misdemeanor traffic offenses? YES.
2. Does the roadside questioning of a motorist detained for a traffic violation constitute a custodial interrogation under *Miranda v. Arizona*? NO.

SUPREME COURT DECISIONS:
1. A person subjected to custodial interrogation must be given *Miranda* warnings regardless of the nature or severity of the offense.
2. The roadside questioning of a motorist detained pursuant to a routine traffic stop does not constitute a custodial interrogation, hence no *Miranda* warnings need be given.

REASON: "In the years since the decision in *Miranda*, we have frequently reaffirmed the central principle established by that case: if the police take a suspect into custody and then ask him questions without informing him of the rights enumerated above, his responses cannot be introduced into evidence to establish his guilt . . ."

"Petitioner asks us to carve an exception out of the foregoing principle. When the police arrest a person for allegedly committing a misdemeanor traffic offense and then ask him questions without telling him his constitutional rights, petitioners argue, his responses should be admissible against him. We cannot agree."

"One of the principal advantages of the doctrine that suspects must be given warnings before being interrogated while in custody is the clarity of that rule. . . . The exception to *Miranda* proposed by petitioner would substantially undermine this crucial advantage of the doctrine. The police often are unaware when they arrest a person whether he may have committed a misdemeanor or a felony . . ."

"Two features of an ordinary traffic stop mitigate the danger that a person questioned will be induced 'to speak where he would not otherwise do so freely.' *Miranda v. Arizona*, 384 U.S. at 476. First, detention of a motorist pursuant to a traffic stop is presumably temporary and brief. The vast majority of roadside detentions last only a few minutes. . . . Second, circumstances associated with the typical traffic stop are not such that the motorist feels completely at the mercy of the police."

CASE SIGNIFICANCE: This case settles two legal issues that had long divided lower courts. It is clear now that once a suspect has been placed under arrest for any offense, be it a felony or a misdemeanor, the *Miranda* warnings must be given before interrogation. It is a rule that is easier for the police to follow than the requirement of determining whether the arrest was for a felony or a misdemeanor before giving the warning. The Court said that the purpose of the *Miranda* warnings, which is to ensure that the police do not coerce or trick captive suspects into confessing, is applicable equally to misdemeanor or felony cases. The second part of the decision is equally important in that it identifies an instance in which the warnings need not be given. There is no custodial interrogation in a traffic stop because it is usually brief and the motorist expects that, although he or she may be given a citation, in the end the motorist will most likely be allowed to continue on his or her way. However, if the motorist who has been temporarily detained is later arrested, the *Miranda* warnings must be given if interrogation is to take place.

Michigan v. Jackson
475 U.S. 625 (1986)

CAPSULE: The police should not initiate an interrogation after the defendant has asserted his or her right to counsel at arraignment or similar proceedings.

FACTS: Jackson was one of four participants in a wife's plan to have her husband killed. When arrested on an unrelated charge, he made a series of statements during a police interrogation prior to his arraignment. At arraignment, Jackson requested the assistance of an attorney and one was appointed for him. The following morning, before Jackson had a chance to consult with counsel, officers obtained another statement confirming that he was the murderer. All of the statements were given after Jackson was advised of his *Miranda* rights and agreed to talk without the presence of counsel. Jackson was charged with and convicted of second degree murder and conspiracy to commit second degree murder.

ISSUE: May an accused who has requested the assistance of counsel during arraignment waive that right at police-initiated post-arraignment custodial interrogations? NO.

SUPREME COURT DECISION: If the police initiate an interrogation after the defendant asserts his or her right to counsel at arraignment or similar proceedings, any waiver of that right for a police-initiated interrogation is invalid.

REASON: "Although the rule of *Edwards v. Arizona*, 451 U.S. 477 (1981), that once a suspect has invoked his right to counsel, police may not initiate interrogation until counsel has been made available to the suspect, rested on the Fifth Amendment and concerned a request for counsel made during custodial interrogation, the reasoning of that case applies with even greater force to this case. The assertion of the right to counsel is no less significant, and the need for additional safeguards no less clear, when that assertion is made at arraignment and when the basis for it is the Sixth Amendment. If police initiate an interrogation after defendant's assertion of his right to counsel, at an arraignment or similar proceeding, as in this case, any waiver of that right for that police-initiated interrogation is invalid."

CASE SIGNIFICANCE: The rule is clear that if a suspect invokes his or her right to remain silent, the police should not and cannot initiate interrogation with the suspect. This rule does not apply if the suspect initiates the conversation on his or her own. If the police violate this rule, the confession obtained will not be admissible in court. The situation in the *Jackson* case is different in that the defendant in this case invoked the right to counsel at arraignment (when the charges are read to the accused in court), not during police interrogation. What was also invoked was not the right to remain silent, but the right to a lawyer. Nonetheless, the Court said that after the accused requested counsel during arraignment, the police should no longer interrogate him, even with the *Miranda* warnings, if the accused has not yet conferred with a lawyer. The rule is clear: Once an accused asks for or has a lawyer, the police must not interrogate the accused except in the presence of a lawyer.

Arizona v. Roberson
486 U.S. 675 (1988)

CAPSULE: An accused who has invoked the right to counsel may not be subjected to a police-initiated interrogation even if the interrogation concerns a different crime.

FACTS: After being arrested at the scene of a burglary, Roberson was advised of his *Miranda* rights and indicated that he wanted to speak to a lawyer before answering any questions. Three days later, a different officer, unaware of Roberson's request for counsel, gave him the *Miranda* warnings and interrogated him concerning a different burglary. Roberson made incriminating statements concerning the crime.

ISSUE: If an accused has invoked the right to counsel, may the police, after giving the *Miranda* warnings again, interrogate the same suspect about a different crime? NO.

SUPREME COURT DECISION: An accused who has invoked the right to counsel may not be subjected to a police-initiated interrogation even if the interrogation concerns a different crime.

REASON: "The *Edwards* rule applies to bar police-initiated interrogation following a suspect's request for counsel in the context of a separate investigation."

"The bright-line prophylactic *Edwards* rule benefits the accused and the State alike. It protects against the inherently compelling pressures of custodial interrogation [on] suspects who feel incapable of undergoing such questioning without the advice of counsel, by creating a presumption that any subsequent waiver of the right to counsel at the authorities' behest was coercive and not purely voluntary. Moreover, it provides clear and unequivocal guidelines that inform police and prosecutors with specificity what they may do in conducting custodial interrogation, and that inform courts under what circumstances statements obtained during interrogation are not admissible."

CASE SIGNIFICANCE: An earlier case, *Edwards v. Arizona*, 451 U.S. 477 (1981), said that if an accused asks for counsel after having been given the *Miranda* warnings, that accused cannot be further interrogated by the police. This case differs from *Edwards* in that:

1. The second interrogation took place three days later (rather than the day after, as in *Edwards*); and

2. The interrogation was for a different offense.

Nonetheless, the Court said that the rule is the same, an accused who had invoked the right to counsel may not be subjected to police interrogation again, even if it is for a different offense. Although the Court did not explicitly say so, it is to be assumed that the exception in *Edwards*, in which interrogations are allowed if the suspect initiates the communication or conversation, also applies to interrogations for a different offense.

Minnick v. Mississippi
498 U.S. 146 (1990)

CAPSULE: Once a suspect requests a lawyer, the interrogation must stop—whether the suspect confers with the lawyer or not.

FACTS: Minnick and a fellow prisoner, Dyess, escaped from a jail in Mississippi and broke into a mobile home in search of weapons. In the course of the burglary, they were interrupted by the arrival of the owner, another man, and an infant. Dyess and Minnick used the stolen weapons to kill the two adults. Dyess and Minnick ultimately split up and Minnick was arrested in California. The day following his arrest, Minnick was told that he would have to talk to FBI agents. After being read his *Miranda* warnings, Minnick refused to sign a waiver form but made some statements to the agents. After making some incriminating statements, the agents reminded Minnick of his *Miranda* rights, at which time Minnick stated "come back Monday when I have a lawyer" and that he would make a more complete statement then. After the FBI interview, an appointed attorney met with Minnick on two or three occasions, although it is unclear whether all of these conferences were in person. Two days later, a deputy from Mississippi arrived to question Minnick. Minnick was again told that he would have to talk to the deputy and that he could not refuse. The deputy advised Minnick of his rights and he again declined to sign a waiver. Minnick did, however, describe the escape and subsequent murders. At trial, Minnick moved to suppress all statements made while in custody. The court suppressed statements made to the FBI because Minnick had not been afforded counsel, but refused to suppress statements made to the deputy.

ISSUE: Once a person invokes *Miranda* rights, can the police initiate an interrogation once counsel has been appointed but is not present during questioning? NO.

SUPREME COURT DECISION: Once a suspect requests a lawyer, the interrogation must stop—whether the defendant confers with the lawyer or not. The Fifth Amendment is violated when the suspect requests a lawyer, is given an opportunity to confer with a lawyer, and then is forced to talk with the police without the lawyer being present. Prior consultation with the lawyer is not enough. The lawyer must be present at all subsequent questionings, otherwise the evidence obtained is not admissible.

REASON: The decision in *Edwards v. Arizona* strengthened *Miranda* by mandating that, once a person invokes his or her rights under *Miranda*, the police cannot initiate further interrogations until counsel had been made available to the person. The lower courts in this case interpreted that to mean that once counsel has been appointed, police could initiate an interrogation and, if the person waived their *Miranda* privileges, statements could be taken and used in court. The Supreme Court disagreed, stating ". . . a fair reading of *Edwards* and subsequent cases demonstrates that we have interpreted the rule to bar police-initiated interrogation unless the accused has counsel with him at the time of questioning. . . . We decline to remove protection from police-initiated questioning based on isolated consultations with counsel who is absent when the interrogation resumes. . . . [T]he need for counsel to protect the Fifth Amendment privilege comprehends not merely a right to consult with counsel prior to questioning, but also to have counsel present during any questioning."

CASE SIGNIFICANCE: This case is a refinement of *Edwards v. Arizona* (451 U.S. 477 [1981]), which held that an accused who invokes the right to remain silent and to have a lawyer present cannot be interrogated further by the police until a lawyer is made available, unless the suspect initiates the conversation. This case, decided nine years later, holds that once a lawyer is assigned, the police cannot force the suspect to answer questions without the lawyer being present, even though there was prior opportunity for the suspect to talk with the lawyer. It is a strict rule aimed at making the *Miranda* rights more meaningful. The fact that the suspect has had the opportunity to confer with the lawyer or that consultation with the lawyer did in fact take place does not give the police authority to ask the suspect questions again. If they want to ask the suspect questions, the lawyer must be present—otherwise, the evidence obtained is not admissible in court. In sum, the rule is: once the suspect invokes the right to have a lawyer, the police must cease interrogation and not initiate it again. The only exceptions are if the suspect initiates such conversation or if the lawyer is present.

Arizona v. Fulminante
499 U.S. 279 (1991)

CAPSULE: The "harmless error" doctrine applies to cases involving the admissibility of involuntary confessions.

FACTS: Fulminante was suspected of having murdered his stepdaughter. His statements to the police concerning her disappearance were inconsistent, but no charges were filed against him. Fulminante left Arizona for New Jersey, where he was later convicted on an unrelated federal charge of possession of a firearm. While incarcerated in a federal prison in New York, Fulminante was befriended by a fellow inmate, Sarivola, who was serving a 60-day sentence for extortion. Sarivola later became a paid informant for the FBI. Sarivola told Fulminante that he knew Fulminante was getting tough treatment from the other inmates because of a rumor that he was a child murderer. Sarivola offered Fulminante protection in exchange for the truth. Fulminante admitted to Sarivola that he had driven his stepdaughter "to the desert on his motorcycle, where he choked her, sexually assaulted her, and made her beg for her life, before shooting her twice in the head."

After Fulminante's release from prison, he also confessed to Sarivola's wife about the same crime. Fulminante was indicted in Arizona for first-degree murder. He sought to exclude the confession to Sarivola, alleging that it was coerced and thus barred by the Fifth and Fourteenth Amendments. He also challenged his confession to Sarivola's wife as "fruit" of the first confession. Both confessions were admitted by the trial court. Fulminante was convicted and sentenced to death.

ISSUES: This case raises a number of issues:

1. Should the "harmless error" doctrine be applied to cases of involuntary confession? YES.

2. Was Fulminante's confession coerced? YES.

3. Was the admission of Fulminante's confession by the trial court a "harmless error" in his conviction? NO—the error was harmful and therefore the conviction had to be reversed.

SUPREME COURT DECISION: The "harmless error" doctrine applies in cases of involuntary confessions. Fulminante's confession was coerced because it was motivated by a fear of physical violence if he were not to be protected by Sarivola. The government had not proved, however, that admitting his confession was not harmless beyond a reasonable doubt; hence Fulminante was entitled to a new trial at which the confessions would not be admitted.

REASON: "Although the question is a close one, we agree with the Arizona Supreme Court's conclusion that Fulminante's confession was coerced. The Arizona Supreme Court found a credible threat of physical violence unless Fulminante confessed. Our cases have made clear that a finding of coercion need not depend upon actual violence by a government agent; a credible threat is sufficient."

"Since five Justices have determined that harmless error analysis applies to coerced confessions, it becomes necessary to evaluate under that ruling the admissibility of Fulminante's confession to Sarivola. *Chapman v. California* (386 U.S., at 24) made clear that 'before a federal constitutional error can be held harmless, the court must be able to declare a belief that it was harmless beyond a reasonable doubt.' The Court has the power to review the record *de novo* in order to determine any error's harmlessness. In so doing, it must be determined whether the State has met its burden to Fulminante's conviction. Five of us are of the view that the State has not carried its burden and accordingly affirm the judgment of the court below reversing petitioner's conviction."

CASE SIGNIFICANCE: This case raised a number of issues on which the Justices were sharply divided. The issues are best discussed separately.

1. On the issue of whether the "harmless error" doctrine should be applied to cases of involuntary confession, the Supreme Court answered yes. The "harmless error" doctrine, enunciated by the Court in *Chapman v. California*, 386 U.S. 18 (1967), holds that an error by a trial court need not lead to the reversal of a conviction as long as the error is harmless. The burden of proving "harmless error" lies with the prosecution and that burden must be established "beyond a reasonable doubt." To establish "harmless error," it is not enough for the prosecution to show that there was other evidence sufficient to support the verdict; rather, it must show that there was no reasonable possibility that a different result would have been reached without the tainted evidence. Under *Fulminante*, an error of a trial judge in admitting an involuntary confession that ought not to have been excluded no longer automatically leads to reversal of defendant's conviction. Lower courts in prior cases applied the automatic reversal rule to confessions, believing that the "harmless error" doctrine did not apply to erroneous admission of confessions because confessions were presumed to be inherently harmful to the defendant. This case applies that doctrine: to all errors made by the judge, including the erroneous admission of confessions.

2. On the issue of whether Fulminante's confession was coerced, the Court answered yes, agreeing with the finding of the Arizona courts that "Sarivola's promise was extremely coercive," and that "the confession was obtained as a direct result of extreme coercion and was tendered in the belief that the defendant's life was in jeopardy if he did not confess." Because the confession was coerced, it could not be admissible in a court of law.

3. On the issue of whether the admission of Fulminante's coerced confession by the trial court was a "harmless error," the Court said it was not. A majority of the Court opined that the prosecution in this case failed to establish that the error committed by the trial court in admitting the evidence was "not harmless beyond a reasonable doubt."

Fulminante is a convoluted case in which the justices split 5 to 4 on the issues identified above. Its importance centers on whether the "harmless error" doctrine applies to trial court errors involving the admission of involuntary confessions. The practice by many appellate courts of automatically reversing any conviction involving the erroneous admission of a confession, regardless of the confession's significance, has now been replaced by the "harmless error" doctrine. Under this rule, reversal of conviction on appeal now involves two steps. The first step is determining whether the confession is voluntary. If it is involuntary, a second step is in order: determining whether the admission of such evidence by the trial court was "harmless error." If the admission constitutes "harmless error" (as determined by the appellate court), the conviction is affirmed. Conversely, if the error is harmful or if the prosecution fails to establish beyond a reasonable doubt that the error is harmless (as in the *Fulminante* case), the conviction is reversed.

Dickerson v. United States
530 U.S. 428 (2000)

CAPSULE: The case of *Miranda v. Arizona* governs the admissibility in federal and state courts of confessions and admissions given during custodial interrogation by the police. Any law passed by Congress that seeks to overturn the *Miranda* decision is unconstitutional.

FACTS: Dickerson was arrested and made incriminating statements to police. Before his trial, he moved that the statements be suppressed because he had not received his *Miranda* warnings prior to being interrogated. His statements were voluntary, but they were made without having been given the *Miranda* warnings. The Federal District Court granted the motion to suppress, but the Court of Appeals overturned it, stating that 18 U.S.C. Section 3501, passed by Congress in response to the *Miranda* decision, prevailed and only required a finding by a court that the confession was given voluntarily. 18 U.S.C. Section 3501 was passed by Congress in 1966 right after the *Miranda* decision came out, but the constitutionality of that law never reached the United States Supreme Court because it was not enforced by the federal government - up until this case. That law sought to overturn the Court decision in Miranda by providing that the admissibility of confessions and admissions in federal court is determined by whether or not they were voluntarily made, not by whether or not they complied with the *Miranda* warnings.

ISSUE: Is a law passed by Congress seeking to overturn the United States Supreme Court ruling in *Miranda v. Arizona* constitutional? NO.

SUPREME COURT DECISION: The case of *Miranda v. Arizona* governs the admissibility in federal and state courts of statements given during custodial interrogation by the police. Any law passed by Congress seeking to overturn the *Miranda* decision is unconstitutional.

REASON: "The law in this area is clear. This Court has supervisory authority over the federal courts, and we may use that authority to prescribe rules of evidence and procedure that are binding in those tribunals. However, the power to judicially create and enforce nonconstitutional 'rules of procedure and evidence for the federal courts exists only in the absence of a relevant Act of Congress.' Congress retains the ultimate authority to modify or set aside any judicially created rules of evidence and procedure that are not required by the Constitution." "But Congress may not legislatively supersede our decisions interpreting and applying the Constitution. This case therefore turns on whether the *Miranda* Court announced a constitutional rule or merely exercised its supervisory authority to regulate evidence in the absence of congressional direction. ". . . we conclude that *Miranda* announced a constitutional rule that Congress may not supersede legislatively."

CASE SIGNIFICANCE: This is a highly significant case because it settled an important issue - whether the *Miranda* decision continues to govern the admissibility of confessions and admissions or whether it could be negated by laws passed by Congress or by State Legislatures. The Court held that *Miranda* is a constitutional rule, not just a rule of evidence, and therefore it cannot be undone by legislation. The *Miranda* decision is here to stay, unless overturned by the Court itself. Had the decision been otherwise, federal cases would have been governed by the provisions of the federal law. Some state legislatures would likely have passed similar legislation, causing the admissibility of statements to be governed by different rules.

    Miranda v. Arizona ruled that statements are admissible only if three questions are answered in the affirmative: (1) were the *Miranda* Warnings given, (2) if they were given, was there a waiver, and (3) was the waiver intelligent and voluntary? Voluntariness is assumed present if the answers to all three questions are affirmative. Statements that are voluntary are not admissible if the *Miranda* warnings were not given. Congress sought to modify that rule by passing legislation stating that the *Miranda* warnings are not necessary if the statement itself is voluntary. The legislation, in effect, wanted to supersede the *Miranda v. Arizona* case. The Court held that Congress could not do that because *Miranda* is not a rule of evidence; instead it is a constitutional rule. If it were a rule of evidence, Congress could have overridden it by legislation, but as a constitutional rule Congress could not override it by legislation. This is significant because since the *Miranda* decision came out in 1966, scholars have debated whether or not *Miranda* is a constitutional rule that could not be superseded by legislation or whether it was merely a rule of evidence. The Court in Dickerson settled that controversy, concluding that *Miranda* is a constitutional rule and is therefore here to stay, unless overturned by the Court. It cannot be superseded by legislation passed by Congress or State Legislatures. This case reaffirms the authority of *Miranda v. Arizona*.

Kaupp v. Texas
538 U.S. 626 (2003)

CAPSULE: A confession must be suppressed if obtained during a detention where officers did not have probable cause for an arrest and where the detention amounted to the functional equivalent of an arrest.

FACTS: Officers investigating the disappearance of a girl focused on her half-brother and Kaupp. Her brother ultimately confessed to killing her, and implicated Kaupp in the murder. Because the brother failed a polygraph test three times and Kaupp had passed his polygraph, officers did not believe they had probable cause for an arrest warrant based solely on the brother's confession. An attempt to get a "pocket warrant" to question Kaupp was also refused by the prosecutor. At least three officers then went to Kaupp's home at 3:00 A.M. and, after his father let them in, went to his bedroom, awakened him with a flashlight, and told him "we need to go and talk." Kaupp was then handcuffed and taken, dressed only in a t-shirt and boxer shorts, to a patrol car. After going to the scene where the body had been recovered, officers then took him to the sheriff's office. There, Kaupp was taken to an interview room where the handcuffs were removed and he was read his *Miranda* warnings. After initially denying any involvement in the crime, he ultimately admitted to having some part, although he did not confess to the murder for which he was later tried. In rejecting Kaupp's motion to suppress his confession, the court held that Kaupp consented to go with the officers when he answered "Okay" when the officers told him "we need to go and talk." The court also agreed with the police that handcuffing was for officer safety and was routine, and that Kaupp did not resist the use of handcuffs or act in other uncooperative ways.

ISSUE: May a confession be admitted in evidence when obtained after officers create a situation where a reasonable person would not have felt free to leave and where the police had no probable cause for an arrest? NO.

SUPREME COURT DECISION: A confession must be suppressed if it is obtained during a detention where officers did not have probable cause for an arrest and where the detention amounted to the functional equivalent of an arrest.

REASON: The Court in this case relied on a number of previous holdings to reinforce the legal factors that represent the functional equivalent of an arrest. Addressing Kaupp's reply of "Okay" to the officers, the Court stated "there is no reason to think Kaupp's answer was anything more than 'a mere submission to a claim of lawful authority,'" and in no way implied consent. The Court also stated that "as for lack of resistance, failure to struggle with a cohort of deputy sheriffs is not a waiver of the Fourth Amendment protection . . ." Again relying on previous cases, the Court stated that, "'at some point in the investigative process, police procedures can qualitatively and quantitatively be so intrusive with respect to a suspect's freedom of movement and privacy interests as to trigger the full protection of the Fourth and Fourteenth Amendments.' It cannot It cannot seriously be suggested that when the detectives began to question Kaupp, a reasonable person in his situation would have thought he was sitting in the interview room as a matter of choice, free to change his mind and go home to bed." Finally, the Court noted that "although certain seizures may be justified on something less than probable cause, see, e.g., *Terry v. Ohio*, 392 U.S. 1 (1968), we have never 'sustained against Fourth Amendment challenge the involuntary removal of a suspect from his home to a police station and his detention there for investigative purposes . . . absent probable cause or judicial authorization." The Court concluded, "since Kaupp was arrested before he was questioned, and because the state does not even claim that the sheriff's department had probable cause to detain him at that point, well-established precedent requires suppression of the confession."

CASE SIGNIFICANCE: The significance of this case lies in its further clarification of what constitutes an arrest when the perceptions of the police and the suspect differ. In this case, a 17-year-old boy was asked by the police to go with them to the police station because "we need to talk." The suspect answered, "Okay," which the police interpreted to mean consent. Ten or 15 minutes into the interrogation at the police station, the defendant implicated himself. The police maintained that the suspect was not under arrest at the time he confessed; therefore, the evidence was admissible. The Court rejected that, saying "a seizure of the person within the meaning of the Fourth and Fourteenth Amendments occurs when, 'taking into account all of the circumstances surrounding the encounter, the police conduct would have communicated to a reasonable person that he was not at liberty to ignore the police presence and go about his business.'" The Court described what happened as follows: "A 17-year-old boy was awakened in his bedroom at three in the morning by at least three police officers, one of whom stated 'we need to go and talk' He was taken out in handcuffs, without shoes, dressed only in his underwear in January, placed in a patrol car, driven to the scene of a crime and then to the sheriff's offices, where he was taken into an interrogation room and questioned. This evidence points to arrest . . ." The Court further said that the suspect's "Okay" response to the invitation by the police did not imply consent; rather, it was "a mere submission to a claim of lawful authority." The confession was inadmissible.

Fellers v. United States
540 U.S. 519 (2004)

CAPSULE: The proper standard to be used when determining whether statements made by a defendant after an indictment are admissible in court is the Sixth Amendment right to counsel, not the Fifth Amendment privilege against self-incrimination.

FACTS: After a grand jury indicted Fellers, officers went to his home to arrest him. While there, after he invited them in, they told Fellers they had come to discuss his involvement in drug distribution, that they had a warrant for his arrest, and that he had been indicted. They then asked Fellers questions concerning the involvement of others in drug distribution. Fellers made incriminating statements concerning other individuals and his involvement with them. Officers then took Fellers to the police station, where he was advised of his *Miranda* rights and signed a waiver of those rights. Fellers reiterated his previous statements and made other statements concerning his involvement in drugs.

ISSUE: What standard should be used to determine the admissibility of statements given to the police after a suspect has been indicted—the Sixth Amendment right to counsel standard or the Fifth Amendment self-incrimination standard?

SUPREME COURT DECISION: The proper standard to determine whether statements made after an indictment should be admitted is the Sixth Amendment protection of right to counsel, not the Fifth Amendment protection against self-incrimination.

REASON: The issue in this case was whether the actions of the officers at Fellers' home were something that could be waived pursuant to *Elstad* or whether it was a Sixth Amendment violation. To address this, the Court stated, "The Sixth Amendment right to counsel is triggered "at or after the time that judicial proceedings have been initiated . . . whether by way of formal charge, preliminary hearing, indictment, information, or arraignment." ' We have held that an accused is denied 'the basic protections' of the Sixth Amendment 'when there [is] used against him at his trial evidence of his own incriminating words, which federal agents . . . deliberately elicited from him after he had been indicted and in the absence of his counsel' " [internal citations removed]. Concluding that the Sixth Amendment applied in this case, the Court stated, "there is no question that the officers in this case 'deliberately elicited' information from petitioner. Indeed, the officers, upon arriving at petitioner's house, informed him that their purpose in coming was to discuss his involvement. . . . Because the ensuing discussion took place after petitioner had been indicted, outside the presence of counsel, and in the absence of any waiver of petitioner's Sixth Amendment rights . . .," the statements made violated the Sixth Amendment. The Court then held that the proper standard to evaluate whether the statements should have been admitted was the Sixth Amendment protection of right to counsel, not a Fifth Amendment analysis under *Elstad*.

CASE SIGNIFICANCE: The defendant in this case claimed that his Sixth Amendment right to counsel and his Fifth Amendment *Miranda* rights were both violated when the statement he made at his home and later at the jail were used against him. Fellers was under indictment when both questionings took place. If the Fifth Amendment privilege against self-incrimination was to be used as the standard for admissibility, then his statement while in jail would have been admissible because he was given the *Miranda* warnings and had waived his Fifth Amendment privilege before giving the confession. However, he claimed that the jail statement was nonetheless inadmissible because it violated his Sixth Amendment right to counsel in that it was the "fruit" of an unlawful interrogation at his home and therefore should be excluded even if he was given the *Miranda* warnings. The Court agreed, saying that in previous cases "this Court has consistently applied the deliberate-elicitation standard in subsequent Sixth Amendment cases . . . and has expressly distinguished it from the Fifth Amendment custodial-interrogation standard." It then added that "there is no question here that the officers 'deliberately elicited information from Fellers at his home.' Because the police officers interrogated Fellers at home without counsel after he was indicted, the absence of his lawyer made his statement in his home inadmissible. Therefore, the subsequent statement in jail was also inadmissible because it was 'fruit of the poisonous tree.'" The lesson for the police in this case is: Once a suspect has been indicted and has a lawyer, the police must refrain from interrogating the suspect even after giving the *Miranda* warnings. The *Miranda* warnings may make the statement admissible under the Fifth Amendment protection against self-incrimination, but the same statement may be inadmissible because it violates the Sixth Amendment right to counsel.

Missouri v. Seibert
542 U.S. 600 (2004)

CAPSULE: Giving the *Miranda* warnings after the police purposefully obtain an unwarned confession violates the *Miranda* rule; therefore, statements made even after the *Miranda* warnings are given are not admissible in court even if they repeat those given before the *Miranda* warnings.

FACTS: Seibert's son had cerebral palsy. When he died in his sleep, Seibert feared charges of neglect because of bedsores on his body. In her presence, two of her teenaged sons and two of their friends planed to burn the family's mobile home to conceal the death of the son. They also planed to leave a mentally ill teenager who was living with the family in the mobile home to avoid the appearance that the son had been left alone. In the fire, the mentally ill teenager died. Five days later, the police awoke Seibert at 3:00 A.M. in the hospital where one of her sons was being treated for burns. She was arrested and taken to the police station. The officer making the arrest was told not to read her the *Miranda* warnings. At the station, Seibert was left in an interrogation room for about 20 minutes, then she was interrogated for about 40 minutes without being read her *Miranda* warnings. After she admitted she knew the teenager was meant to die in the fire, she was given a 20-minute break. The officer then turned on a tape recorder, gave Seibert the *Miranda* warnings, obtained a signed waiver of rights, and then resumed the interrogation. At the beginning of the interrogation, the officer confronted Seibert with her pre-warning statements and essentially walked her back through the statements she made prior to her *Miranda* warnings. At a suppression hearing to exclude the statements, the officer admitted he made a conscious decision to withhold the *Miranda* warnings based on an interrogation technique he was taught by police trainers—which was to question first, give the warnings, then repeat the questioning "until I get the answer she's already provided once."

ISSUE: Are statements made after a suspect is given the *Miranda* warnings that repeat a statement given when officers intentionally did not give *Miranda* warnings admissible in court? NO.

SUPREME COURT DECISION: Giving the *Miranda* warnings after an interrogation and an unwarned confession has first been obtained by the police does not effectively comply with *Miranda's* constitutional requirement even if it repeats the statements made before the warnings were given; therefore, statements obtained are not admissible in court.

REASON: "The object of question-first is to render *Miranda* warnings ineffective by waiting for a particularly opportune time to give them, after the suspect has already confessed. . . . The threshold issue when interrogators question first and warn later is thus whether it would be reasonable to find that in these circumstances the warnings could function effectively as *Miranda* requires. Could the warnings effectively advise the suspect that he had a real choice about giving an admissible statement at that juncture? Could they reasonably convey that he could choose to stop talking even if he had talked earlier? For unless the warnings could place a suspect who has just been interrogated in a position to make such an informed choice, there is no practical justification for accepting the formal warnings as compliance with *Miranda*, or for treating the second state of interrogation as distinct from the first, unwarned and inadmissible segment. . . . By any objective measure, applied to the circumstances exemplified here, it is likely that if the interrogators employ the technique of withholding warnings until after interrogation succeeds in eliciting a confession, the warnings will be ineffective in preparing the suspect for successive interrogations, close in time and similar in content. . . . Upon hearing the warnings only in the aftermath of interrogation and just after making a confession, a suspect would hardly think he had a genuine right to remain silent, let alone persist in so believing once the police began to lead him over the same ground again. . . . Thus, when the *Miranda* warnings are inserted in the midst of coordinated and continuing interrogation, they are likely to mislead and 'depriv[e] a defendant of knowledge essential to his ability to understand the nature of his rights and the consequences of abandoning them' *Moran v. Burbine*, 475 U.S. 412 (1986)."

CASE SIGNIFICANCE: The Court in this case struck down an established practice in some police departments. In an earlier case, *Oregon v. Elstad*, the Court admitted a confession obtained after the police gave the *Miranda* warnings—even though the suspect had previously made statements before the warnings were given. This practice was subsequently used by police training organizations, such as the Police Law Institute, in what became known as the "question-first" technique of interrogation. In this procedure, police first interrogate a person without the *Miranda* warnings. Once a confession is obtained, the *Miranda* warnings are then given, the officer resumes the interrogation, and obtains a warned confession similar to the unwarned confession that was given. In *Seibert*, the Court held this practice violated *Miranda* and therefore held the evidence inadmissible.

The Court said that there were several distinctions between this case and *Elstad* (where the evidence obtained was admissible despite a prior unwarned statement). These included "the completeness and detail of the question and answers in the first round of interrogation, the overlapping content of the two statements, the timing and setting of the first and the second statements, the continuity of police personnel, and the degree to which the interrogator's questions treated the second round as continuous with the first." The over-riding consideration in these types of "two-interrogation" cases is whether the two interrogations (the unwarned and the warned) can be seen as sepa-rate and distinct interrogations where a reasonable person would believe he or she is free to disregard the first and assert his or her rights on the second. In the *Seibert* case, the Court stated, "At the opposite extreme are the facts here [as opposed to the facts in the *Elstad* case], which by any objective meas-ure reveal a police strategy adapted to undermine the *Miranda* warnings. The unwarned interrogation was conducted at the stationhouse, and the ques-tioning was systematic, exhaustive, and managed with psychological skill. When the police were finished there was little, if anything, of incriminating potential left unsaid. The warned phase of questioning proceeded after a pause of only 15 to 20 minutes, in the same place as the unwarned segment. When the same officer who had conducted the first phase recited the *Miranda* warn-ings, he said nothing to counter the probable misimpression that the advice that anything Seibert said could be used against her also applied to the details of the inculpatory statement previously elicited. In particular, the police did not advise that her prior statement could not be used."

The end result is that the issue of whether a subsequent warned admis-sion or confession is admissible after the suspect has given an unwarned admission or confession depends on the facts and circumstances of the case. If the facts and circumstances are closer to *Elstad*, the statement may be admissible, but if they are closer to *Seibert*, the statement may not be admissible.

Confessions and Admissions: Cases Weakening *Miranda*

15

Introduction

Since 1966, when *Miranda* was decided, the Supreme Court has continued to refine the *Miranda* rule—either affirming or weakening it by carving out instances in which the *Miranda* rule does or does not apply. This chapter briefs some of the more significant cases dealing with the general rule that the *Miranda* warnings must be given whenever there is a "custodial interrogation."

As the cases briefed in this chapter indicate, the main exceptions to the police giving *Miranda* warnings to a suspect are:

1.   when there is concern for public safety;

2.   statements made when the mental state of the defendant interfered with his "rational intellect" and "free will" are not automatically excludable. Instead, their admissibility is governed by state rules of evidence;

3.   when the suspect believes that the interrogation will focus on minor crimes, but the police later shift the questioning to cover a different and more serious crime;

4.   when giving an oral confession;

5.   after a knowing and voluntary waiver of *Miranda* rights, law enforcement officers may continue questioning unless the suspect clearly requests an attorney;

6.   the *Miranda* warnings need not be given in the exact form as worded in *Miranda v. Arizona,* as long as the warnings convey to the suspect his or her rights.

The *Miranda* case, decided by a 5 to 4 vote, was intensely controversial when it came out in 1966, particularly in the law enforcement community. Over the years, however, reservations about the adverse effects of *Miranda* in police work continued to diminish. At present, its acceptance is assured even among those who administer it. The *Miranda* rule has become an integral part of policing.

The leading cases briefed in this chapter are *New York v. Quarles* and *Duckworth v. Eagan.* A more recent significant case, *United States v. Patane* (2004), holds that failure to give a suspect the *Miranda* warnings does not require suppression of the physical fruits of a suspect's unwarned but voluntary statements.

South Dakota v. Neville
459 U.S. 553 (1983)

CAPSULE: The admission into evidence of a suspect's refusal to submit to a blood-alcohol test does not violate the suspect's privilege against self-incrimination.

FACTS: South Dakota law permits a person suspected of driving while intoxicated to submit to a blood-alcohol test and authorizes revocation of the driver's license of any person who refuses to take the test. The statute permits such refusal to be used against the driver as evidence of guilt during the trial. Neville was arrested by the police for driving while intoxicated. He was asked to submit to a blood-alcohol test and warned that he could lose his license if he refused to take the test. He was not warned, however, that the refusal could be used against him during trial. Neville refused to take the test. During trial, Neville sought to exclude the evidence obtained, claiming that it violated his right to protection against compulsory self-incrimination.

ISSUE: Does a state law that allows the admission into evidence of a suspect's refusal to submit to a blood-alcohol test violate the suspect's Fifth Amendment right against self-incrimination? NO.

SUPREME COURT DECISION: The admission into evidence of a defendant's refusal to submit to a blood-alcohol test does not violate the suspect's Fifth Amendment right against self-incrimination. A refusal to take such a test, after a police officer has lawfully requested it, is not an act coerced by the officer, and thus is not protected by the Fifth Amendment. A law that allows the accused to refuse to take a blood-alcohol test and provides that such refusal may be admitted in evidence against him or her is constitutional.

REASON: "The simple blood-alcohol test is so safe, painless, and commonplace that respondent concedes, as he must, that the state could legitimately compel the suspect, against his will, to accede to the test. Given, then, that the offer of taking a blood-alcohol test is clearly legitimate, the action becomes no less legitimate when the State offers a second option of refusing the test, with the attendant penalties for making that choice. Nor is this a case where the State has subtly coerced respondent into choosing the option it had no right to compel, rather than offering a true choice. To the contrary, the State wants respondent to choose to take the test, for the inference of intoxication arising from a positive blood-alcohol test is far stronger than that arising from a refusal to take the test. . . . We recognize, of course, that the choice to submit or refuse to take a blood-alcohol test will not be an easy or pleasant one for a suspect to make. But the criminal process often requires suspects and defendants to make difficult choices. We hold, therefore, that a refusal to take a blood-alcohol test, after a police officer has lawfully requested it, is not an act coerced by the officer, and thus is not protected by the privilege against self-incrimination."

CASE SIGNIFICANCE: This case legitimizes the practice, established by law in many states, of giving suspected DWI offenders a choice to take or refuse blood-alcohol tests, but to use the refusal as evidence of guilt later in court. The defendant in this case argued that introducing such evidence in court, in effect, coerces the suspect to waive constitutional protection against self-incrimination because of the consequence. The Court rejected this contention, saying that any incrimination resulting from a blood-alcohol test is physical in nature, not testimonial, and hence is not protected by the Fifth Amendment; therefore, a suspect has no constitutional right to refuse to take the test. The Court said that the offer to the suspect to take the test is clearly legitimate and becomes no less legitimate when the state offers the option of refusing the test but prescribes consequences for making that choice. The Court added that the failure by the police to warn Neville that his refusal to take the test could be used as evidence against him during the trial was not so fundamentally unfair as to deprive him of "due process" rights. The evidence obtained could, therefore, be admissible during trial.

New York v. Quarles
467 U.S. 649 (1984)

CAPSULE: Concern for public safety represents an exception to the *Miranda* rule.

FACTS: Officers were approached by a woman claiming that she had just been raped by an armed man. She described him, and said that he had entered a nearby supermarket. The officers drove the woman to the supermarket and one officer went in while the other radioed for assistance. The officer in the supermarket quickly spotted Quarles, who matched the description provided by the woman, and a chase ensued. The officer ordered Quarles to stop and place his hands over his head. The officer frisked Quarles and discovered an empty shoulder holster. After handcuffing Quarles, the officer asked him where the gun was. Quarles nodded in the direction of some empty cartons and responded, "the gun is over there." The gun was retrieved from the cartons and Quarles was placed under arrest and read his *Miranda* warnings. Quarles indicated that he would answer questions without an attorney present and admitted that he owned the gun.

ISSUE: Were the suspect's initial statements and the gun admissible in evidence despite the failure of the officer to give him the *Miranda* warnings prior to asking questions that led to the discovery of the gun? YES.

SUPREME COURT DECISION: Responses to questions asked by a police officer that are reasonably prompted by concern for public safety are admissible in court even though the suspect was in police custody and was not given the *Miranda* warnings.

REASON: "We hold that on these facts there is a 'public safety' exception to the requirement that *Miranda* warnings be given before a suspect's answers may be admitted into evidence, and that the availability of that exception does not depend upon the motivation of the individual officers involved. In a kaleidoscopic situation such as the one confronting these officers, where spontaneity rather than adherence to a police manual is necessarily the order of the day, the application of the exception which we recognize today should not be made to depend on *post hoc* findings at a suppression hearing concerning the subjective motivation of the arresting officer. Undoubtedly most police officers, if placed in Officer Kraft's position, would act out of a host of different, instinctive, and largely unverifiable motives—their own safety, the safety of others, and perhaps as well the desire to obtain incriminating evidence from the suspect."

CASE SIGNIFICANCE: *New York v. Quarles* carves out a "public safety" exception to the *Miranda* rule. The Supreme Court said that the case presents a situation in which concern for public safety must be paramount to adherence to the literal language of the rules enunciated in *Miranda*. Here, although Quarles was in police custody and therefore should have been given the *Miranda* warnings, concern for public safety prevailed. In this case, said the Court, the gun was concealed somewhere in the supermarket and therefore posed more than one danger to the public. The Court hinted, however, that the "public safety" exception needs to be interpreted narrowly and added that police officers can and will distinguish almost instinctively between questions necessary to secure their own safety or the safety of the public and questions designed solely to elicit testimony evidence from a suspect. Whether the police will be able to do this remains to be seen.

Oregon v. Elstad
470 U.S. 298 (1985)

CAPSULE: A confession made after proper *Miranda* warnings and waiver of rights is admissible even if the police obtained an earlier voluntary but unwarned admission from the suspect.

FACTS: Officers went to a burglary suspect's home with a warrant for his arrest. Elstad's mother answered the door and led the officers to her son's room. One officer waited with Elstad while the other explained his arrest to the mother. The officer told Elstad that he was implicated in the burglary, to which he responded "Yes, I was there." Elstad was then taken to the police station where he was advised of his *Miranda* rights for the first time. Elstad indicated that he understood his rights and wanted to talk to the officers. He then made a full statement that was typed, reviewed, and read back to Elstad for corrections, then signed by the officer and Elstad. Elstad was charged with and convicted of first degree burglary.

ISSUE: Do voluntary but unwarned statements made prior to *Miranda* warnings render all subsequent statements inadmissible under the Fifth Amendment's protection from self-incrimination? NO.

SUPREME COURT DECISION: If a confession is made after proper *Miranda* warnings and waiver of rights, the Fifth Amendment does not make it inadmissible solely because the police obtained an earlier voluntary but unwarned admission from the suspect.

REASON: "Far from establishing a rigid rule, we direct courts to avoid one; there is no warrant for presuming coercive effect where the suspect's initial inculpatory statement, though technically in violation of *Miranda*, was voluntary. The relevant inquiry is whether, in fact, the second statement was also made voluntarily. As in any such inquiry, the finder of fact must examine the surrounding circumstances and the entire course of police conduct with respect to the suspect in evaluating the voluntariness of his statements. The fact that a suspect chooses to speak after being informed of his rights is, of course, highly probative. We find that the dictates of *Miranda* and the goals of the Fifth Amendment proscription against use of compelled testimony are fully satisfied in the circumstances of this case by barring the use of the unwarned statement in the case in chief. No further purpose is served by imputing 'taint' to subsequent statements obtained pursuant to a voluntary and knowing waiver."

CASE SIGNIFICANCE: This case partly weakens the *Miranda* doctrine by holding that "a suspect who has once responded to unwarned yet noncoercive questioning is not thereby disabled from waiving his or her rights and confessing after he or she has been given the requisite *Miranda* warnings." The suspect in this case alleged that the "statement he made in response to questioning at his house (without *Miranda* warnings) 'let the cat out of the bag,' . . . and tainted the subsequent confessions as 'fruit of the poisonous tree.'" In most cases, the courts have held that any evidence obtained as a result of an illegal act by the police is inadmissible in court because it is, indeed, fruit of the poisonous tree. Such was not the case here, however, because, while the statement, "Yes, I was there," from Elstad was inadmissible because it was in response to a police question asked before the *Miranda* warnings were given, such an act by the police was not, in itself, illegal. As long as subsequent facts prove that the second statement, after *Miranda* warnings were given, was valid, the fact that no warnings were given earlier does not render the second statement inadmissible. The police should note, however, that the rule still holds that if the police commit an illegal act, any evidence obtained as a result of that illegal act is inadmissible as "fruit of the poisonous tree."

Colorado v. Connelly
479 U.S. 157 (1986)

CAPSULE: Statements made when the mental state of the defendant interfered with his "rational intellect" and "free will" are not automatically excludable. Their admissibility is governed by state rules of evidence.

FACTS: Connelly approached a uniformed Denver police officer and confessed that he had murdered someone in Denver in 1982 and wanted to talk to the officer about it. The officer advised Connelly of his *Miranda* rights. Connelly indicated that he understood his rights and wanted to talk about the murder. After a homicide detective arrived, Connelly was again advised of his *Miranda* rights and again indicated that he understood them and still wanted to speak with the police. Connelly was then taken to the police station, where he told officers that he had come from Boston to confess to the murder. He made a full statement of the facts, and agreed to take the officers to the scene of the murder. When he became visibly disoriented, he was sent to a state hospital where, in an interview with a psychiatrist, Connelly revealed that he was following the advice of God in confessing to the murder. He was found incompetent to assist in his own defense but competent to stand trial.

ISSUE: Is a suspect's waiver of the *Miranda* rights that is not fully rational (because he was allegedly "following the advice of God") valid? YES.

SUPREME COURT DECISION: The admissibility of statements made when the mental state of the defendant interfered with his "rational intellect" and "free will" is governed by state rules of evidence rather than previous Supreme Court decisions regarding coerced confessions and the *Miranda* waivers. Such evidence therefore is not automatically excluded; its admissibility instead depends upon state rules.

REASON: "We have . . . observed that 'jurists and scholars have recognized that the exclusionary rule imposes a substantial cost on the societal interest in law enforcement by its proscription of what concededly is relevant evidence.' . . . Moreover, suppressing respondent's statements would serve absolutely no purpose in enforcing constitutional guarantees. The purpose of excluding evidence seized in violation of the Constitution is to substantially deter future violations of the Constitution. . . . Only if we were to establish a brand new constitutional right—the right of a criminal defendant to confess to his crime only when totally rational and properly motivated—could respondent's present claim be sustained."

CASE SIGNIFICANCE: The Supreme Court indicated in this case that confessions and admissions are involuntary and invalid under the Constitution only if coercive police activity is involved. If the waiver is caused by anything other than police behavior, admissibility of the confession should depend on the state's rules of evidence. It is clear in this case that the *Miranda* warnings were repeatedly given and that there was a waiver. Such waiver, however, was later challenged as involuntary because it was promoted by a "voice of God." The Court said that this was not sufficient to render the waiver involuntary because the police did not act improperly or illegally. As long as police behavior is legal, a waiver is considered voluntary under the Constitution and its admissibility is governed by state law. This means that if state law allows its admissibility, such evidence can be used.

Colorado v. Spring
479 U.S. 564 (1987)

CAPSULE: The waiver of *Miranda* rights is valid even if the suspect believes that the interrogation will focus on minor crimes but the police later shift the questioning to cover a different and more serious crime.

FACTS: Spring and a companion shot and killed a man during a hunting trip in Denver. An informant told federal agents that Spring was engaged in interstate trafficking in stolen firearms and that he had participated in the murder. Pursuant to that information, agents set up an undercover operation and arrested Spring in Kansas City. Agents advised Spring of his *Miranda* rights upon arrest. At the agent's office, Spring was again advised of his *Miranda* rights and signed a statement that he understood and waived his rights. Agents then asked Spring about his involvement in the firearms transactions leading to his arrest. He was also asked if he had ever shot a man, to which he responded affirmatively, but denied the shooting in question. Thereafter, Colorado officials questioned Spring. He was again read his *Miranda* warnings and again signed a statement asserting that he understood and waived his rights. This time, Spring confessed to the Colorado murder. A written statement of his confession was prepared, which Spring read, edited, and signed. Spring was charged with and convicted of first degree murder.

ISSUE: Must a suspect be informed of all crimes of which he or she is to be questioned before there can be a valid waiver of the Fifth Amendment privilege against self-incrimination? NO.

SUPREME COURT DECISION: A suspect's waiver of *Miranda* rights is valid even if he or she believes that the interrogation will focus on minor crimes but the police shift the questioning to cover a different and more serious crime.

REASON: "Respondent's March 30 decision to waive his Fifth Amendment privilege was voluntary absent evidence that his will was overborne and his capacity for self-determination critically impaired because of coercive police conduct. His waiver was also knowingly and intelligently made, that is, he understood that he had the right to remain silent and that anything he said could be used as evidence against him. The Constitution does not require that a suspect know and understand every possible consequence of a waiver of the Fifth Amendment privilege. Here, there was no allegation that respondent failed to understand that privilege or that he misunderstood the consequences of speaking freely."

CASE SIGNIFICANCE: The confession was held valid in this case because there was no deception or misrepresentation by the police in obtaining the confession. Here, the police first questioned Spring about firearms transactions (a lesser offense) and, after he incriminated himself on these, the police asked him about a more serious offense, the murder, and Spring again incriminated himself. Spring, in challenging the validity of the waiver, felt that he should have been informed first of the offense for which he would be interrogated. The Court said that the police did not have to do so as long as there was no intention on the part of the police to mislead or deceive Spring. The principle is that a valid waiver of the *Miranda* rights allows the police to ask questions of the suspect about any crime as long as the interrogation does not involve misrepresentation or deception. There is no need to repeat the *Miranda* warnings if the suspect is asked about a different crime.

Connecticut v. Barrett
479 U.S. 523 (1987)

CAPSULE: A suspect's oral confession is admissible even if the suspect tells the police that he or she will not make a written statement without a lawyer present.

FACTS: Barrett was arrested in connection with a sexual assault. Upon arrival at the police station, Barrett was advised of his *Miranda* rights and signed a statement acknowledging the understanding of his rights. Barrett stated that he would not give a written statement in the absence of counsel, but that he would talk to the police about the incident. In two subsequent interrogations, Barrett was again advised of his rights and signed a statement of understanding. On both occasions he gave an oral statement admitting his involvement in the assault but refused to make a written statement. Because of a malfunction in the tape recorder, an officer reduced the confession to writing based on his recollection of the conversation. Barrett was charged with and convicted of sexual assault.

ISSUE: Is there a valid waiver of the *Miranda* rights if a defendant requests assistance of counsel and refuses to make written statements, but makes oral statements voluntarily to the police? YES.

SUPREME COURT DECISION: The oral confession made by a suspect is admissible as evidence in court even if the suspect tells the police that he would talk with them but would not make a written statement without a lawyer present. The waiver of *Miranda* rights by Barrett is valid because he was not "threatened, tricked, or cajoled" into speaking to the police.

REASON: "Respondent's statements to the police made it clear his willingness to talk about the sexual assault, and, there being no evidence that he was 'threatened, tricked, or cajoled' into speaking to the police, the trial court properly found that his decision to do so constituted a voluntary waiver of his right to counsel. Although the *Miranda* rules were designed to protect defendants from being compelled by the government to make statements, they also gave defendants the right to choose between speech and silence."

"Respondent's invocation of his right to counsel was limited by its terms to the making of written statements, and did not prohibit all further discussions with the police. Requests for counsel must be given broad, all-inclusive effect only when the defendant's words, understood as ordinary people would understand them, are ambiguous. Here, respondent clearly and unequivocally expressed his willingness to speak to police after the sexual assault."

CASE SIGNIFICANCE: The issue in this case was the validity of the waiver of *Miranda* rights. The defendant told the police that he would talk with them, but would not make a written statement without a lawyer present. Ordinarily, a waiver is unconditional; here, the waiver was conditional in that the suspect did agree to make oral statements without a lawyer present. He later challenged his incriminating oral statements as inadmissible because he had asked for a lawyer, even though he agreed to make an oral statement. The Supreme Court rejected the challenge, saying that the sole test for the admissibility of an oral confession was voluntariness. There was a voluntary waiver of rights here, although the defendant refused to make a written statement. What this case tells the police is that the waiver of rights does not have to be complete or unconditional to be valid. Refusal to have a statement in writing does not make a confession inadmissible, as long as the police can establish that the *Miranda* warnings were given and the waiver was intelligent and voluntary.

Patterson v. Illinois
487 U.S. 285 (1988)

CAPSULE: A valid waiver after the *Miranda* warnings constitutes a waiver of the right to counsel as well as the privilege against self-incrimination.

FACTS: After being informed by the police that he had been charged with murder, Patterson, who was in police custody, twice indicated his willingness to discuss the crime with the authorities. He was interrogated twice, and on both occasions was read a form waiving his *Miranda* rights. He initialed each of the five specific warnings on the form and then signed it. He then gave incriminating statements to the police about his participation in the crime. He was tried and convicted of murder.

ISSUE: Is a waiver of rights after the *Miranda* warnings a waiver of the Sixth Amendment right to counsel as well as a waiver of the Fifth Amendment privilege against self-incrimination? YES.

SUPREME COURT DECISION: A defendant who has been given the *Miranda* warnings has been sufficiently made aware of the Sixth Amendment right to counsel so that any waiver of that right is valid if it is a knowing and intelligent waiver.

REASON: "This Court has never adopted petitioner's suggestion that the Sixth Amendment right to counsel is 'superior' to or 'more difficult' to waive than its Fifth Amendment counterpart. Rather, in Sixth Amendment cases, the court has defined the scope of the right to counsel by a pragmatic assessment of the usefulness of counsel to the accused at the particular stage of the proceedings in question, and the dangers to the accused of proceedings without counsel at that stage. . . . *Miranda* warnings are sufficient for this purpose in post-indictment questioning context, because, at that stage, the role of counsel is relatively simple and limited, and the dangers and disadvantages of self-representation are less substantial and more obvious to an accused than they are at trial."

CASE SIGNIFICANCE: Many police officers believe that *Miranda v. Arizona* is a right to counsel case. It is not. Instead, it is a right against self-incrimination case, meaning that the main reason *Miranda* warnings must be given by the police is because these warnings protect a suspect's right against self-incrimination. The statement that "you have the right to a lawyer" is given primarily because a lawyer can help protect a suspect's self-incrimination privilege. In this case, Patterson conceded that he validly waived his Fifth Amendment right when he signed the waiver, but asserted that such waiver did not mean a waiver of his Sixth Amendment right to counsel, a right given the accused after charges are filed, as they were in this case. In essence, Patterson maintained that he ought to have been specifically informed of his right to counsel (apart from the *Miranda* warnings) and that there must be a separate waiver for that right. The Court disagreed, saying that the *Miranda* warnings were sufficient to inform Patterson of both rights and that his statements were, therefore, admissible in evidence.

Duckworth v. Eagan
492 U.S. 195 (1989)

CAPSULE: The *Miranda* warnings need not be given in the exact form as worded in *Miranda v. Arizona*; what is needed is that they simply convey to the suspect his or her rights.

FACTS: Duckworth, when first questioned by Indiana police in connection with a stabbing, made incriminating statements after having signed a waiver form that provided, among other things, that if he could not afford a lawyer, one would be appointed for him "if and when you go to court." Twenty-nine hours later, he was interrogated again and signed a different waiver form. He confessed to the stabbing and led officers to a site where they recovered relevant physical evidence. Over respondent's objection, his two statements were admitted into evidence at trial. Duckworth was charged with and convicted of attempted murder. He challenged his confession as inadmissible, saying that the first waiver form did not comply with the requirements of *Miranda*; therefore, his confessions were not admissible.

ISSUE: Was the waiver form used by the police in this case (which informed the suspect that an attorney would be appointed for him "if and when you go to court") sufficient to comply with the requirements of *Miranda v. Arizona*? YES.

SUPREME COURT DECISION: The *Miranda* warnings need not be given in the exact form as outlined in the case; they must simply convey to the suspect his or her rights. The initial warning given to Duckworth in this case, namely: the right to remain silent, that anything said could be used against him in court, that he had the right to talk to a lawyer for advice before and during questioning even if he could not afford to hire one, that he had the right to stop answering questions at any time until he talked to a lawyer, and that the police could not provide him with a lawyer, but one would be appointed for him, "if and when you go to court," complied with all the requirements of the *Miranda* case. The evidence obtained was, therefore, admissible.

REASON: "We think it must be relatively commonplace for a suspect, after receiving *Miranda* warnings, to ask *when* he will obtain counsel. The 'if and when you go to court' advice simply anticipates the question. Second, *Miranda* does not require that attorneys be producible on call, but only that the suspect be informed, as here, that he has the right to an attorney before and during questioning, and that an attorney would be appointed for him if he could not afford one. The Court in *Miranda* emphasized that it was not suggesting that 'each police station must have a "stationhouse lawyer"' present at all times to advise prisoners.' If the police cannot provide appointed counsel, *Miranda* requires only that the police not question a suspect unless he waives his right to counsel. Here, respondent did just that."

CASE SIGNIFICANCE: This case clarifies two unclear points in the *Miranda* case. First, must the police use the exact wording in the *Miranda* decision to warn a suspect of his or her rights? The Court said no. It is sufficient that the warnings, however worded, "reasonably convey to a suspect his rights." Note, however, that although the warnings need not be adopted verbatim from the *Miranda* case, the substance of the warnings, as indicated above, must be conveyed to the suspect. The second point addresses whether the police must immediately produce a lawyer if a suspect asks for one. The Court also said no. There is no requirement that the police produce a lawyer on call. The police need to inform the suspect that he or she has the right to an attorney and to an appointed attorney if he or she cannot afford one. If the suspect wants a lawyer and the police cannot immediately provide one, the interrogation simply stops; there is no obligation to provide a lawyer immediately. If the interrogation continues, however, any evidence obtained cannot be used in court.

Pennsylvania v. Muniz
496 U.S. 582 (1990)

CAPSULE: The police may validly ask routine questions of persons suspected of driving while intoxicated and videotape their responses without giving them the *Miranda* warnings.

FACTS: An officer stopped Muniz's vehicle and directed him to perform three standard field tests. Muniz performed these tests poorly and informed the officer that he failed the tests because he had been drinking. The officer then arrested Muniz and took him into custody. After informing him that his actions and voice would be videotaped, Muniz was processed through procedures for receiving persons suspected of driving while intoxicated. Without being given his *Miranda* warnings, he was asked seven questions regarding his name, address, height, weight, eye color, date of birth, and age. He was also asked, and was unable to give, the date of his sixth birthday.

An officer directed Muniz to perform each of the sobriety tests he had performed during the initial stop, which he again completed poorly. While performing these tests, Muniz attempted to explain his difficulties in completing the tasks and often requested further instruction on the tests.

An officer then asked Muniz to submit to a Breathalyzer test and read him the law regarding sanctions for failing or refusing the test. After asking several questions and commenting on his state of inebriation, Muniz refused to submit to the test. At this point, Muniz was read his *Miranda* warnings for the first time. He then waived his rights and admitted in further questioning that he had been driving while intoxicated. The evidence obtained by the police in the form of Muniz's responses and the videotape of Muniz's performance during booking was submitted into court over his objection and he was convicted of driving under the influence of alcohol.

ISSUE: Do the police need to give drunk driving suspects the *Miranda* warnings when asking routine questions and videotaping the proceeding? NO.

SUPREME COURT DECISION: The police may ask persons suspected of driving while intoxicated routine questions and videotape their responses without giving *Miranda* warnings. The questions and videotape do not elicit testimonial responses that are protected by the Fifth Amendment.

REASON: "The privilege against self-incrimination protects an 'accused from being compelled to testify against himself, or otherwise provide the state with evidence of a testimonial or communicative nature,' but not from being compelled by the state to produce 'real or physical evidence.' To be testimonial, the communication must, explicitly or implicitly, relate to a factual assertion or disclose information."

"Muniz's answers to direct questions are not rendered inadmissible by *Miranda* merely because the slurred nature of his speech was incriminating. Requiring a suspect to reveal the physical manner in which he articulates words, like requiring him to reveal the physical properties of the sound of his voice, by reading a transcript, does not, without more, compel him to provide a 'testimonial' response for the purposes of the privilege."

"However, Muniz's response to the sixth birthday question was incriminating not just because of his delivery, but because the content of his answer supported an inference that his mental state was confused. His response was testimonial because he was required to communicate an expressed or implied assertion of the fact or belief and, thus, was confronted with the 'trilemma' of truth, falsity, or silence, the historical abuse against which the privilege against self-incrimination was aimed."

CASE SIGNIFICANCE: This case aids the police in obtaining evidence for prosecutions in drunk driving cases. Another case, decided by the Court a few days earlier, holds that sobriety checkpoints in which the police stop every vehicle do not violate the Constitution (*Michigan Department of State Police v. Sitz*, 496 U.S. 444 [1990]). Within a week's time, the Court gave the police a virtual one-two punch in DWI cases.

This case holds that the police may ask questions of a drunk driving suspect and videotape the whole proceeding without giving the suspect the *Miranda* warnings. This case, however, addresses only "routine" questions (namely: eye color, date of birth, and current age). Questions that are not routine were not addressed in this case. The fact that the answers to the seven questions were slurred and therefore incriminating did not render the evidence inadmissible.

Four justices who voted with the majority said that this decision constitutes a new exception to the *Miranda* rule, and that this routine booking exception is justified because the questions asked are not intended to obtain information for investigatory purposes. Four other justices, however, said that the *Miranda* rule simply did not apply to such questions and therefore did not consider the ruling an exception to the *Miranda* rule. Despite this disagreement, the fact remains that, when asking routine questions, the *Miranda* warnings need not be given and the videotaping of the proceedings is constitutional.

From the perspective of police officers, this case means that they now have greater leeway in handling DWI cases. From a legal perspective, however, the main issue is what kind of self-incriminating evidence is admissible in court. The rule is that the Fifth Amendment prohibition against self-incrimination (which is protected by the *Miranda* rule) prohibits only testimonial or communicative self-incrimination and does not prohibit physical self-incrimination. The asking of routine questions, the answers to which were slurred, and the videotaping of the proceedings were self-incriminatory, but such incrimination was physical; the *Miranda* warnings were, therefore, not needed and the evidence was admissible in court. Note, however, that Muniz's answer to the question about the date of his sixth birthday was excluded because "the content of his answer supported the inference that his mental state was confused." In sum, if the evidence obtained was *physical* instead of *mental* in nature, the evidence was admissible in court, even without the *Miranda* warnings being given.

McNeil v. Wisconsin
501 U.S. 171 (1991)

CAPSULE: An accused's request for a lawyer at a bail hearing after being charged with an offense does not constitute an invocation of the Fifth Amendment right to counsel under *Miranda* for other offenses for which the accused has not yet been charged.

FACTS: McNeil was arrested in Omaha, Nebraska pursuant to a warrant charging him with an armed robbery in a suburb of Milwaukee, Wisconsin.

In that case, McNeil asked for and was represented by a public defender at a bail hearing for that offense. While in detention because of that charge, he was asked by the police about a murder and related crimes in a nearby town. McNeil was advised of his *Miranda* rights; he signed forms waiving them and then made statements incriminating himself in those crimes. Over the next four days, McNeil was interviewed twice more, each time being read his *Miranda* warnings and signing statements that he waived his rights. Ultimately, McNeil confessed to the murder, attempted murder, and armed burglary. McNeil sought to suppress his confession, saying that his request for a lawyer during the bail hearing for the armed robbery charge constituted an invocation of his *Miranda* rights, thus precluding any further police interrogation.

ISSUE: Does an accused's request for counsel at a bail hearing constitute an invocation of his Fifth Amendment right to counsel under *Miranda* for other unrelated offenses for which he had not yet been charged? NO.

SUPREME COURT DECISION: An accused's request for a lawyer at a bail hearing, after being charged with an offense, does not constitute an invocation of the Fifth Amendment right to counsel under *Miranda* for other offenses for which he had not yet been charged.

REASON: "In *Michigan v. Jackson*, 475 U.S. 625 (1986) we held that once this right to counsel has attached and has been invoked, any subsequent waiver during a police-initiated custodial interview is ineffective. . . . In *Edwards v. Arizona*, 451 U.S. 477 (1981), we established a second layer of prophylaxis for the *Miranda* right to counsel: once a suspect asserts the right, not only must the current interrogation cease, but he may not be approached for further interrogation until counsel has been made available to him. . . . The *Edwards* rule, moreover, is not offense-specific: once a suspect invokes the *Miranda* right to counsel for interrogation regarding one offense, he may not be reapproached regarding any offense unless counsel is present. . . . The Sixth Amendment right, however, is offense-specific. It cannot be invoked once for all future prosecutions, for it does not attach until a prosecution is commenced. . . . To exclude evidence pertaining to charges as to which the Sixth Amendment right to counsel had not attached at the time the evidence was obtained, simply because other charges were pending at that time, would unnecessarily frustrate the public's interest in the investigation of criminal activities." [Citations omitted.]

CASE SIGNIFICANCE: In several decisions that followed *Miranda v. Arizona*, the Supreme Court strengthened *Miranda* by holding that once a person has invoked his or her right to counsel, the person could not be subjected to any further police-initiated questioning for any crime (*Edwards v. Arizona*) and unless counsel is present (*Minnick v. Mississippi*). This case is slightly different in that the accused maintained that when he invoked the right to counsel during a bail hearing for armed robbery, he was in effect also invoking his *Miranda* rights for the other offenses with which he had not yet been charged; therefore, police interrogation for the other offenses could not take place. The Court disagreed, saying that his invocation of *Miranda* during that bail hearing did not apply to the other cases with which he had not yet been charged, particularly because he voluntarily waived his *Miranda* rights when interrogated by the police concerning those cases. The Court said that "requesting the assistance of an attorney at a bail hearing does not satisfy the minimum requirement of some statements that can reasonably be construed as an expression of a desire for counsel in dealing with custodial interrogation by the police." In other words, the request for counsel at a bail hearing is different from a request for counsel when being interrogated by the police for a crime.

Davis v. United States
512 U.S. 452 (1994)

CAPSULE: After a knowing and voluntary waiver of *Miranda* rights, law enforcement officers may continue questioning until and unless the suspect clearly requests an attorney.

FACTS: Davis and Keith Shackleford were playing pool on October 2, 1988. Shackleford lost a game and a $30 wager but refused to pay. Shackleford was later beaten to death with a pool cue. An investigation into the murder revealed Davis' presence on the evening of the murder and that he was absent without authorization from his Naval duty station the next morning. The investigation also found that only privately owned pool cues could be taken from the club and that Davis had two of them, one of which was subsequently found to have a blood stain on it. Investigative agents were told by others that Davis had either admitted committing the murder or had recounted details that clearly indicated his involvement. On November 4, 1988, Davis was interviewed by Naval Investigative Service agents. As required by military law, the agents advised Davis that he was a suspect, that he was not required to make a statement, that any statement made could be used against him at a trial, and that he was entitled to speak to an attorney and to have the attorney present during questioning. Davis waived his rights to remain silent and to counsel both orally and in writing. An hour and a half into the interview, Davis stated "Maybe I should talk to a lawyer." When agents inquired if Davis was asking for an attorney, he replied that he was not. After a short break, agents reminded Davis of his rights and the interview continued. After another hour, Davis said "I think I want a lawyer before I say anything else." At that time, questioning ceased. At his court-martial hearing, a motion to suppress the statements obtained prior to requesting an attorney was denied and Davis was convicted of murder.

ISSUE: After a knowing and voluntary waiver of the *Miranda* rights, does a suspect's statement during custodial interrogation that does not qualify as an unambiguous invocation of the right to counsel require officers to cease questioning? NO.

SUPREME COURT DECISION: "Invocation of the *Miranda* [*v. Arizona*, 384 U.S. 436, (1966)] right to counsel 'requires, at a minimum, some statement that can reasonably be construed to be an expression of a desire for the assistance of an attorney.' *McNeil v. Wisconsin*, 501 U.S. 171 (1991) at 178. But if a suspect makes a reference to an attorney that is ambiguous or equivocal in that a reasonable officer in light of the circumstances would have understood only that the suspect *might* be invoking the right to counsel, our precedents do not require the cessation of questioning."

REASON: "The rationale underlying *Edwards* [*v. Arizona*, 451 U.S. 477 (1981)] is that the police must respect a suspect's wishes regarding his right to have an attorney present during custodial interrogation. But when the officers conducting the questioning reasonably do not know whether or not the suspect wants a lawyer, a rule requiring the immediate cessation of questioning 'would transform the *Miranda* safeguards into wholly irrational obstacles to legitimate police investigative activity' *Michigan v. Mosley*, 423 U.S. 96, 102 (1975) . . ."

CASE SIGNIFICANCE: This 5 to 4 decision by the Court represents a modification of the *Edwards* rule. The *Edwards* case stated that once a suspect asks for a lawyer, questioning by the police must cease. In this case, the suspect argued that the statement, "Maybe I should talk to a lawyer" constituted an invocation of the right to a lawyer under *Miranda*, hence police interrogation should have stopped. The Court disagreed, saying that the statement was an ambiguous request for counsel and therefore did not trigger the protections under *Edwards* or *Miranda*. Had the request been unambiguous to a reasonable investigator, the result would have been different. A statement such as, "I want a lawyer before I say anything else," would likely have been considered an unambiguous request. That the case was decided on such a close vote indicates that the other justices did not think that the preceding phrase, "Maybe . . ." made all that difference in the tone of the request. This case holds that the request for the right to counsel must be clear and unambiguous (as judged from the perspective of a reasonable interrogator) where there was a previous valid and intelligent waiver, before the *Edwards* rule applies.

United States v. Patane
542 U.S. 630 (2004)

CAPSULE: Failure to give a suspect the *Miranda* warnings does not require suppression of the physical fruits of the suspect's unwarned but voluntary statements.

FACTS: Patane was arrested for harassing his ex-girlfriend. He was released on bond, subject to a restraining order that prohibited him from contacting her. Patane violated the restraining order by contacting his ex-girlfriend by phone. An officer investigating the matter was provided information by a probation officer that Patane illegally possessed a pistol. The officer went to Patane's home and inquired about his attempts to contact his girlfriend. The officer then arrested Patane for violating the restraining order. When another officer attempted to read Patane his *Miranda* warnings, Patane interrupted and said he knew his rights. Neither officer attempted to further warn Patane about his Miranda rights. The officer then asked Patane about the pistol. Patane was initially reluctant to discuss the matter, but upon the officer's insistence told him where the pistol was located. He then gave the officer permission to retrieve the pistol and it was seized by the officer. Patane was arrested for being a felon in possession of a firearm.

ISSUE: Does the failure to give a suspect the *Miranda* warnings require suppression of the physical fruits of the unwarned but voluntary statements? NO.

SUPREME COURT DECISION: Failure to give a suspect the *Miranda* warnings does not require suppression of the physical fruits of the suspect's unwarned but voluntary statements.

REASON: The Court based its ruling on three foundations: the relationship between the self-incrimination clause and physical evidence, the requirement to provide *Miranda* warnings for physical evidence, and the relationship to the exclusionary rule.

On the self-incrimination clause, the Court stated, ". . . the *Miranda* rule is a prophylactic employed to protect against violation of the Self-Incrimination Clause. The Self-Incrimination Clause, however, is not implicated by the admission into evidence of the physical fruit of a voluntary statement. . . . The core protections afforded by the Self-Incrimination Clause is a prohibition on compelling a criminal defendant to testify against himself at trial." The court in *Elstad*, upon which Patane partially based his arguments, agreed that the Fifth Amendment was not concerned with non-testimonial evidence.

Even if this were so, the Court stated that "[o]ur cases make clear the related point that a mere failure to give *Miranda* warning does not, by itself, violate a suspect's constitutional rights or even the *Miranda* rule. . . . And although it is true that the Court requires the exclusion of the physical fruit of actually coerced statements, it must be remembered that statements taken without sufficient *Miranda* warnings are presumed to have been coerced only for certain purposes and then only when necessary to protect the privilege against self-incrimination. . . . It follows that police do not violate a suspect's constitutional rights (or the *Miranda* rule) by negligent or even deliberate failures to provide the suspect with the full panoply of warnings prescribed by *Miranda*. Potential violations occur, if at al, only upon the admission of unwarned statements into evidence at trial. And at this point, 'the exclusions of unwarned statements . . . is a complete and sufficient remedy' for any perceived *Miranda* violation. . . . Finally, nothing in *Dickerson*, including its characterization of *Miranda* as announcing a constitutional rule, 530 U.S., at 444, changes any of these observations."

Turning to the exclusionary rule, the Court reiterated that the exclusionary rule was created to control police conduct. The court noted that the *Miranda* rule is not aimed at police conduct, and police do not violate the Constitution by mere failure to warn. "Thus, unlike unreasonable searches under the Fourth Amendment or actual violation of the Due Process clause or the Self-Incrimination Clause, there is, with respect to mere failures to warn, nothing to deter. There is therefore no reason to apply the 'fruit of the poisonous tree' doctrine of *Wong Sun*, 371 U.S., at 448."

CASE SIGNIFICANCE: This case involved the suppression of physical, not testimonial, evidence obtained without the suspect being given the *Miranda* warnings. It did not involved the admissibility of statements or confessions obtained without the *Miranda* warnings (as is the issue in most *Miranda* cases); instead, it focused on the admissibility of the pistol that was obtained without the suspect being given the *Miranda* warnings and after he had asserted that he knew his rights. The Court held that the physical evidence obtained was admissible on the grounds that it did not violate the constitutional guarantee against self-incrimination because the evidence involved was physical, not testimonial (spoken). Neither was there any need to apply the "fruit of the poisonous tree" doctrine (which holds that evidence obtained from other evidence illegally obtained is not admissible in court) because the "fruit of the poisonous tree" doctrine involves a violation of the Fourth Amendment protection against unreasonable searches and seizures and is unrelated to the *Miranda* rule, which was the issue in this case.

What Constitutes Interrogation for *Miranda* Purposes? 16

Introduction

The *Miranda* warnings must be given whenever there is a "custodial interrogation." *Custodial* means that the person is under arrest or is deprived of freedom in a significant way. *Interrogation* means that the suspect is asked questions by the police that tend to link the suspect to a crime.

There are instances in which the police must give the *Miranda* warnings even if no actual interrogation or questioning takes place. The case that set this rule is *Brewer v. Williams*, 430 U.S. 387 (1977), more commonly known as the "Christian burial" case. In that case, the Supreme Court ruled that the police must give the *Miranda* warnings even if no questioning takes place if the behavior of the police constitutes the functional equivalent of an interrogation, meaning that the behavior is likely to elicit a confession even in the absence of questioning.

In *Brewer*, the officers gave the suspect the "Christian burial" speech in which the officer called the suspect "Reverend" and indicated that the parents of the missing girl ought to have the opportunity to give a Christian burial to their child, who had been kidnapped on Christmas Eve. The suspect then confessed. The Court said that, although there was no actual interrogation, the police officers' behavior amounted to the "functional equivalent" of an interrogation because it was likely to elicit a confession.

No other Supreme Court case has directly applied the functional equivalent test. Instead, the Court has held in two subsequent cases that the following instances did not constitute the functional equivalent of an interrogation:

1. When officers, who had the suspect in the backseat of the car, talked between themselves about how terrible it would be if one of the handicapped students from a school near the crime scene were to find a loaded shotgun (supposedly the weapon used in the shotgun robbery of a taxicab driver) and get hurt. This led the suspect to interrupt the police and tell them the location of the shotgun; and

2. When the police recorded a conversation, in the presence of an officer, between a suspect and his wife.

In sum, interrogation takes place when the police ask questions of a suspect that tend to link him or her to a crime. There are instances, however, when the *Miranda* warnings must be given even if the police are not asking questions of a suspect, as illustrated in the *Williams* case. Because this case has not been used by the Court in any other case it has thus far decided, its effect as an exception to the interrogation requirement is minimal.

The leading cases briefed in this chapter on custodial interrogation for *Miranda* purposes are *Brewer v. Williams* and *Rhode Island v. Innis*.

Brewer v. Williams
430 U.S. 387 (1977)

CAPSULE: Under the *Miranda* rule, interrogations can be "actual" (as when questions are asked) or the "functional equivalent" thereof.

FACTS: The day before Christmas, a ten-year-old girl disappeared from a YMCA building in Des Moines, Iowa. A short time later, Williams, an escapee from a mental hospital and a religious person, was seen leaving the YMCA with a large bundle wrapped in a blanket. A 14-year-old boy who helped him carry the bundle reported that he had seen "two legs in it and they were skinny and white." Williams' car was found the next day 160 miles east of Des Moines. Items of clothing belonging to the missing child and a blanket like the one used to wrap the bundle were found at a rest stop between the YMCA in Des Moines and Davenport, where the car was found. Assuming that the girl's body could be found between the YMCA and the car, a massive search was conducted. Meanwhile, Williams was arrested by police in Davenport and was arraigned. Williams' counsel was informed by the police that Williams would be returned to Des Moines without being interrogated. During the trip, an officer began a conversation with Williams in which he said that the girl ought to be given a Christian burial before a snowstorm, which might prevent the body from being found. As Williams and the officer neared the town where the body was hidden, Williams agreed to take the officer to the child's body. The body was found about two miles from one of the search teams. At the trial, a motion to suppress the evidence was denied and Williams was convicted of first-degree murder.

ISSUE: Was what the police did in talking to Williams about a "Christian burial" equivalent to interrogating a suspect without giving him his right to counsel? YES.

SUPREME COURT DECISION: Interrogation takes place, not only when direct questions are asked, but also when, as in this case, the police officers, knowing the defendant's religious interest, make remarks designed to appeal to that interest and therefore induce a confession. In this case, the police officer's "Christian burial" speech was equivalent to an interrogation; therefore, Williams was entitled to the assistance of counsel at that time.

REASON: "There can be no serious doubt . . . that Detective Leaming deliberately and designedly set out to elicit information from Williams just as surely as—and perhaps more effectively than—if he had formally interrogated him. Detective Leaming was fully aware before departing from Des Moines that Williams was being represented in Davenport by [lawyer] Kelly and in Des Moines by [lawyer] McKnight. Yet he purposely sought during

Williams' isolation from his lawyers to obtain as much information as possible. Indeed Detective Leaming conceded as much when he testified at Williams' trial."

CASE SIGNIFICANCE: There are two important principles for the police in this case. The first is that once a suspect has been formally charged with an offense and has a lawyer, he or she should not be interrogated unless there is a valid waiver. The second is that conversations with or appeals to the suspect that may induce a confession constitute an interrogation that then requires both *Miranda* warnings and the right to counsel.

This case declares that "interrogation" by the police does not simply mean asking direct questions. In this case, the police had been told by the lawyers for the suspect that he was not to be interrogated while being transported from Davenport to Des Moines. The police assured the lawyers that Williams would not be interrogated. There was, in fact, no interrogation, but the police officer gave Williams what became known as the "Christian burial speech" in which he addressed Williams as "Reverend" and pleaded that "the parents of this little girl should be entitled to a Christian burial for the little girl who was snatched away from them on Christmas Eve and murdered." The Court said that the speech was the functional equivalent of an interrogation and therefore violated the suspect's right to counsel.

Rhode Island v. Innis
446 U.S. 291 (1980)

CAPSULE: The conversation in this case was merely a dialogue between police officers and did not constitute the "functional equivalent" of an interrogation, hence no *Miranda* warnings were needed.

FACTS: Police arrested Innis for the abduction and killing of a taxicab driver. The officer advised Innis of his *Miranda* rights and did not converse with him. When a sergeant and captain arrived at the scene, Innis was again advised of his *Miranda* rights. He replied that he understood his rights and wanted to speak to an attorney. Innis was placed in a police car to be transported to the police station. En route, two of the officers engaged in a conversation between themselves concerning Innis' shotgun, which had not been recovered. When one of the officers expressed concern that children from a nearby school for the handicapped might find the weapon and hurt themselves, Innis interrupted the conversation, saying that the officers should return to the scene so that he could show them where the shotgun was hidden. Upon returning to the scene, Innis was again advised of his *Miranda* rights. He again stated that he understood his rights but wanted to remove the gun before one of the children found it. He then led the police to the shotgun. Innis was charged with and convicted of robbery, kidnapping, and murder.

ISSUE: Did the conversation between the two police officers that prompted Innis to lead them to the shotgun constitute a custodial interrogation in the absence of his lawyer? NO.

SUPREME COURT DECISION: "Interrogation" refers not only to express questioning, but also the "functional equivalent" of questioning that involves any words or actions by the police that they should know are reasonably likely to elicit an incriminating response. In this instance, no such interrogation occurred—the conversation was merely a dialogue between two police officers; therefore, the evidence obtained by the police was admissible.

REASON: "Here there was no express questioning of respondent; the conversation between the two officers was, at least in form, nothing more than a dialogue between them to which no response from respondent was invited. Moreover, respondent was not subjected to the 'functional equivalent' of questioning since it cannot be said that the officers should have known that their conversation was reasonably likely to elicit an incriminating response from respondent. There is nothing in the record to suggest that the officers were aware that respondent was peculiarly susceptible to an appeal to his conscience concerning the safety of handicapped children, or that the police knew that respondent was unusually disoriented or upset at the time of his arrest. Nor does the record indicate that, in the context of a brief conversation, the officers should have known that respondent would suddenly be moved to make a self-incriminating response."

CASE SIGNIFICANCE: The *Miranda* case says that the *Miranda* warnings must be given whenever a suspect is subjected to "custodial interrogation." Subsequent cases have held that there is interrogation not only if questions are asked of a suspect, but also if police behavior amounts to the "functional equivalent" of actual questioning. An example is *Brewer v. Williams*, 430 U.S. 387 (1977), in which the police officers, knowing the defendant's religious interest, made remarks designed to appeal to that interest and thus induced a confession even without directly asking the suspect questions. What the police did in this case, however, was not the "functional equivalent" of interrogation. As the Court said, "the conversation between the two officers was, at least in form, nothing more than a dialogue between them to which no response from respondent was invited." It is important for police officers to know that "interrogation" does not necessarily mean asking questions of the suspect. There are situations in which the behavior of the police constitutes the "functional equivalent" of an interrogation (as in *Brewer*), but that was not the case here.

Arizona v. Mauro
481 U.S. 520 (1987)

CAPSULE: A conversation between a suspect and his wife, which was recorded in the presence of an officer, did not constitute the "functional equivalent" of an interrogation.

FACTS: The police received a call that a man had just entered a store claiming that he had killed his son. When officers reached the store, Mauro admitted to committing the act and directed officers to the body. He was then arrested and advised of his *Miranda* rights. He was taken to the police station where he was again given the *Miranda* warnings. Mauro told officers that he did not wish to make any more statements until a lawyer was present. At that time, all questioning ceased. Following questioning in another room, Mauro's wife insisted on speaking with him. Police allowed the meeting on the condition that an officer be present and tape the conversation. The tape was used to impeach Mauro's contention that he was insane at the time of the murder. Mauro was charged with and convicted of murder and child abuse.

ISSUE: Does a conversation between a suspect and a spouse that is recorded by an officer constitute an interrogation under *Miranda v. Arizona*? NO.

SUPREME COURT DECISION: A conversation between a suspect and a spouse, which is recorded in the presence of an officer, does not constitute the functional equivalent of an interrogation under *Miranda* or *Innis*. Evidence obtained during the conversation is, therefore, admissible in court.

REASON: "The purpose of *Miranda* . . . is to prevent the government from using the coercive nature of confinement to extract confessions that would not be given in an unrestrained environment. This purpose is not implicated here, since respondent was not subjected to compelling influences, psychological ploys, or direct questioning. There is no evidence that the police allowed the wife to meet with respondent in order to obtain incriminating statements. Moreover, police testimony, which the trial court found credible, indicated a number of legitimate reasons for an officer's presence at the meeting, including the wife's safety and various security considerations. Furthermore, an examination of the situation from respondent's perspective demonstrated the improbability that he would have felt he was being coerced to incriminate himself simply because he was told his wife would be allowed to speak to him."

CASE SIGNIFICANCE: This case further explains the meaning of the term "interrogation" as used in *Miranda*. In an earlier case (*Rhode Island v. Innis*), the Court said that "interrogation" does not have to mean the actual asking of questions by the police; rather, it includes instances that amount to the "functional equivalent" of interrogation, meaning "words or actions by the police which they know are reasonably likely to elicit an incriminating response." The term "functional equivalent" is subjective and difficult to determine. Whatever its meaning may be, what the police did in this case (allowing the wife to talk with the husband and recording the conversation) was not the "functional equivalent" of an interrogation; hence, anything the suspect said during that conversation could be used against him in court. The police in this case merely "arranged a situation" in which there was a likelihood that the suspect would say something incriminating.

Right to Counsel
Related to Policing 17

Introduction

The right to counsel in criminal prosecutions is guaranteed by the Sixth Amendment, which states that "in all criminal prosecutions, the accused shall enjoy the right . . . to have the Assistance of Counsel for his defense." Although generally associated with trial, the right to counsel has been interpreted to apply to "every critical stage" of the criminal proceeding. Some encounters with the police are considered a critical stage of an investigation and therefore require the presence of a lawyer if the evidence obtained is to be admissible in court.

The seminal case on the right to counsel is *Powell v. Alabama*, 287 U.S. 45 (1932), in which the Supreme Court held that the trial in state court for a capital offense without a defense attorney violated the right to due process. The Court held that "[w]ithout counsel, though he [the defendant] may not be guilty, he faces the danger of conviction because he does not know how to establish his innocence."

The first major right to counsel case involving the police was *Escobedo v. Illinois*, 378 U.S. 478 (1964), in which the Court said that the suspect in a serious offense is entitled to a lawyer during interrogation at a police station. *Escobedo* is credited with "having brought the right to counsel out into the police station" instead of being confined to the courtroom. Two years later, in *Miranda v. Arizona*, the Court extended the right to counsel and the privilege against self-incrimination when it said that those rights apply whenever there is "custodial interrogation," even if the interrogation took place outside a police station. *Miranda*, then, brought the right to counsel out into the streets.

In *Massiah v. United States*, 377 U.S. 201 (1964), incriminating statements obtained while the defendant was questioned after the defendant had been charged with a crime and had obtained an attorney, but without an attorney present, were held not admissible in court. In *United States v. Henry*, the Court said that a defendant's right to counsel is violated if the police intentionally create a situation that is likely to elicit incriminating statements.

The cases briefed in this section establish that the right to counsel is a basic right that must be observed by the police if the contact can be characterized as a critical stage, as the above cases illustrate. One the other hand, questioning during stops or while issuing traffic citations do not trigger the right to counsel because they are not critical stages in a criminal prosecution.

The important cases briefed in this chapter on the right to counsel related to policing are *Massiah v. United States* and *United States v. Henry*.

Powell v. Alabama
287 U.S. 45 (1932)

CAPSULE: The trial in state court of nine youths for a capital offense without a defense attorney violated their right to due process.

FACTS: Nine black youths were charged with the rape of two white girls while on a train in Alabama. All were illiterate. The atmosphere in the town was such that the boys had to be held in a different town under military guard during the proceedings. The judge appointed "all members of the bar" to assist the boys during the proceedings; however, they were not represented by any attorney by name until the day of the trial. Each of the trials lasted only a day and resulted in a conviction. The youths were given the death penalty.

ISSUE: Were the defendants in this case denied their constitutional rights to counsel and due process? YES.

SUPREME COURT DECISION: "In a capital case, where the defendant is unable to employ counsel, and is incapable adequately of making his own defense because of ignorance, feeblemindedness, illiteracy, or the like, it is the duty of the court, whether requested or not, to assign counsel for him as a necessary requisite of due process of law; and that duty is not discharged by an assignment at such a time or under such circumstances as to preclude the giving of effective aid in the preparation and trial of the case."

REASON: "Even the intelligent and educated layman has small and sometimes no skill in the science of the law. Left without aid of counsel, he may be put on trial without proper charge, and convicted upon incompetent evidence irrelevant to the issue or otherwise against him. Without counsel, though he may not be guilty, he faces the danger of conviction because he does not know how to establish his innocence."

CASE SIGNIFICANCE: The Sixth Amendment to the Constitution provides that "in all criminal prosecutions, the accused shall enjoy the right . . . to have the assistance of counsel for his defense." This case provides the often-quoted reason, (penned by Justice Sutherland), for this constitutional provision. Without a lawyer, an accused may be convicted, not because he or she is guilty, but because "he does not know how to establish his innocence." The right to counsel is a basic and fundamental right under the Constitution and must be respected by the police. Note that, in this case, the Court used the due process clause of the Fourteenth Amendment rather than the Sixth Amendment right to counsel to overturn the convictions. This is because, in 1932, when the case was decided, the provisions of the Bill of Rights had not yet been extended to state proceedings. Were this case to be decided today, the Sixth Amendment right to counsel provision would have been used.

Gideon v. Wainwright
372 U.S. 335 (1963)

CAPSULE: A lawyer must be appointed for an indigent who is charged with a felony offense in state court.

FACTS: Gideon was charged in a Florida state court with breaking and entering a poolroom with intent to commit a misdemeanor, an act classified as a felony offense under Florida law. Appearing in court without funds and without a lawyer, Gideon asked the court to appoint a lawyer for him. The court refused, saying that under Florida law the only time the court could appoint a lawyer to represent an accused was when the crime charged was a capital offense. Gideon conducted his own defense and was convicted.

ISSUE: Does the Constitution require appointment of counsel for an indigent person who is charged in a state court with a felony offense? YES.

SUPREME COURT DECISION: The Sixth Amendment requires that a person charged with a felony offense in a state court be appointed counsel if he or she cannot afford it.

REASON: "The right of one charged with crime to counsel may not be deemed fundamental and essential to fair trials in some countries, but it is in ours. From the very beginning, our state and national constitutions and laws have laid great emphasis on procedural and substantive safeguards designed to assure fair trials before impartial tribunals in which every defendant stands equal before the law. This noble ideal cannot be realized if the poor man charged with a crime has to face his accusers without a lawyer to assist him . . ."

CASE SIGNIFICANCE: This case mandates that when an indigent person is charged with a felony in a state court, counsel must be provided. This settled a controversy among lower courts, which had inconsistent rulings on the type of offense an indigent had to be charged with in order to be entitled to a lawyer. An earlier decision (*Betts v. Brady*, 316 U.S. 455 [1942]), which held that the requirement that counsel be provided to all indigent defendants in federal felony trials, did not extend to the states. This was overruled in the *Gideon* case when the Supreme Court held that the rule applied to criminal proceedings in state courts as well. Since 1963, both federal and state felony defendants must be given court-appointed counsel if indigent. Note that the *Gideon* case required the appointment of counsel for indigents only in felony cases. This was later extended to misdemeanor cases in *Argersinger v. Hamlin*. Although not a case directly involving the police, the *Gideon* case is included here because it is helpful for the police to know what types of indigent offenders are entitled to a court-appointed lawyer during trial.

Escobedo v. Illinois
378 U.S. 478 (1964)

CAPSULE: A suspect in a serious offense is entitled to a lawyer during interrogation at a police station.

FACTS: Escobedo was arrested without a warrant and interrogated in connection with a murder. En route to the police station, officers told Escobedo that he had been named as the murderer and that he should admit to the crime. Escobedo replied that he wished to speak to an attorney. Shortly after Escobedo arrived at the police station, his retained lawyer arrived and asked permission from various police officials to speak with his client. His request was repeatedly denied. Escobedo also asked several times during an interrogation to speak to his attorney and was told that the attorney did not want to see him. Escobedo subsequently admitted to some knowledge of the murder and implicated himself as the murderer. Escobedo was charged with and convicted of murder.

ISSUE: Is a suspect entitled to a lawyer, if he or she requests one, during interrogation at a police station? YES.

SUPREME COURT DECISION: A suspect is entitled to a lawyer during interrogation at a police station. Denial of counsel in this case was a violation of the suspect's constitutional right to counsel because the investigation had focused on the suspect, he had been taken into custody, and he had requested and been denied an opportunity to consult with his lawyer.

REASON: "We hold, therefore, that, where, as here, the investigation is no longer a general inquiry into unsolved crime but has begun to focus on a particular suspect, the suspect has been taken into police custody, the police carry out a process of interrogations that lends itself to eliciting incriminating statements, the suspect has requested and been denied an opportunity to consult with his lawyer, and the police have not effectively warned him of his absolute right to remain silent, the accused has been denied 'the Assistance of Counsel' in violation of the Sixth Amendment to the Constitution as 'made obligatory upon the States by the Fourteenth Amendment,' and that no statement elicited by the police during the interrogation may be used against him at a criminal trial."

CASE SIGNIFICANCE: This was an easy case for the Supreme Court to decide because the police had indeed grossly violated Escobedo's right to counsel. *Escobedo*, however, left two issues unsettled:

1. Is the right to counsel available only when the suspect is accused of a serious offense, when he or she is being questioned at the police station, and when he or she has asked to see a lawyer?

2. What did the Court mean when it said that the right to counsel could be invoked when the investigation had "begun to focus" on a particular suspect?

Because of its peculiar facts, the *Escobedo* case raised more questions than it answered. Lower court decisions disagreed on the meaning of *Escobedo*, leading to conflicting interpretations. Further guidance from the Supreme Court was necessary, which led to the decision in *Miranda v. Arizona* (see brief on page 198). Because of the *Miranda* decision, the impact of *Escobedo* has been lessened because *Escobedo* only brought the right to counsel to the police station, whereas *Miranda* took it out into the streets.

Massiah v. United States
377 U.S. 201 (1964)

CAPSULE: Incriminating statements are not admissible in court if the defendant was questioned without an attorney present after the defendant was charged with a crime and obtained a attorney.

FACTS: Customs officials received information that Massiah was transporting drugs from South America aboard a ship on which he was a merchant seaman. Officials searched the ship and found 300 pounds of cocaine. Massiah was indicted for possession of narcotics aboard a United States vessel. While out on bail, officials enlisted the aid of one of Massiah's confederates. The informant allowed officials to install a transmitter under the front seat of his automobile, then engaged Massiah in a conversation that could be overheard by officials. These incriminating statements were admitted over Massiah's objection at trial, and he was convicted.

ISSUE: Are statements obtained through electronic eavesdropping and the use of an informant, which are elicited after the filing of formal charges and in the absence of an attorney, a violation of the Sixth Amendment's right to counsel? YES.

SUPREME COURT DECISION: Evidence in the form of incriminating statements is not admissible in court if the defendant was questioned without an attorney by police agents after the defendant was charged and had obtained a lawyer. The evidence is inadmissible, not because there was a violation of the right against unreasonable searches and seizures, but because the right to counsel under the Sixth Amendment has been violated.

REASON: "We hold that the petitioner was denied the basic protections of the guarantee [of the Sixth Amendment] when there was used against him at his trial evidence of his own incriminating words, which federal agents had deliberately elicited from him after he had been indicted and in the absence of his counsel. It is true that in *Spano* [*v. New York*, 360 U.S. 315 (1959)], the defendant was interrogated in a police station while in this case the damaging testimony was elicited from the defendant without his knowledge while he was free on bail. But, as Judge Hays pointed out in his dissent in the Court of Appeals decision, 'if such a rule is to have any efficacy it must apply to indirect and surreptitious interrogations as well as those conducted in the jailhouse.' In this case, Massiah was more seriously imposed upon . . . because he did not even know that he was under interrogation by a government agent."

CASE SIGNIFICANCE: This case, although involving electronic surveillance, is really a right to counsel case. The Court discussed the electronic surveillance issue only briefly. It reserved most of its discussion to the right to counsel issue, concluding that, while evidence was obtained validly with the use of radio equipment, it had to be excluded because the suspect's right to counsel was violated. It is important to note that here the suspect had been formally charged in court and had obtained an attorney. If these factors had not been present, the evidence would have been admissible.

United States v. Henry
447 U.S. 264 (1980)

CAPSULE: A defendant's right to counsel is violated if the police intentionally create a situation that is likely to elicit incriminating statements.

FACTS: Henry was indicted for armed robbery and incarcerated. While in jail, government agents contacted an informant who was a cellmate of Henry and instructed him to be alert to any statements made by Henry, but not to initiate any conversations regarding the robbery. After the informant had been released from jail, he was contacted by the agents and paid for information he provided them concerning incriminating statements Henry made to him in reference to the robbery. There was no indication that the informant would have been paid had he not provided such information. Henry was convicted of robbery, based partly on the testimony of the informant.

ISSUE: Is a defendant denied the right to counsel under the Sixth Amendment if the government uses a paid informant to create a situation likely to induce incriminating statements? YES.

SUPREME COURT DECISION: The government violates a defendant's Sixth Amendment right to counsel by intentionally creating a situation likely to elicit incriminating statements.

REASON: "The question here is whether under the facts of this case a Government agent 'deliberately elicited' incriminating statements from Henry. . . . Three factors are important. First, Nichols [the informant] was acting under instructions as a paid informant for the Government; second, Nichols was ostensibly no more than a fellow inmate of Henry; and third, Henry was in custody under indictment at the time he was engaged in conversation with Nichols."

"The Government argues that federal agents instructed Nichols not to question Henry about the robbery. Yet according to his own testimony, Nichols was not a passive listener; rather, he had 'some conversations with Mr. Henry' while he was in jail and Henry's incriminatory statements were 'the product of this conversation.'"

CASE SIGNIFICANCE: This is a right to counsel rather than a privilege against self-incrimination case. The evidence obtained was excluded because what the government did violated the suspect's right to a lawyer, not because what the government did amounted to a form of interrogation. The Court said that, here, the government created a situation likely to induce the suspect to make incriminating statements without the assistance of counsel. Some observers find it difficult to accept this logic particularly because the informant was instructed to simply listen to incriminating statements Henry made and not to interrogate him at all. Nonetheless, the Court said that incriminating statements were "deliberately elicited" by the informant, which the police cannot do in the absence of a lawyer. Great weight was given by the Court to the fact that the informant was acting under government instruction and that Henry was in custody under indictment at the time the incriminating statements were made. Moreover, the informant in fact engaged Henry in conversations that produced the incriminating statements.

This case was not decided under *Miranda v. Arizona*, but under *Massiah v. United States*. In *Massiah*, the Court said that when a police informant carries into a suspect's car an electronic device that transmits the conversation to the police outside, the evidence is not admissible if the defendant was questioned without a lawyer after one had been retained. The police ought to be careful when interviewing or interrogating a suspect who has retained a lawyer. In these cases, courts frown upon such interrogations, not because no *Miranda* warnings were given, but because a suspect has the right to have counsel present whenever he or she is questioned by the police. In sum, once a suspect has a lawyer, the police must leave the subject alone.

Entrapment 18

Introduction

Entrapment is a defense in criminal law that questions the propriety of police action. It is defined as the act of government officers or agents in inducing a person to commit a crime that is not contemplated by the person for the purpose of instituting a criminal prosecution against him or her. A person entrapped is not guilty of a criminal offense because of the presumption that the legislators did not intend to allow government agents to lure otherwise innocent persons into committing a crime so that they can be prosecuted.

Entrapment is a valid defense in a criminal case, but the act by the police of merely providing an opportunity for a person to commit a crime is not. That line, however, is sometimes difficult to draw and becomes a matter of proof during trial.

Entrapment tests may be divided into two general categories: the subjective test and the objective test. The *subjective* test focuses on a defendant's predisposition, and holds that entrapment exists only if the accused had no predisposition to commit the offense but did so because of inducement by the government agent. If the accused was predisposed to commit the offense charged, there is no entrapment because the accused is an "unwary criminal," and not an "unwary innocent." Under this test, a known prostitute cannot successfully claim entrapment, regardless of police conduct, because she or he had the predisposition.

In contrast, the *objective test* focuses on the conduct of the government agent by asking: Were the activities of the government agent so instigative that they could well have induced an innocent person to commit the crime? Under this test, the accused's past conduct is irrelevant; what is relevant is the conduct of the government agent. Under the objective test, a known prostitute can successfully claim entrapment if the conduct of the government agent induced him or her to commit the offense charged.

The entrapment test that courts use is typically determined by the criminal code. The two tests are not mutually exclusive. Some jurisdictions combine an element of both, as in laws providing that the predisposition of a defendant defeats an entrapment defense, except in cases in which the conduct of the government agent is outrageous—in which case even a predisposed defendant can successfully claim the entrapment defense.

The latest significant case on entrapment is *Jacobson v. United States*, 503 U.S. 540 (1992). In *Jacobson*, the Court held that government entrapment exists if government agents originate a criminal design, implant in an innocent person's mind the disposition to commit a criminal act, and then induce the commission of the crime. More importantly, *Jacobson* holds that, in entrapment cases, the government has the burden of proving "beyond a reasonable doubt" the defendant's predisposition to commit the offense.

If the government fails to prove predisposition, the defendant wins because of the presumption that the defendant is an "unwary innocent" instead of an "unwary criminal."

The leading cases briefed in this chapter are *Sherman v. United States*, *United States v. Russell*, and *Jacobson v. United States*.

Sherman v. United States
356 U.S. 369 (1958)

CAPSULE: A defendant is entrapped when the government induces him or her to commit a crime that he or she would not have otherwise committed.

FACTS: A government informant met Sherman in a doctor's office, where both were being treated for drug addiction. On several subsequent chance meetings, the informant asked Sherman if he knew a source of drugs. Sherman avoided the issue, but after several requests, Sherman offered to supply narcotics. Several times thereafter, Sherman supplied the informant with drugs for cost plus expenses. The informant notified FBI agents of the transactions and set up narcotics deals on three more occasions, which agents observed. Sherman was arrested, tried, and convicted of drug offenses.

ISSUE: Were the actions of the government informant such that they induced Sherman to commit crimes that he would have otherwise been unwilling to commit, resulting in entrapment? YES.

SUPREME COURT DECISION: There is entrapment when the government induces an individual to commit a crime that he or she otherwise would not have attempted.

REASON: "The case at bar illustrates an evil which the defense of entrapment is designed to overcome. The government informer entices someone attempting to avoid narcotics not only into carrying out an illegal sale but also returning to the habit of use. Selecting the proper time, the informer then tells the government agent. The setup is accepted by the agent without even a question as to the manner in which the informer encountered the seller. Thus the government plays on the weakness of an innocent party and beguiles him into committing crimes which he otherwise would not have attempted. Law enforcement does not require methods such as this."

CASE SIGNIFICANCE: This case sets the current test used by many courts for entrapment, namely: there is entrapment if the government induces an individual to commit a crime that he or she otherwise would not have committed. In this case, the informant asked Sherman if he knew a drug supplier and then whether Sherman himself would provide the narcotics. Sherman first avoided the issue, but then gave in after repeated requests. It is clear that, in this case, Sherman would not have committed the crime had the government officials, in effect, not forced him to do so. This case also decided that the accused bears the burden of proving entrapment and that the factual issue of whether the defendant was actually entrapped is a question of fact, not a question of law, and is, therefore, for the jury to decide.

United States v. Russell
411 U.S. 423 (1973)

CAPSULE: Supplying one of the necessary ingredients for the manufacture of a prohibited drug does not constitute entrapment.

FACTS: Russell and two others were indicted and convicted of illegally manufacturing and selling methamphetamine, a prohibited drug. Shapiro, an agent of the Federal Bureau of Narcotics and Dangerous Drugs, had met earlier with the three accused and told them that he represented a group desiring to obtain control of the manufacture and distribution of the drug. Shapiro offered to supply them with phenyl-2-propanone, a chemical required to manufacture methamphetamine. In return, Shapiro wanted to receive one-half of the speed made with the ingredient supplied. Shapiro later received his share and also bought some of the remainder from Russell. There was testimony at the trial that phenyl-2-propanone was generally difficult to obtain because, at the request of the Bureau of Narcotics and Dangerous Drugs, some chemical supply firms had voluntarily ceased to sell the chemical. On appeal, Russell conceded that the jury could have found him predisposed to commit the offenses with which he was charged, but argued that he was entrapped as a matter of law.

ISSUE: Did the act by the undercover government agent of providing an essential chemical for the manufacture of a prohibited drug constitute entrapment? NO.

SUPREME COURT DECISION: The act by a government agent of supplying one of the necessary ingredients for the manufacture of a prohibited drug does not constitute entrapment. That conduct stops short of being a violation of "fundamental fairness" that would shock "the universal sense of justice." This is a case of an accused who was an "unwary criminal" and not an "unwary innocent," for whom the entrapment defense would have been available.

REASON: "While we may some day be presented with a situation in which the conduct of law enforcement agents is so outrageous that due process principles would absolutely bar the government from invoking judicial processes to obtain conviction, the instant case is distinctly not of that breed. Shapiro's contribution of propanone to the criminal enterprise already in process was scarcely objectionable. The chemical is, by itself, a harmless substance and its possession is legal. While the government may have been seeking to make it more difficult for drug rings, such as that of which respondent was a member, to obtain the chemical, the evidence described above shows that it nonetheless was obtainable. The law enforcement conduct here stops short of violating that 'fundamental fairness, shocking to the universal sense of justice,' mandated by the due process clause of the Fifth Amendment."

CASE SIGNIFICANCE: The *Russell* case illustrates the majority view on the entrapment defense. This view focuses on the predisposition of the defendant to commit the alleged act, rather than on an analysis of the conduct of the government. Under this view, the entrapment defense applies only if the accused has no predisposition to commit the crime, but does so because of inducement by a government agent. The Court minimized the importance of Shapiro's supplying the accused with an essential ingredient for the manufacture of the prohibited drug, saying that the chemical was a harmless substance and its possession was legal. Besides, although it was difficult to obtain the chemical, the evidence showed that it was, nonetheless, obtainable; therefore, the conduct of the government agent stopped short of violating the "fundamental fairness" mandated by the due process clause of the Fifth Amendment. In using this language, the Court strongly implies that, even under the majority test, there may be conduct by the government that may entrap a person who is predisposed to commit a crime. The Court, however, did not give any example of that type of prohibited government conduct. Note that, had the Court here used the minority (objective) test, the accused most probably would have been acquitted.

Hampton v. United States
425 U.S. 484 (1976)

CAPSULE: There is no entrapment when a government informant supplies heroin to a suspect who is predisposed to commit the crime.

FACTS: Hampton was convicted of two counts of distributing heroin in violation of federal law. The conviction arose from two sales of heroin by Hampton to agents of the Drug Enforcement Administration. The sales were arranged by an acquaintance of Hampton who was also a DEA informant. Hampton claimed entrapment, stating that he neither intended to sell, nor knew that he was dealing in heroin and that all of the drugs he sold were supplied by the acquaintance who was also a government informant.

ISSUE: Is there entrapment when a government informant supplies heroin to a suspect, who then sells it to government agents? NO.

SUPREME COURT DECISION: There was no entrapment here because the government informant supplied heroin to a suspect who had the predisposition to commit the crime. The entrapment defense applies only if the accused had no predisposition to commit the crime but was induced to do so by government agents.

REASON: "Here . . . the police, the government informant, and the defendant acted in concert with one another. If the result of the governmental activity is to 'implant in the mind of an innocent person the disposition to commit the alleged offense and induce its commission,' the defendant is protected by the defense of entrapment. If the police engaged in illegal activity in concert with a defendant beyond the scope of their duties, the remedy lies not in freeing the equally culpable defendant but in the prosecuting the police under the applicable provisions of state or federal law."

CASE SIGNIFICANCE: To civil libertarians, this decision is shocking, that there is no entrapment even when a government informant supplies an illegal substance to an accused who then sells it to government agents. This case expanded the ruling in *Russell* (see brief on page 258). In the *Russell* case, the government informant provided the defendant with a difficult-to-obtain but legal item. In this case, however, the item provided was heroin, an illegal drug.

There are two views on the entrapment defense. The *Hampton* case reiterates the majority view, which focuses on the conduct of the defendant, rather than on the conduct of the government agents. Under this test, if the defendant is predisposed to commit the crime, there is no entrapment, regardless of the conduct of the government agents. Using this test, there was no entrapment in this case although the conduct of the government informant in providing the accused with heroin was extreme, if not gross. In contrast, the minority view rejects the predisposition test and focuses solely on the conduct of the government. If the conduct of the government is outrageous, the accused is entitled to the entrapment defense even if he or she is predisposed to commit the crime. Under this minority view, Hampton could have successfully claimed entrapment because the conduct of the government was indeed outrageous. The Court, however, rejected this view (as it did in the *Russell* case) and took into account Hampton's predisposition. The current majority view on entrapment is: if a suspect is predisposed to commit the crime, there is no entrapment, regardless of the conduct of the government. Note, however, that state law or court decisions determine the entrapment rule in a particular state; the *Hampton* rule only applies in federal cases. State entrapment defenses depend on whether a state uses the majority or minority view. Police officers must be familiar with state law on the entrapment defense.

Mathews v. United States
485 U.S. 58 (1988)

CAPSULE: The entrapment defense may be raised even if the defendant denies one or more elements of the crime charged.

FACTS: A government informant, under the surveillance of FBI officers, requested a loan from Mathews in return for Small Business Association benefits. When the two met to exchange the money, Mathews was arrested for accepting a bribe in exchange for government services. The trial court denied Matthew's motion seeking to raise the affirmative defense of entrapment because he would not admit all the elements of the crime. Mathews was ultimately found guilty of accepting an unlawful gratuity.

ISSUE: Can a defendant in a federal criminal prosecution deny an element of a crime and still raise the entrapment defense? YES.

SUPREME COURT DECISION: Even if the defendant in a federal criminal case denies one or more elements of the crime, the affirmative defense of entrapment may be raised if there is sufficient evidence from which a reasonable jury could conclude that there was entrapment.

REASON: "There is no merit to the Government's contention that, because entrapment presupposes the commission of a crime, defendant should not be allowed both to deny the offense or an element thereof, and to rely on the inconsistent, affirmative defense of entrapment."

CASE SIGNIFICANCE: The *Mathews* case resolves an issue that generated inconsistent decisions among the various federal courts of appeals. In previous cases, the Third, Sixth, and Seventh Circuits allowed the entrapment defense only if the defendant admitted to committing all the elements of the crime charged. By contrast, the Ninth and District of Columbia Circuits allowed the raising of the entrapment defense even if the accused denied any or all elements of the offense charged. The Circuits that allowed the entrapment defense only if the defendant admitted to having committed all the elements of the crime charged maintained that a defendant's denial of one of the elements was inconsistent with the entrapment defense, saying that there was no entrapment if one of the elements of the offense was not in fact committed. These same courts reasoned that to allow a defendant to assert inconsistent defenses encouraged perjury and confused the court. The Court in *Mathews* rejected these claims, saying that the issue was not whether defendant's claims were inconsistent, but whether sufficient grounds existed from which a reasonable jury could find entrapment. That is a question for the trial judge to decide.

Jacobson v. United States
503 U.S. 540 (1992)

CAPSULE: Government entrapment exists if government agents originate a criminal design, implant in an innocent person's mind the disposition to commit a criminal act, and then induce the commission of the crime so that the government can prosecute.

FACTS: In February 1984, Jacobson ordered two magazines from an adult bookstore titled *Bare Boys I* and *Bare Boys II*, which contained photographs of nude preteen and teenage boys. The boys in the magazines were not engaged in sexual activity, and Jacobson's purchase was not illegal at that time. Subsequently, the Child Protection Act of 1984 was passed, which criminalized the receipt through the mail of a "visual depiction [that] involves the use of a minor engaging in sexually explicit conduct . . ."

In January 1985, the month that the law became effective, a postal inspector found Jacobson's name on a mailing list from the bookstore in which he had ordered the books and sent him a letter and application for membership from a fictitious organization espousing the rights of people to "read what we desire . . . discuss similar interests with those who share our philosophy, and . . . to seek pleasure without restrictions being placed on us by outdated puritan morality." Jacobson enrolled in the organization and returned a questionnaire, responding in part that he "enjoyed" preteen sexual materials but that he was opposed to pedophilia.

Over the next 26 months, different government agencies re-contacted Jacobson through five fictitious organizations and a bogus pen pal (a postal inspector). In one of these contacts, the Customs Service sent Jacobson a brochure advertising photographs of young boys engaging in sex. Jacobson placed an order through this organization, but the order was never filled. In May of 1987, the Postal Service sent Jacobson a brochure from a fictitious Canadian company with the opportunity to order a catalogue of pornographic materials. Jacobson responded to the brochure and a catalogue was sent. From the catalogue, Jacobson ordered the magazine *Boys Who Love Boys*.

The magazines were delivered and Jacobson was arrested. In Jacobson's home, government agents found only the two original magazines and the materials sent from the various fictitious organizations. Jacobson was convicted of receiving child pornography through the mail.

ISSUE: Did the government operations, lasting over two years, in which a person was repeatedly contacted in relation to criminal activities, offer enough inducement to cause the "unwary innocent" to commit a crime, such that it constituted entrapment? YES.

SUPREME COURT DECISION: "In their zeal to enforce the law, . . . Government agents may not originate a criminal design, implant in an innocent person's mind the disposition to commit a criminal act, and then induce commission of the crime so that the government may prosecute."

REASON: "Had the agents in this case simply offered petitioner the opportunity to order child pornography through the mails, and the petitioner—who must be presumed to know the law—had promptly availed himself of the criminal opportunity, it is unlikely that his entrapment defense would have warranted a jury instruction. But this was not what happened here. By the time petitioner finally placed his order, he had already been the target of 26 months of repeated mailings and communications from Government agents and fictitious organizations. Therefore, although he had become predisposed to break the law by May 1987, it is our view that the Government did not prove that this predisposition was independent and not the product of the attention that the government had directed at the petitioner since January 1985." [Citations omitted.]

CASE SIGNIFICANCE: The importance of this case to law enforcement lies in the Court's view of the concept of entrapment. The Court reversed the defendant's conviction in this case on the grounds that the "prosecution failed, as a matter of law, to adduce evidence to support the jury verdict that Jacobson was predisposed, independent of the Government's acts and beyond a reasonable doubt, to violate the law by receiving child pornography through the mails." Implicit in the decision is the requirement that, in entrapment cases, the government has the burden of proving "beyond a reasonable doubt" defendant's predisposition to commit the offense independent of the government's acts.

The entrapment rule states that "Government agents may not originate a criminal design, implant in an innocent person's mind the disposition to commit a criminal act, and then induce commission of the crime so that the Government may prosecute" (*Sorrells v. United States,* 287 U.S., at 442). In this case, there were repeated efforts by two government agencies, spanning a period of two and one-half years and using five fictitious organizations and a bogus pen pal, to probe into the defendant's willingness to break the law by ordering sexually explicit photographs of children through the mail. The Court said that this was tantamount to implanting in the defendant's mind the desire to commit a criminal act. Such presumption could have been rebutted had the government established beyond a reasonable doubt that the defendant was predisposed to commit the act, but the government failed to prove that. It must be noted, however, that there is a big difference between implanting in defendant's mind the desire to commit a criminal act and merely affording opportunities of facilities for the commission of the act. The first leads to a valid entrapment defense, the second does not.

Legal Liabilities 19

Introduction

Being sued is an occupational hazard in policing. American society is litigious, and the police are an attractive target because they wield power and are public employees. Most lawsuits against the police do not succeed, but some are high-profile cases that generate media attention and result in huge damage awards. The American public remembers the Rodney King case, the New York City cases, and the Detroit cases. In the Rodney King and New York City cases, huge damage awards were given to the plaintiffs. Suing the police sometimes pays. It does not come as a surprise that there is hardly any major law enforcement agency in the United States that has not been sued.

The police may be liable under state law and under federal law. These two types of liabilities may be sub-classified into three general categories: civil liabilities, criminal liabilities, and administrative liabilities. Plaintiffs usually prefer the civil liabilities route for a number of reasons. Civil cases are easier to win than criminal cases, they result in a monetary award, and they do not need the intervention of the prosecutor's office to file the case.

The Supreme Court has addressed a number of issues involving police liability. The issues range from who can be sued, when the police can be sued, who can be held liable and under what circumstances, for what specific acts police officers may be held liable, what defenses are available in police liability cases, and what level of negligence is required for police administrators and their employers to be held liable.

The cases briefed in this chapter represent the more significant cases decided by the Supreme Court on police civil liability. Among these decisions are:

1. Police officers enjoy absolute immunity from civil liability when testifying, even if the testimony is perjured;

2. Inadequate police training can lead to liability under federal law, but only if it amounts to deliberate indifference;

3. Neither the state nor state officials acting in their official capacity may be sued under federal law in state court;

4. State officials sued in their individual capacity are liable for civil rights violations; and

5. A municipality may be held liable for a sheriff's single negligent decision to hire an officer, but only if the hiring constitutes deliberate indifference, interpreted to mean that what happened was the plainly obvious consequence of the decision to hire the officer.

There are no indications that lawsuits against the police will abate soon. The law and case law on police liability are complex and constantly evolving. The briefs below should be considered introductory, albeit leading, cases on the subject of police liability. Many more issues on police liability have been decided by lower courts, and even more issues remain to be decided.

The leading cases briefed in this chapter are *City of Canton v. Harris*, *Board of the County Commissioners of Bryan County, Oklahoma v. Brown*, and *County of Sacramento v. Lewis*. Three new cases were added by the Court to the police legal liabilities jurisprudence in 2004 and 2005. They are: *Chavez v. Martinez* (2004), *Muehler v. Mena* (2005), and *Town of Castle Rock v. Gonzales* (2005).

Owen v. City of Independence
445 U.S. 622 (1980)

CAPSULE: A municipality may be held liable in a § 1983 lawsuit and cannot claim the good faith defense.

FACTS: The City Council of Independence, Missouri, decided that reports of an investigation of the police department should be released to the news media and turned over to the prosecutor for presentation to the grand jury, and that the city manager take appropriate action against the persons involved in the wrongful activities. Acting on this, the city manager dismissed the chief of police. No reason was given for the dismissal. The chief of police received only a written notice stating that the dismissal was made in accordance with a specified provision of the city charter. The chief of police filed a Title 42 U.S.C. § 1983 lawsuit against the city manager and members of the city council, alleging that he was discharged without notice of reasons and without a hearing, thereby violating his constitutional rights to procedural and substantive due process. The district court decided for the city manager and council members.

ISSUE: Are municipalities and municipal officials entitled to the "good faith" defense if a right is violated while officials are following the provisions of a city policy or custom? NO.

SUPREME COURT DECISION: A municipality has no immunity to liability under § 1983 flowing from violations of an individual's constitutional rights and may not assert the "good faith" defense that is available to its officers.

REASON: "We believe that today's decision, together with prior precedents in this area, properly allocates these costs among the three principals in the scenario of the Section 1983 cause of action: the victim of the constitutional deprivation; the officer whose conduct caused the injury; and the public, as represented by the municipal entity. The innocent individual who is harmed by an abuse of governmental authority is assured that he will be compensated for his injury. The offending official, so long as he conducts himself in good faith, may go about his business secure in the knowledge that a qualified immunity will protect him from personal liability for damages that are more appropriately chargeable to the populace as a whole. And the public will be forced to bear only the costs of injury inflicted by the 'execution of a government's policy or custom, whether made by its lawmakers or by those whose edicts or acts may fairly be said to represent official policy.'"

CASE SIGNIFICANCE: The *Owen* case makes clear that the municipality may be liable if a person's constitutional right is violated (in this case the right to due process prior to dismissal) by public officials who are acting in accordance with agency policy as contained in the city charter. Because they were acting in accordance with the provisions of the city charter, the city manager and members of the city council enjoyed a "good faith" defense, but the city did not. The implication is that municipalities must make sure that their policy does not violate individual rights. The fact that something is official policy does not mean that it is automatically valid. The Court said that individual blameworthiness is no longer the acid test of liability, substituting in its place the principle of "equitable loss-spreading," in addition to fault, as a fact in distributing the costs of official misconduct.

Briscoe v. LaHue
460 U.S. 325 (1983)

CAPSULE: Police officers enjoy absolute immunity from civil liability when testifying, even if the testimony is perjured.

FACTS: Briscoe was convicted in a state court of burglary. He then filed a Title 42 U.S.C. § 1983 suit in the District Court alleging that LaHue, a police officer, had violated his right to due process by committing perjury in the criminal proceeding leading to his conviction.

ISSUE: May a police officer be liable in a § 1983 case for giving perjured testimony? NO.

SUPREME COURT DECISION: Police officers enjoy absolute immunity from civil liability when testifying, even if the testimony is perjured.

REASON: "The common law provided absolute immunity from subsequent damages liability for all persons—governmental or otherwise—who are integral parts of the judicial process. . . . When a police officer appears as a witness, he may reasonably be viewed as acting like any witness sworn to tell the truth, in which event he can make a strong claim to witness immunity. Alternatively, he may be regarded as an official performing a critical role in the judicial process, in which even he may seek the benefit afforded to other governmental participants in the same proceeding. Nothing in Section 1983 language suggests that a police officer witness belongs in a narrow, special category lacking protection against damages suits."

CASE SIGNIFICANCE: This decision assures police officers that they cannot be held liable under 42 U.S.C. § 1983 (the usual type of civil liability cases filed against government officials) for giving false testimony against a defendant in a criminal trial. The Court gives two reasons for this absolute immunity. First, the officer is just like any other witness who is sworn to tell the truth, and therefore enjoys witness immunity. Second, the officer is a public official performing a critical role in the judicial process. The decision does not mean, however, that officers have complete freedom to tell falsehoods in court. The officer who does so may be held liable under the state penal code, usually for perjury. Note that only when testifying in court does an officer enjoy absolute immunity. In all other aspects of police work, an officer enjoys only qualified (good faith) immunity.

Malley v. Briggs
475 U.S. 335 (1986)

CAPSULE: A police officer is entitled only to qualified immunity, not to absolute immunity, in § 1983 cases.

FACTS: On the basis of two monitored telephone calls pursuant to a court-authorized wiretap, Rhode Island state trooper Malley prepared felony complaints charging Briggs and others with possession of marijuana. The complaints were given to a state judge, together with arrest warrants and supporting affidavits. The judge signed the warrants, and the defendants were arrested. The charges, however, were subsequently dropped when the grand jury refused to return an indictment. The defendants then brought an action under 42 U.S.C. § 1983, alleging that Malley, in applying for the arrest warrants, had violated their rights against unreasonable searches and seizures.

ISSUE: Is absolute immunity afforded a defendant police officer in Title 42 U.S.C. § 1983 actions when it is alleged that the officer caused the plaintiffs to be unconstitutionally arrested by presenting a judge with a complaint and a supporting affidavit that failed to establish probable cause? NO.

SUPREME COURT DECISION: A police officer is not entitled to absolute immunity, but only qualified immunity to liability for damages in § 1983 cases.

REASON: "Although we have previously held that police officers sued under Section 1983 for false arrest are qualifiedly immune, petitioner urges that he should be absolutely immune because his function in seeking an arrest warrant was similar to that of a complaining witness. The difficulty with this submission is that complaining witnesses were not absolutely immune at common law. In 1871, the generally accepted rule was that one who procured the issuance of an arrest warrant by submitting a complaint could be held liable if the complaint was made maliciously and without probable cause. Given malice and the lack of probable case, the complainant enjoyed no immunity. The common law thus affords no support for the petitioner."

CASE SIGNIFICANCE: Officer Malley argued that he be given absolute immunity because his function in seeking an arrest warrant was similar to that of a complaining witness. The Court said that complaining witnesses were not absolutely immune at common law. If malice and lack of probable cause are proved, the officer enjoys no absolute immunity. The Court also rejected the officer's argument that policy considerations require absolute immunity for the officer applying for a warrant, saying that, as the qualified immunity defense has evolved, it provides ample protection to all but the plainly incompetent or those who knowingly violate the law. The Court considered this protection sufficient because, under current standards, the officer is not liable anyway if he or she acted in an objectively reasonable manner. The *Malley* case, therefore, makes clear that under no circumstances will the Court extend the "absolute immunity" defense (available to judges, prosecutors, and legislators) to police officers. The only exception is when the officer is testifying in a criminal trial. This means that officers enjoy only qualified immunity, but that they will not be liable if they act in an objectively reasonable manner.

City of Canton v. Harris
489 U.S. 378 (1989)

CAPSULE: Inadequate police training may serve as the basis for municipal liability under Title 42 § 1983, but only if it amounts to "deliberate indifference."

FACTS: Harris was arrested and taken to the police station in a patrol wagon. Upon arrival at the station, Harris was found sitting on the floor of the wagon. When asked if she needed medical help, her reply was incoherent. Harris fell twice more during her stay at the station. She was ultimately left lying on the floor to prevent her from falling again. The officers did not offer medical assistance. When she was released an hour later, she was taken by an ambulance provided by her family to a hospital where she was diagnosed as having several emotional ailments and was hospitalized. Harris filed a 42 U.S.C. § 1983 lawsuit against the city for failure to provide her with adequate medical care while in police custody.

ISSUE: Can a municipality be held liable in a § 1983 suit for constitutional violations resulting from a failure to properly train municipal employees? YES.

SUPREME COURT DECISION: Inadequate police training may serve as the basis for municipal liability under § 1983, but only if the failure to train amounts to deliberate indifference to the rights of persons with whom the police come into contact and the deficiency in the training program is closely related to the injury suffered.

REASON: "Only where a failure to train reflects a 'deliberate' or 'conscious' choice by the municipality can the failure be properly thought of as actionable city 'policy.' . . . [T]he focus must be on whether the program is adequate to the tasks the particular employees must perform, and if it is not, on whether such inadequate training can justifiably be said to represent 'city policy.' Moreover, the identified deficiency in the training program must be closely related to the ultimate injury. Thus, respondent still must prove that the deficiency in training actually caused the police officers' indifference to her medical needs. To adopt lesser standards of fault and causation would open municipalities to unprecedented liability under Section 1983; would result in *de facto respondeat superior* liability, a result rejected in *Monell* [*v. New York City Department of Social Services*, 436 U.S. 658 (1978)]; would engage federal courts in an endless exercise of second-guessing municipal employee training programs, a task that they are ill-suited to undertake; and would implicate serious questions of federalism."

CASE SIGNIFICANCE: This case settles an issue that has long bothered lower courts: "can a municipality be held liable for failure to train?" The Court in this case answered "yes," but subject to strict requirements. These requirements are:

1. The failure to adequately train reflects a "deliberate" or "conscious" choice by the municipality;

2. Such inadequate training represents city policy; and

3. The identified deficiency in the training program must be closely related to the ultimate injury.

What this means is that not every injury caused by police officers leads to municipal liability for failure to train. It is only when the three requirements above are met that municipal liability ensues. These three requirements are usually difficult for plaintiffs in § 1983 cases to establish, hence discouraging the "deep pockets" approach (in which the municipality is involved in the lawsuit because of a greater ability to pay than the police officer) often used in civil rights liability cases. No liability on the part of the municipality for failure to train does not mean that the officer cannot be held liable. There are instances in which an officer may be liable even if the municipality is not liable for failure to train.

Will v. Michigan Department of State Police
491 U.S. 58 (1989)

CAPSULE: Neither the state nor state officials, acting in their official capacity, may be sued under § 1983 in state court.

FACTS: Will filed a Title 42 U.S.C. § 1983 lawsuit alleging that he was denied a promotion, in violation of his constitutional rights, because his brother had been a student activist and the subject of a "red squad" file maintained by the department. He named as defendants the Michigan Department of State Police and the Director of the State Police in his official capacity.

ISSUE: May state officials, acting in their official capacity, be sued under Title 42 § 1983 in a state court? NO.

SUPREME COURT DECISION: Neither the state nor state officials acting in their official capacity may be sued under § 1983 in a state court. A suit against state officials in their official capacity is a suit against the state itself and, therefore, will not succeed because a state cannot be sued under § 1983.

REASON: "Section 1983 provides a federal forum to remedy many deprivations of civil liabilities. The Eleventh Amendment bars such suits unless the State has waived its immunity. . . . Given that a principal purpose behind the enactment of Section 1983 was to provide a federal forum for civil rights claims, and that Congress did not provide such a federal forum for civil rights claims against States, we cannot accept petitioner's argument that Congress intended nevertheless to create a cause of action against States to be brought in State courts, which are precisely the courts Congress sought to allow civil rights claimants to avoid through Section 1983."

CASE SIGNIFICANCE: This decision has limited significance because it applies only to state law enforcement officials, not local police. Public officials can be sued either in their public or private capacity. If sued in their public capacity, the agency will most likely pay if the officer is held liable, as long as the officer acted within the scope of his or her authority. If sued in their private capacity, liability is personal with the officer so the agency will most likely refuse to pay. Plaintiffs prefer to sue officials in their public (official) capacity because of the "deep pockets" theory. The *Will* case says that state officials cannot be sued under § 1983 in their official capacity because the Eleventh Amendment exempts states from liability in such lawsuits, unless the liability is waived by the state. This decision extends state immunity to state public officials when sued in their official capacity on the grounds that such lawsuits are, in fact, lawsuits against the state. The following points need to be emphasized, however, in connection with this decision. These are:

1. Although state officials cannot now be sued in their official capacity in a § 1983 lawsuit, they can be sued in their personal capacity, although that approach is less attractive to plaintiffs;

2. State officials can be sued in their official or personal capacity in a state tort case because the *Will* case only applies to § 1983 cases;

3. The *Will* case applies only to state public officials. Most law enforcement officers are municipal or county officials and, therefore, may be sued in either their public or private capacity under § 1983. This is because the Eleventh Amendment grants immunity to states, not local government;

4. State officials have immunity from § 1983 cases in federal courts. The *Will* case says that they now have immunity in § 1983 cases filed in state courts. The problem, however, is that many states have waived sovereign immunity and, therefore, expose state officials to possible liability.

Hafer v. Melo
502 U.S. 21 (1991)

CAPSULE: State officials sued in their individual capacity are liable for civil rights violations.

FACTS: Hafer was elected to the post of Auditor General of Pennsylvania. As a part of her campaign platform, she promised to fire 21 employees of the Auditor General's office who allegedly secured their jobs through payments to a former employee of the office. After Hafer took office she did fire 18 people, including Melo. Melo and the others filed suit under 42 U.S.C. § 1983, seeking monetary damages. The District Court dismissed all claims, holding that such claims were barred under *Will v. Michigan Department of State Police*, which held that state officials acting in their official capacity are outside the class of "persons" subject to § 1983 claims. The Court of Appeals reversed the ruling of the District Court, holding that *Will* did not apply in this case because Hafer had acted under the color of law in firing the employees, but was being sued in her personal capacity.

ISSUE: Can state officials be held personally liable for damages under Title 42 U.S.C. § 1983 based upon actions taken in their official capacity? YES.

SUPREME COURT DECISION: State officials sued in their individual capacities are "persons" within the meaning of § 1983, and therefore may be held liable for civil rights violations.

REASON: "State officers sued for damages in their official capacity are not 'persons' for the purposes of the suit because they assume the identity of the government that employs them. By contrast, officers sued in their personal capacity come to court as individuals. . . . [T]he phrase 'acting under official capacities' is best understood as a reference to the capacity in which the state officer is sued, not the capacity in which the officer inflicts the alleged injury."

CASE SIGNIFICANCE: In an earlier case, *Will*, the Court held that neither the state nor state officials acting in their official capacities may be sued under § 1983 because a suit against state officials in their official capacity is, in fact, a suit against the state itself; therefore, it will not succeed because a state cannot be sued under § 1983 unless immunity has been waived. *Will*, however, merely says that state officials cannot be sued in their *official* capacity in a § 1983 suit filed in a *state* court. It has long been settled that state officials cannot be sued in their *official* capacity in a § 1983 suit filed in a *federal* court. This case held that state officials could be sued in their *personal* capacity in a *federal* court.

In this case, the auditor general who fired the plaintiffs and was subsequently sued, maintained that she was acting within her official capacity and therefore could not be sued under § 1983 because such action fell within the authority of her office. The Court rejected that defense, saying that this lawsuit that was filed by plaintiffs who sought to hold the defendant liable in her *personal* capacity and not in her *official* capacity. The fact that she was acting within her official capacity when she fired the plaintiffs did not make any difference because she was not sued for having acted in that capacity but instead as an individual whose actions allegedly violated the due process rights of the plaintiffs. Thus, although public officials acting in their public capacity may be protected from lawsuits under § 1983 (civil rights violations), they can be sued as private individuals who can be held personally responsible for what they do.

Collins v. City of Harker Heights
503 U.S. 115 (1992)

CAPSULE: A city's failure to warn employees about known hazards in the workplace does not violate the due process clause of the Fourteenth Amendment.

FACTS: Collins, a sanitation department employee of Harker Heights, died of asphyxia after entering a manhole to unstop a sewer line. His widow brought suit against the city under 42 U.S.C. § 1983, alleging that Collins had a right under the Fourteenth Amendment due process clause to be "free from unreasonable risks of harm," and that the city had violated that right by not training its employees about the dangers of working in sewers and not providing safety equipment and training.

ISSUE: Did the city's alleged failure to warn or train its employees about known hazards in the workplace violate the due process clause of the Fourteenth Amendment? NO.

SUPREME COURT DECISION: The due process clause of the Fourteenth Amendment does not impose a federal obligation upon municipalities to provide minimum levels of and security in the workplace. Because the city's alleged failure to warn or train its employees about known hazards in the workplace did not violate the due process clause of the Constitution, it could not be the basis of a § 1983 lawsuit.

REASON: "Petitioner's submission that the city violated a federal constitutional obligation to provide its employees with certain minimal levels of safety and security is unprecedented. It is quite different from the constitutional claim advanced by plaintiffs in several of our prior cases who argued that the State owes a duty to take care of those who have already been deprived of their liberty. . . . Neither the text nor the history of the Due Process Clause supports petitioner's claim that the governmental employer's duty to provide its employees with a safe working environment is a substantive component of the Due Process Clause."

CASE SIGNIFICANCE: One of the elements of a § 1983 case is that there must have been a violation of a constitutional or federally protected right (the other being that the offending person must have been acting under color of law). Plaintiffs in this case alleged that failure on the part of the city to train and warn them about the dangers of the workplace constituted a violation of their right to due process and therefore could be the basis for a lawsuit against the city. The Court rejected that claim, saying that the due process clause did not impose an independent substantive duty on the city to provide certain levels of safety and security in the workplace. Moreover, the municipality's failure to train its employees or to warn them about known dangers was not so arbitrary or conscience-shocking as to be a violation of a constitutional right.

Had the Court's decision been otherwise, cities and municipalities would have been wide open to lawsuits stemming from failure to warn or train employees about the hazards of the workplace. This would have had a significant impact on the obligation of local government to train and to warn, as in policing. Under this case, such failure to warn or train about workplace hazards could still be the basis for a lawsuit as violative of due process rights, but only if such omission is "arbitrary or conscience-shocking."

Board of the County Commissioners of Bryan County, Oklahoma v. Brown
520 U.S. 397 (1997)

CAPSULE: A county cannot be held liable under § 1983 for a single hiring decision made by a county official.

FACTS: In the early hours of the morning, Brown and her husband approached a police checkpoint and then turned around to avoid it. Deputy Morrison and Reserve Deputy Burns pursued the vehicle for more than four miles at speeds in excess of 100 miles per hour. When the Browns stopped, Morrison pointed his gun at the truck and ordered them to raise their hands. Burns, who was unarmed, went to the passenger side of the truck and ordered Brown out of the vehicle. When Brown did not respond after the second request, Burns pulled Brown from the truck by the arm and swung her to the ground. The fall caused severe injuries to Brown's knees, possibly requiring knee replacement. Brown sued Burns, the county Sheriff, and the county for her injuries under 42 U.S.C. § 1983, claiming that the Sheriff had failed to adequately review Burn's background because he had a history of misdemeanor offenses, including assault and battery, resisting arrest, driving while intoxicated, and public drunkenness.

ISSUE: Can a county be held liable in a § 1983 case involving excessive use of force for a single hiring decision made by a county official? NO.

SUPREME COURT DECISION: County liability for a sheriff's decision to hire does not ". . . depend on the mere probability that any officer inadequately screened will inflict any constitutional injury. Rather, it must depend on a finding that *this* officer was highly likely to inflict the *particular* injury suffered by the plaintiff."

REASON: "Where a claim of municipal liability rests on a single decision, not itself representing a violation of federal law and not directing such a violation, the danger that a municipality will be held liable without fault is high. Because the decision necessarily governs a single case, there can be no notice to the municipal decision maker, based on previous violations of federally protected rights, that his approach is inadequate. Nor will it be readily apparent that the municipality's action caused the injury in questions because the plaintiff can point to no other incident tending to make it more likely that the plaintiff's own injury flows from the municipality's action, rather than from some other intervening cause" (520 U.S. at 408-409). "Where a plaintiff presents a § 1983 claim premised upon the inadequacy of an official's review of a prospective applicant's record, however, there is a particular danger that a municipality will be held liable for an injury not directly caused by a deliberate action attributable to the municipality itself" (520 U.S. at 410).

CASE SIGNIFICANCE: This case relieves some pressure from counties for liability when hiring police officers. In *Canton v. Harris*, the Court ruled that § 1983 liability could be incurred from a single act of an officer if there was a finding of failure to adequately train the officer. The plaintiff in this case attempted to extend that theory to a single hiring decision made by the Sheriff. The Court ruled, however, that hiring is different from training. In training, there is "policy or custom" involved in how the municipality views effective training of officers. That view can also be traced directly to any possible constitutional injury. Hiring decisions are different. Failure to adequately screen an applicant may represent poor judgment on the part of the municipal official, but it does not rise to the level of "deliberate indifference" required for liability to arise. Municipalities and municipal officials can be assured, then, that as long as a hiring decision does not rise to the level of deliberate indifference that can be traced directly to the officer's future actions involving a constitutional violation, the municipality is free from liability.

McMillian v. Monroe County, Alabama
520 U.S. 781 (1997)

CAPSULE: Whether a sheriff is an agent of the county or of the state is determined by the state's constitution, laws, or other regulations. In this case, Alabama law indicates that sheriffs are agents of the state and not of the county.

FACTS: McMillian was convicted of murder and sentenced to death based on the testimony of a co-conspirator. His conviction was later overturned after a ruling that those involved in the investigation had suppressed statements from the co-conspirator that contradicted his trial testimony and other exculpatory evidence. McMillian then brought suit against the investigators, the County Sheriff and Monroe County under 42 U.S.C. § 1983. The case against the county was based on the assumption that the Sheriff was acting as an agent of the county when he and others intimidated the co-conspirator "into making false statements and suppress[ing] exculpatory evidence."

ISSUE: Is a sheriff in Alabama a representative of the county? NO.

SUPREME COURT DECISION: Whether a sheriff is an agent of the county or an agent of the state is determined by the state's constitution, laws, and other regulations. Alabama law indicates that sheriffs are agents of the state and not of the county.

REASON: "In determining a local government's § 1983 liability, a court's task is to identify those who speak with final authority for the local governmental actor concerning the action alleged to have caused the violation at issue. *Jett v. Dallas Independent School Dist.,* 491 U.S. 701, 703. . . . In deciding this dispute, the question is not whether . . . sheriffs act as county or state officials in all of their official actions, but whom they represent in a particular area or on a particular issue. *Ibid.* This inquiry is dependent on the definition of the official's functions under relevant state law."

CASE SIGNIFICANCE: This case probably creates as many issues for law enforcement as it solves. The Supreme Court said in this case that a sheriff may be an agent of the county in some states and an agent of the state in other states; that issue being determined by the state itself. Additionally, the sheriff may be an agent of the county when performing certain tasks and an agent of the state when performing other tasks. This is important, because it determines who else, other than the sheriff, can be sued for what a sheriff does. The only time this will probably be an issue is when a county is sued for the actions of the sheriff. When that occurs, according to the Court, it is up to the courts to decide, based on the state constitution, laws, etc., whether the sheriff was acting in his or her official capacity as an agent of the county or the state.

County of Sacramento v. Lewis
523 U.S. 833 (1998)

CAPSULE: In high-speed vehicle pursuit cases, liability in § 1983 cases ensues only if the conduct of the officer "shocks the conscience." The lower standard of "deliberate indifference" does not apply.

FACTS: Deputy Smith and another officer responded to a disturbance call. Upon returning to their vehicles, the other officer observed a motorcycle (not related to the disturbance call) traveling at a high rate of speed. The officer attempted to stop the motorcycle by turning on his blue lights, shouting at the driver, and moving his patrol car closer to Smith's. The driver of the motorcycle did not stop, swerved between the two patrol cars and sped off. Smith then switched on his blue lights and began to pursue the motorcycle. The pursuit lasted for approximately 75 seconds as the two traveled a little more than a mile through a residential area at speeds in excess of 100 mph. The pursuit ended when the motorcycle overturned while attempting to make a sharp left turn. The driver of the motorcycle and Lewis, a passenger, were thrown from the motorcycle. Smith had been travelling at about 100 feet from the motorcycle and was unable to stop before hitting Lewis, knocking him about 70 feet down the road and inflicting massive injuries. Lewis was pronounced dead at the scene. Lewis' family filed suit under 42 U.S.C. § 1983, alleging a deprivation of Lewis' Fourteenth Amendment substantive due process right to life.

ISSUE: Does a police officer violate the Fourteenth Amendment's guarantee of substantive due process by causing death through deliberate or reckless indifference to life in a high-speed automobile chase aimed at apprehending a suspected offender? NO.

SUPREME COURT DECISION: Only "conduct that shocks the conscience" leads to liability under § 1983 in high-speed pursuit cases. "Only a purpose to cause harm unrelated to the legitimate object of arrest will satisfy the element of arbitrary conduct shocking to the conscience, necessary for a due process violation." ". . . [H]igh-speed chases with no intent to harm suspects physically or to worsen their legal plight do not give rise to liability under the Fourteenth Amendment, redressible by an action under § 1983."

REASON: "The Fourth Amendment covers only 'searches and seizures,' U.S. Const., Amdt. 4, neither of which took place here. No one suggests that there was a search, and our cases foreclose finding a seizure." "Our cases dealing with abusive executive action have repeatedly emphasized that only the most egregious official conduct can be said to [rise to a Constitutionally objectionable standard]." "To this end, for half a century now we have spoken of the cognizable level of executive abuse of power as that which shocks the conscience."

CASE SIGNIFICANCE: This case fills a substantial void by clarifying the issue of a Fourth Amendment seizure versus a Fourteenth Amendment substantive due process violation when the police pursue a person suspected of a crime. Through the years, the Court has held that deadly force issues generally involve a "seizure" of the person; thus making these kinds of cases Fourth Amendment issues (see *Tennessee v. Garner*, 471 U.S. 1 [1985] and *Brower v. County of Inyo*, 489 U.S. 593 [1989]). But what is the prevailing Constitutional issue prior to the police "seizing" the person? In *California v. Hodari D.*, 499 U.S. 621 (1991), the Court ruled that a person was not "seized" unless some physical force was applied (also relying on a statement from *Brower* that there must be "a termination of freedom of movement through means intentionally applied"). There was dissension in the lower courts, however, concerning what represented "seizure" in instances of police automobile pursuits, and the proper standard to be applied for possible liability in these cases. This case settled both of those issues and set forth a flexible standard that, when a police pursuit in which no physical force or "means intentionally applied" occurs, there is not a "seizure"; and if no seizure occurs to bring the action to the level of a Fourth Amendment issue, then the Fourteenth Amendment standard applies, which is a standard of conduct shocking to the conscience. This set a high standard to be met by persons bringing § 1983 cases based on high-speed police pursuits that result in fatal injuries. With this decision, it is not enough that the officers may have acted recklessly or with indifference for life, the plaintiffs must prove that the officer acted with "a purpose to cause harm unrelated to the legitimate object of arrest."

Saucier v. Katz
533 U.S. 194 (2001)

CAPSULE: A ruling on qualified immunity is not intertwined with a ruling on the violation of a constitutional right and should be made early in the proceedings so that, if established, the cost and expense of trial are avoided.

FACTS: The Vice President was to speak at a military base. Katz was concerned that a hospital at the base would be used for conducting experiments on animals, and planned to protest the speech. Katz brought a 4 x 3 foot sign to the speech and kept it concealed under his coat because he was aware that persons had been asked to leave the base in the past for certain behaviors such as distributing handbills. Katz sat in the front row, next to a waist-high fence that separated the seating area from the stage. As the Vice President began to speak, Katz began to unfold the banner and walk toward the fence. Two military police officers, who had been specifically warned about Katz, intercepted him and rushed him out of the area (partially dragging him). Katz argued that they then shoved him into a police van, causing him to fall. Katz was taken to a police station and then released. Katz brought suit claiming excessive use of force. The District Court held that "in the Fourth Amendment context, the qualified immunity inquiry is the same as the inquiry made on the merits," and, thus, is a decision to be made during the trial.

ISSUE: Is an officer's qualified immunity defense an issue that is to be decided separately from the issue of an actual violation of a constitutional right? YES.

SUPREME COURT DECISION: A ruling on the qualified immunity defense is not intertwined with a ruling on an actual constitutional violation (in this case the use of excessive force) and should be made early in the proceedings so that the cost and expense of trial are avoided.

REASON: "In a suit against an officer for an alleged violation of a constitutional right, the requisites of a qualified immunity defense must be considered in the proper sequence. Where the defendant seeks qualified immunity, a ruling on that issue should be made early in the proceedings so that the costs and expenses of trial are avoided where the defense is dispositive. Qualified immunity is 'an entitlement not to stand trial or to face the other burdens of litigation.' *Mitchell v. Forsyth*, 472 U.S. 511, 536 (1985). The privilege is 'an *immunity from suit* rather than a mere defense to liability; and like an absolute immunity, it is effectively lost if a case is erroneously permitted to go to trial.' *Ibid*. As a result, 'we repeatedly have stressed the importance of resolving immunity questions at the earliest possible stage in litigation" *Hunter v. Bryant*, 502 U.S. 224, 227 (1991)."

CASE SIGNIFICANCE: This decision favors police officers who are sued in federal court under federal law (Section 1983) for alleged violations of constitutional rights. A popular defense is these cases is that the officer enjoys qualified immunity and therefore cannot be held liable. Qualified immunity under federal law provides that the officer is not held liable unless he or she violated a clearly established constitutional rule of which a reasonable person would have known. The Court in this case held that if qualified immunity is established early in the proceedings, then the case should be dismissed and the officer does not have to go through trial. The Ninth Circuit, from where this case was appealed, held that the issue of qualified immunity and the actual violation of a constitutional right were so intertwined that a dismissal of the case after a finding of qualified immunity was not proper. This would have prolonged the case. The Court disagreed, ruling that these two issues are different and that if qualified immunity is established by the officer early, then the case should be dismissed and the trial avoided. Thus qualified immunity, once established, immunizes the officer from trial and civil liability under Section 1983. This ruling is significant because it spares officers the burden of having to go through the whole trial once qualified immunity is established early in the case, usually in a motion to dismiss. Therefore, in a Section 1983 case filed in federal court, the case is to be dismissed if the defense establishes qualified immunity, meaning that the officer did not violate a clearly established constitutional right of which a reasonable person would have known.

Chavez v. Martinez
538 U.S. 760 (2004)

CAPSULE: "Statements compelled by police interrogation may not be used against a defendant in a criminal case, but it is not until such use that the Self-Incrimination Clause is violated."

FACTS: Officers were questioning an individual about suspected drug activity when they heard a bicycle approaching on a darkened path. They ordered the rider, Martinez, to dismount the bicycle, spread his legs, and place his hands behind his head. He complied, and an officer found a knife in his waistband during a pat-down search. An altercation ensued with the police and Martinez was shot several times. Chavez, a patrol supervisor, arrived several minutes later and accompanied Martinez to the hospital. Chavez interviewed Martinez in the hospital while he was receiving medical treatment. The interview lasted 10 minutes over a 45-minute period, with Chavez leaving the emergency room periodically to allow medical personnel to attend to Martinez. During the interview, Martinez admitted to taking a gun from one of the officer's holsters, and he admitted to heroin use. At one point, Martinez stated "I am not telling you anything until they treat me," but Chavez nonetheless continued the interview. At no point was Martinez given his *Miranda* warnings. Martinez was never charged with a crime and his answers were never used against him in any criminal prosecution. Martinez filed a § 1983 suit against Chavez, claiming his Fifth and Fourteenth Amendment rights were violated by the interrogation.

ISSUE: Do statements taken in violation of *Miranda* violate the Fifth Amendment protection against self-incrimination even if they are not used in a criminal trial? NO.

SUPREME COURT DECISION: "Statements compelled by police interrogation may not be used against a defendant in a criminal case, but it is not until such use that the Self-Incrimination Clause is violated." Therefore, the police in this case are not liable in a Section 1983 case because no constitutional right of the suspect was violated.

REASON: In this case, the Court reemphasized that statements made in violation of the Fifth Amendment cannot be used against the person in legal proceedings, "but it is not until their use in a criminal case that a violation of the Self-Incrimination Clause occurs. . . . Here, Martinez was never made to be a 'witness' against himself in violation of the Fifth Amendment's Self-Incrimination Clause because his statements were never admitted as testimony against him in a criminal case." The Court stated that, although conduct by police prior to trial may cause the constitutional violation (such as taking an illegal confession), it is not until the trial itself that the privilege applies. The Court argued that there are several instances where witnesses can be compelled to testify without violating the Fifth Amendment, such as testifying before a grand jury or the compelled testimony of a witness who has been granted immunity. "Even for persons who have a legitimate fear that their statements may subject them to criminal prosecution, we have long permitted the compulsion of incriminating testimony so long as those statements (or evidence derived from those statements) cannot be used against the speaker in any criminal case." Turning specifically to the facts here, the Court held, "the fact that Martinez did not *know* his statements could not be used against him does not change our view. . . . [and] Chavez's failure to read *Miranda* warnings to Martinez did not violate Martinez's constitutional rights and cannot be the grounds for a § 1983 action." The Court further stated "our views on the proper scope of the Fifth Amendment's Self-Incrimination Clause do not mean that police torture or other abuse that results in a confession is constitutionally permissible so long as the statements are not used at trial . . ." What the Court ruled here was simply that the officer's conduct did not interfere with Martinez's medical attention to a level where it constituted a violation of Martinez's constitutional right.

CASE SIGNIFICANCE: This case is best understood as a Section 1983 civil liability case for a possible violation of a suspect's constitutional right. A Section 1983 case, filed by a plaintiff primarily seeking monetary compensation from a police officer, succeeds only if there is a proven violation of a constitutional right or of a right guaranteed by federal law. The suspect in this case filed a Section 1983 case alleging his constitutional privilege against self-incrimination was violated when he was not given the *Miranda* warnings and the interrogation continued despite his telling the police that "I am not telling you anything until they treat me." The Court held that "mere compulsive questioning" by the police does not violate the Constitution, neither does police questioning constitute a criminal case. It is true that statements compelled through police interrogation cannot be used against a defendant in a criminal trial, "but it is not until such use that the Self-Incrimination Clause is violated." The Court concluded that "failure [by the police] to read *Miranda* warnings to Martinez did not violate Martinez's constitutional rights and cannot be grounds for a Section 1983 action. And the absence of a "criminal case" in which Martinez was compelled to be a witness against himself defeats his core Fifth Amendment claim." The police officer in this case could possibly have been held liable administratively for violating agency rules (if agency rules prohibited such type of questioning), but could not be held liable under Section 1983, a civil liability case, which succeeds only if the police violate a constitutional right or a right guaranteed by federal law.

Muehler v. Mena
544 U.S. ___, 125 S. Ct. 1465 (2004)

CAPSULE: Detaining occupants of the premises in handcuffs for a certain period of time while executing a search warrant does not by itself violate the Fourth Amendment prohibition against unreasonable searches and seizures.

FACTS: Based on information concerning gang-related, drive-by shootings, officers obtained a search warrant for a home known to be occupied by gang members. Believing one or more of the suspects in the home might be armed and dangerous, a SWAT team was called to assist in the search. Officers executed the warrant at 7:00 A.M. Mena was awakened by officers and placed in handcuffs at gunpoint. Mena and three other individuals were taken to a converted garage where they were held during the search. They remained in handcuffs, but were allowed to move around in the garage. Aware that this gang had illegal immigrants as members, the Immigration and Naturalization Service was also alerted. During the detention of Mena and the others, INS agents asked for identifying information and immigration documentation. Mena's status as permanent resident was confirmed by her papers. The search revealed several weapons, ammunition, drugs, and gang paraphernalia. Mena was released before officers left the area. She later filed a § 1983 lawsuit, claiming she was detained for an unreasonably long time and in an unreasonable manner in violation of the Fourth Amendment.

ISSUE: May police handcuff occupants of a home for the duration of a lawfully conducted search? YES.

SUPREME COURT DECISION: Officers may detain in handcuffs occupants of the premises during a search without violating the Fourth Amendment.

REASON: "In *Michigan v. Summers*, 452 U.S. 692 (1981), we held that officers executing a search warrant for contraband have the authority 'to detain the occupants of the premises while a proper search is conducted.' *Id.*, At 705. Such detentions are appropriate, we explained, because the character of the additional intrusion caused by the detention is slight and because the justifications for detention are substantial. . . . Against this incremental intrusion, we posited three legitimate law enforcement interests that provide substantial justification for detaining an occupant: 'preventing flight in the event that incriminating evidence is found,' 'minimizing the risk of harm to the officers,' and 'facilitating the orderly completion of the search.' . . . The officers' use of force in the form of handcuffs to effectuate Mena's detention in the garage, as well as the detention of the three other occupants, was reasonable because the governmental interests outweigh the marginal intrusion. . . . In such inherently dangerous situations, the use of handcuffs minimized the risk of harm to both officers and occupants. [and] . . . the need to detain multiple occupants made the use of handcuffs all the more reasonable." Finally, the Court ruled, that "the 2- to 3-hour detention in handcuffs in this case does not outweigh the government's continuing safety interests."

CASE SIGNIFICANCE: Mena filed a Section 1983 case seeking monetary damages from the police, alleging a violation of her constitutional right against unreasonable searches and seizures. She claimed she was illegally detained in handcuffs and for an unreasonably long time. The Court rejected both claims, holding that the detention was consistent with previous cases where the "Court held that officers executing a search warrant for contraband have the authority 'to detain the occupants of the premises while a proper search is conducted.'" Detention in handcuffs by the police was justified in these cases as "minimizing the risk of harm to officers." In this case, there was a valid search in which the police were authorized to "use reasonable force to effectuate the detention." The Court added that "[t]he use of force in the form of handcuffs to detain Mena was reasonable because the governmental interest in minimizing the risk of harm to both officers and occupants, at its maximum when a warrant authorizes a search for weapons and a wanted gang member resides on the premises, outweighs the marginal intrusion." On the allegation that the detention was unreasonably long, the Court replied, "Although the duration of a detention can affect the balance of interest, the 2- to 3-hour detention in handcuffs in this case does not outweigh the government's continuing safety interests." In sum, the Court held that no prior specific rules determine when detention of suspects is unreasonable. The use of handcuffs and the reasonableness of the length of the detention are determined by the circumstances of that case. In this particular case, the circumstances surrounding the search justified the use of handcuffs and the length of the detention.

Town of Castle Rock v. Gonzales
545 U.S. ___, 125 S. Ct. 2796 (2005)

CAPSULE: The wrongful failure by the police to arrest a husband who violated a restraining order does not amount to a violation of a constitutional due process right under the Fourteenth Amendment and therefore does not result in civil liability under federal law (Section 1983).

FACTS: Pending a divorce, Gonzales obtained a restraining order against her estranged husband that required him to stay 100 yards away from the house where she lived with their three children, except for specified visitation. The order commanded all law enforcement officials to ". . . use every reasonable means to enforce this restraining order," and either to arrest or to seek an arrest warrant when there was ". . . information amounting to probable cause that the restrained person has violated or attempted to violate any provision of this order." Three weeks after the order was issued, the husband took his daughters from the front yard of their house without Gonzales's awareness or permission. When Gonzales noticed the girls were missing she called the Castle Rock Police Department, which dispatched two officers. She showed them the restraining order, but the officers stated that there was nothing they could do about the order, and that she should call the police department again if her children had not been returned by that evening. Gonzales called her husband who said the children were at an amusement park with him. Gonzales called the police department again and asked that they have someone check for her husband's truck at the amusement park, or "put out an [all points bulletin]" for him. She was again told to wait until that evening to see if the girls were returned. Gonzales called the police department again at 10:00 P.M. and was told to call back at midnight. She called at midnight from her husband's apartment and was told to wait for an officer to arrive. No officer arrived, and at 12:50 A.M. she went to the police department and filed an incident report. The officer receiving the report took no action. At 3:20 A.M., the husband went to the police station, opened fire with a pistol purchased that evening, and was killed when police shot back. Police found in the husband's truck the bodies of his three daughters, who he had previously killed. Gonzales filed a Section 1983 suit against the city for failure to protect her children and to take action on the restraining order.

ISSUE: Is a town civilly liable under federal law (Section 1983) for having a custom or policy that tolerates non-enforcement by its police department of court restraining orders? NO.

SUPREME COURT DECISION: A town cannot be held civilly liable under federal law (Section 1983) for wrongfully and intentionally having a custom or policy that tolerates non-enforcement of court restraining orders. Such practice does not amount to a violation of due process rights and therefore do not result in civil liability.

REASON: The Court in this case relied on previous Supreme Court decisions. Such cases applied the due process clause of the Fourteenth Amendment through Section 1983 to determine what interests were protected in particular cases. The Court noted that the due process clause protects "property," so Gonzales was required to have a property interest in the enforcement of the restraining order for the due process clause to be applicable. Such property interests are enforced by federal law under the due process clause, but are created by state law. The court of appeals found in this case that Colorado had created such a property interest for persons like Gonzales by the using the language "shall arrest or . . . [shall] seek a warrant for the arrest of the restrained person" on the order. The Supreme Court rejected this logic because police officers traditionally had discretion not to enforce even "mandatory enforcement" laws. If the interest is one that government officials may grant or deny at their discretion, then under previous cases it is not a property interest. The Colorado statute had not specifically given or attempted to give Gonzales a property right; but even if it had, it would have been an indirect benefit. The due process clause protects property rights in "direct benefits" such as money from Medicaid, but not an "indirect benefit" such as enforcement of standards of care in a nursing home. The Court concluded that because it had not found any property interest that could be protected by the due process clause, it did not have to evaluate whether the actions of police in this case constituted a custom or policy of the Town of Castlerock.

CASE SIGNIFICANCE: This case is significant because it further clarifies when a government agency might be held civilly liable under federal law (Section 1983). Gonzales filed this case as a violation of the due process clause. The Court ruled that, to have a claim under the due process clause, a person must have a true property interest, not simply "an abstract need or desire," and the person must have "more than a unilateral expectation of it." The Court pointed out that ". . . the Due Process Clause does not protect everything that might be described as a benefit." In determining whether this case represented a benefit, the Court ruled that "our cases recognize that a benefit is not a protected entitlement if government officials may grant or deny it in their discretion." In examining the law in this case, the Court held that it did not appear that the state law made enforcement of court restraining orders mandatory. Because of these circumstances, Gonzales did not have a Section 1983 claim because her rights under the due process clause were not violated.

Index